THE QUALITY OF LIFE

THE QUALITY OF LIFE

Valuation in Social Research

HN
25
.M85
1989
West

RAMKRISHNA MUKHERJEE

SAGE Publications
New Delhi/Newbury Park/London

First published in 1989 by

Sage Publications India Pvt Ltd
M–32 Greater Kailash Market I
New Delhi 110 048

Sage Publications Inc
2111 West Hillcrest Drive
Newbury Park, California 91320

Sage Publications Ltd
28 Banner Street
London EC1Y 8QE

Published by Tejeshwar Singh for Sage Publications India Pvt Ltd, photo-typeset by Mudra Typesetters, Pondicherry and printed at Chaman Offset Printers.

ISBN 0–8039–9587–3 (U.S.)
81–7036–126–5 (India)

To the memory of
Syed Nesar Ahmad
who died in the 1986 PAN AM hijacking
disaster at Karachi

• Contents •

• List of Tables •

• List of Figures •

• Acknowledgements •

This study grew out of two quality of life surveys in India in 1980 and 1982, and a status report on the quality of life research in 1984. The two surveys and the status report were commissioned by the Sector of Social Sciences and their Applications of the Division for Socio-economic Analysis of the UNESCO, Paris. The first survey report was published in 1983 in Socio-economic Studies No. 5 of the UNESCO, Paris, entitled *Quality of Life: Problems of Assessment and Measurement*. The second survey report was circulated as a mimeograph by the UNESCO, Paris, in 1983, under reference number SS.83/Conf./CS/13/4. The status report was mimeographed by the UNESCO, Paris, in 1984, for limited circulation, under reference number SHS/SEA/WS/84. My thanks are due to the UNESCO, Paris, and its aforementioned Division and Sector for the support and encouragement I have received towards writing this book.

My thanks are also due to several other research organizations and individual scholars: Professor Alex C. Michalos for his comments on the status report, and Professor Pradip K. Bose for his comments on this volume; The National Institute for Educational Planning and Administration (NIEPA), New Delhi, for assistance in organizing the field investigation for the 1982 quality of life survey, at the initiative of its Director (Professor Moonis Raza); The Centre for Social Studies, Surat, for computer analysis of the data according to the design outlined in Table 3.27 of Chapter 3, at the initiative of its Director (Professor Ghanshyam Shah) and Professor Pradip K. Bose; Dr. Suraj Bandyopadhyay and Mr. Dipankar Chatterjee for their assistance in content analysis of the programmes and election manifestos of the Indian political parties around 1970 and in 1977, respectively, which in the final form is placed in Chapter 2; Dr. Prafulla Chakrabarti for pretesting the questionnaire-schedule for the 1980 survey of quality of life, and Mr. Krishnendu Bhattacharya for his assistance in collecting and analyzing the 1980 survey data beyond his contractual obligations; and, Mr. Ranjit K. Santra for his assistance in preparing this volume for publication, beyond his secretarial commitments.

May 1988   RAMKRISHNA MUKHERJEE
Calcutta

• Preface •

The expression *quality* of life suggests the antonym *quantity* of life and prompts debate on the efficiency of the qualitative rather than quantitative appraisal of the aspects of reality concerned, or the converse. The debate is crystallized by the object-subject dichotomy of the aspects of reality viewed and the viewers of different aspects of reality, under the impression that the object may be quantified (partly or fully) but the subjective variation is basically qualitative. The debate extends to the ideologies of objectivism and subjectivism because of the duality arising from our encounter and experience that the world exists without oneself but one can appreciate the world only by oneself. Ultimately, the quality—quantity and subject—object dichotomies, stimulated by the philosophies of subjectivism and objectivism, provoke polemics for castigating the contenders as mystique or positivist.

The present study does not indulge in such polemics, nor is it concerned with a philosophical discourse on objectivism (defined as knowledge superior to Ego) and subjectivism (defined as without external or objective test of truth). In place of any abstract discussion or summary labelling, the study examines the relationships within and across the subjects and the objects in the light of a successive relation that can be drawn between the qualitative and the quantitative appraisals of the quality of life as knowledge accumulates on the phenomenon.

With this objective in view, the study also eschews empiricism as an ideology because that may lead to the quest for 'pure' knowledge. As knowledge is acquired from the manifestation of reality, it cannot pre-empt its source. Therefore, knowledge can more and more approximate reality but cannot grasp it fully and finally, nor can it reproduce reality in its pristine form and content. The present study, therefore, accepts this limiting condition to the quality of life research.

However, reality is invariably appraised by means of the observations made, the deductions drawn from the observations, and the inferences posited with reference to the items of information observed and the deductions made therefrom. The observable items of information and

the deductions made therefrom may be negated by an inference drawn
from another perspective of observation and deduction, as in the case
of Yagnavalka's declaration *'neti, neti'* (not this, nor that) in order to
establish the 'true' reality of the Supreme Being (Hume 1958: 97, 125,
132, 143, 147). Nonetheless, the process of observation, deduction,
and inference is *sui generis* to the appraisal of reality and is manifest by
an enquirer while it may remain latent with an enquired person. This
process, and not its initial form or the end product, is most efficiently
rendered by the empirical method. The present study, therefore,
follows the empirical methodology.

The empirical method may be considered inadequate to the appraisal
of the quality of life because observation, which initiates the visible
process of accumulation of knowledge on reality, follows from contemplation of the enquirer or the enquired. It thus introduces a factor
which seems to be qualitatively *a priori* to observation. However,
contemplation may or may not be quantitative in its initial state, fully
or partly, but it is not *a priori*. It bears manifest or latent antecedence
of observation, deduction, and inference. Otherwise, *what, how*, and
why may one contemplate?

The point, therefore, is not of inadequacy of the empirical method
but of its application in such a manner that there is no hiatus between
contemplation and the consequent action, both succeeding from respective sequences of observation, deduction, and inference. As the
sequences are expressed by the perception and the behaviour of each
individual, the scope of the present study is so defined.

From the perspective of an enquirer, his/her perception and
behaviour are not only manifest but he/she may employ deductive
principles to elicit the perception and behaviour of the enquired
persons. The procedure would make him or her vulnerable to the
charge of being a positivist, especially if the statistical techniques of
deduction are employed for the appraisal of reality. But if an enquirer
follows the principles of induction and inference on a probability basis
and applies the principles to the appraisals of the enquirers, the charge
of being a positivist may not be so easily applicable. The empirical
method may be employed either way, i.e., in a deductive-positivistic or
an inductive-inferential manner, as discussed and illustrated (Mukherjee
1978). The present study has adopted the second alternative.

The adoption of the inductive-inferential method of empirical research will bring the enquirers and the enquired together because both
will be concerned with, theoretically, an infinite but enumerable space

of information on social reality with a view to appraising the quality of
life, all available and possible selection (i.e., primary valuation) of the
items of information as quality of life data, and their secondary valuation
of the data items as desirable, undesirable, or of no significance for
attaining a better quality of life. Therefore, this method of empirical
research should establish an unequivocal relation within and across
the subjects and the objects of enquiry.

Even so, charges may be levelled that positivism would linger
because the deductions and the inferences may exclude the singular
appraisals of the quality of life by some individuals, as being random
variations in the value space structured in the above manner, while one
such indubitably subjective appraisal may be more efficient than those
deduced or inferred.

One should bear in mind in this context that any evaluation of the
quality of life acquires relevance only when it is mediated through
society and attains group affiliation with respect to some or all its
attributes. Yagnavalka's valuation would have had no relevance at all if
his portrayal of the 'illusory' and the 'real' quality of life was not
subscribed by a number of subjects, wholly or by a selection of the
objects it incorporates. The same is true for the valuations of any great
thinker and/or activist, such as, of Gandhi, Rousseau, Tolstoy, Marx,
etc.

Correspondingly, an object would not acquire relevance unless it is
socially mediated. For example, from whichever perspective the
phenomenon of madness may be observed, deduced, and inferred, the
phenomenon would not acquire any relevance for consideration unless
it exists socially by group affiliation to the object of madness.

This means that by repeatability for the subjects and the objects, the
test of relevance assures the validity of an evaluation and leads the
researcher toward examining its necessity, efficiency, and sufficiency
for depicting a phenomenon. In other words, objectification of the
subjective is inherent to understanding social reality and appraising
the quality of life. Therefore, *commonality* in the perception and
behaviour of the enquirers and the enquired, which registers their
contemplation (rationality) and its expression (action), forms the base
for the appraisal of the quality of life.

Thus designed, the base for the appraisal of the quality of life
provides scope for the singular valuations to establish their validity
because the commonalities discerned at a time-point do not exclude
the possibility of any singular valuation forming a commonality later;

nor are the commonalities immutable, indestructible, or irreversible in the future context. At the same time, a systematic and rigorous search for commonalities with regard to the subjects and the objects of enquiry would safeguard the researcher from straying toward positivism or mysticism.

Therefore, rather than searching for any absolute truth, true reason, universal laws, or pure knowledge, the present study is concerned with eliciting the commonalities in the valuation of the quality of life under the three dimensions of variability in the place, the time, and the people, as enumerated by the *Sāṅkhya* school of Indian philosophy.

Commonality denotes objectivity by presenting the 'oneness' of a set of objects with reference to a set of subjects. By thus reducing Ego-variability toward zero, the present study is concerned with the *extent of objectivity from subjectivity* of respective Ego, and the quantification of the extent of objectivity. The attempt should pave the way toward resolving the apparently irreconcilable bipolarity of objects and subjects, and of quality and quantity.

Quality in its elemental form is denoted by minimally exclusive variations with respect to the enquirers and the enquired. At that primeval state, the variable properties of a phenomenon form an amorphous information space which is not conducive to a coherent accumulation of knowledge on the phenomenon. The prime necessity is therefore of organizing the information space by conceiving it as comprising known and *knowable* properties, so that, empirical research may systematically elicit these properties to represent the phenomenon more and more precisely and comprehensively. Thus organized, the course of research would reveal distinctive commonalities in the evaluation of the phenomenon by the enquired and the enquirers.

To begin with, the commonalities may be nominally distinguished as 'this' or 'that' by the presence or absence of some of the properties of a phenomenon. However, as knowledge accumulates on these properties, the nature and extent of their presence or absence in respective commonalities are precisely rendered. On that basis, and at the end of a progressive sequence of quantification of the properties beyond their omnibus presence or absence, the commonalities may be comprehensively interrelated by the unit-interval distances they register.

This point is discussed and demonstrated in this study. However, that will not put an end to the debate on quality and quantity, and in favour or against 'positivism' in social research, because some singular (i.e., individualized) items of information will no doubt be lost in the course of identification, distinction, and interrelation of the commonalities in the progressive sequence from quality to quantity. Therefore, the point is: Are these individual-wise *unique* variations indicative of *mot juste* of the phenomenon?

If a unique individual variation would denote a phenomenon with more precision than its other properties, then the phenomenon would not require further investigation. But social research has progressed far enough to preclude a discussion like Lenin's and Plekhanov's on Mikhailovskhy's and Danielson's unique characterization of Russian society (Lenin 1894, 1899; Plekhanov 1895) or the caste system in India as being the product of 'Brahmanical theodicy' (Weber 1958b: 131). However, leaving aside a unique appreciation of a phenomenon, it is possible that, rather than remaining as an extraneous variation, what is uniquely individualistic today may assume a *group character* tomorrow and form a discernible commonality. Therein lies the need for the never-ending course of empirical research which will involve the enquirers and the enquired in ascertaining, at a time and in the time sequence, the nature and the extent of objectivity (commonality) from subjectivity in appreciating a phenomenon.

Even so, the point of *mot juste* of a phenomenon may never be fully answered because, at its best possible accumulation, knowledge forms an asymptotic relation with reality. Therefore, the appreciation of a phenomenon should either be left to a mystique (in any case, an impressionist) or empirical research should be so designed that, in the first place, more and more mutually distinct but interrelated commonalities are deciphered among the enquired and the enquirers along with the progressive sequence of qualitative to quantitative appreciation of the variations within and across them. This means that empirical research must provide an unconstrained scope for the identification of commonalities with respect to a phenomenon, i.e., beyond those *deduced* by one or another enquirer according to his/her synoptic appreciation of the phenomenon.

An enquirer is a component of a theoretically conceived infinite but enumerable space of all enquirers. Correspondingly, those enquired by an enquirer form a selected set out of all possible persons for enquiry. Moreover, the selected enquired persons are categorized into groups in the light of *a priori* knowledge of the enquirer on the phenomenon examined, while the knowable properties of the phenomenon may align them in group formations different from the predetermined one. Thus, empirical research is concerned with three mutually distinct but interrelated spaces of the enquirers, the enquired, and the known and knowable properties of the phenomenon examined. The orientation to research should therefore be *inductive* for an unconstrained exploration of the three spaces with a view to identify, distinguish, and interrelate commonalities among the enquirers and the enquired in the light of evermore precise and comprehensive knowledge on the known and the knowable properties of the phenomenon.

In this context, the predetermined grouping of the enquired persons by an enquirer imposes a constraint which is seldom taken into account, while it adversely affects the appraisal of the dynamics of a phenomenon. This point is particularly discussed and illustrated in this study.

The commonalities with respect to the enquirers and the enquired are formed by the properties of the phenomenon selected by respective enquirers and enquired out of the known and knowable information space on the phenomenon. The selection conveys primary valuation by an enquirer or the enquired of distinctive items of information for representing the phenomenon. The information-items are thus transformed into data, and the sets of data structuring the commonalities register the valuations of the phenomenon by respective enquirers and the enquired.

Additionally, the quality of life research is concerned with secondary valuations of the data-items as desirable, undesirable, or of no consequence to improving the quality of life. Similar secondary valuations of a phenomenon are found in case the value-input to a phenomenon by the enquirer or the enquired is obvious. However, both the primary and the secondary valuations of a phenomenon are *ordinal* valuations made by the enquirers and the enquired in the course of identifying, distinguishing, and interrelating the commonalities with respect to the phenomenon. The point, therefore, is of *relative* validity, relevance, necessity, and efficiency of the revealed commonalities in the context of presenting the phenomenon.

Academic discourse rests on this issue for the accumulation of knowledge by rejecting the less to the least valid, relevant and necessary valuations of commonalities for the appraisal of a phenomenon, and investigating the *relative efficiency* of the remaining commonalities for representing the phenomenon. Usually, however, this course of rejection and accretion rests upon polemics on which commonalities denote the *mot juste* of a phenomenon. But polemics on the ordinal valuations of enquirers for forming commonalities of the enquired ones would generate more heat than shed light unless there is a common yardstick for the evaluation of all ordinal valuations made by the enquirers and the enquired.

The common yardstick must be acceptable to humankind as a whole. Therefore, it may be provided by four human-specific *cardinal* valuations; namely, survival of the species, security in the life-span of individuals, material prosperity to ensure survival and security and attaining a wholesome life, and mental progress to unfold the potentials of respective humans.

The cardinal valuations may be better formulated. Also, the methodology of eliciting the ordinal valuations may be better than that demonstrated in this book. However, the point is that social research implies progression of objectivity from subjectivity in reference to quality and quantity, and systematic treatment of the ordinal value-inputs of the enquirers and the enquired in the light of cardinal valuations for humanity. These are the essential points dealt with in this book with reference to the quality of life research which evidently highlights these points.

· 1 ·

· Approach ·

AN ALL-INCLUSIVE NOTION

Although the quality of life research is only two decades old, it has spread all over the globe and the venture has become so popular that the politicians, who previously spoke of welfare of the masses, now speak of the quality of life of the people. However, the parameters of the quality of life are unspecified. Researches are conducted on various aspects of life, with the admission that the manifestation of life and of the immanent life processes denote an infinite but enumerable field of concerns. Therefore, the quality of life is treated as an all-inclusive notion of life and living (Szalai 1980).

A common attempt to delimit the field of concern with the quality of life is by attending to the living conditions of the people. The attempt has made the field of enquiry more and more visible, but has not foreclosed its limits. This is noticeable from the labels used from earlier times to depict the people's living conditions, such as, the standard, the level, and the style of living. The labels tend to follow a sequence and register new inputs for the appreciation of the quality of life: from an exclusively quantitative and assumed objective base to an increasingly complex blend of quantity and quality, and of the objective behavioural and the subjective perceptual variables.

Investigations into the standard of living of the people have now been conducted for many decades. The standard is usually constructed from quantitative variations in the *object of enquiry* which is given by a list of information items, such as, consumption of food, clothes, use of various kinds of durable goods like furniture and fittings, possession of items like radio, TV, and other housing and necessities and amenities of life (see, United Nations 1951).

The level of living is used as an interchangeable label with the standard of living, but there is also the attempt to designate a qualitative distinction of the standard of living. The distinction is applied to the *subject of enquiry*, such as, the level or the standard of living of the middle class, the working class, and the peasantry. The distinction is also applied to the object of enquiry by treating the items of information under headings sharply differentiated by quality; such as, from food, clothing, health, housing, education, leisure, and security, to 'human freedom' (see, United Nations 1954). The notion of quality is thus introduced into the information space in addition to the quantitative and assumed objective variations in living conditions. So far, however, quality is treated as a *classificatory* and not a *measure* variable, even for the object of enquiry.

Quality becomes a measure variable for the object of enquiry with the use of the label 'style of living', because 'style' introduces the concept of culture which bears Tylor's (1898: I. 1) classic definition of 'that complex whole which includes knowledge, belief, art, morals, law, custom, and any other capabilities and habits acquired by man as a member of society.' The individuals' style of living in a group will thus be represented by some qualitative attributes of culture, which will be introduced as object of enquiry along with the quantitative attributes denoting the standard of living, while the groups (the subject of enquiry) may be categorized under different levels of living in the manner illustrated.

For example, 'dress' may be a qualitative, classificatory heading for the object of enquiry under the level of living, and given by the number of different varieties of clothing worn by an individual. Now, the style of living will be measured by the qualitative attributes of the model, the design, etc., of the clothing. Similar treatment will be applicable to other items of information which are categorized by quality and employed as classificatory headings of the object of enquiry for denoting the level of living.

However, the coexistence of quality and quantity as measure variables for the object of enquiry is not the only consequence of introducing the concept of culture to depict the conditions of living. Culture introduces, in its turn, other labels like the 'mode of life', the 'way of life' (Ryabushkin et al. 1983). These labels are usually employed for a group of individuals registering a particular mode or way of life, while the label, style of living, is equally meaningful with reference to an individual or a group. Therefore, the groups of individuals previously classified by qualitative distinctions (e.g., the middle class, the working class, and the peasantry) will now form subgroups by the qualitative measure variables of the mode or the way of life.

Thus, quality as a measure variable would refer to both the subject and the object of enquiry. On one side, subgroups will be formed under the subject of enquiry by the blending of the quantitative variables of the standard of living and the qualitative variables of the style of living and other expressions of culture. On the other, all these quantities and qualities will be considered as items of information of the object of enquiry, which are also classified, as noted, under the levels of living.

The blending of quality and quantity as measure variables has yielded new group formations of living conditions like the *nouveau riche* from the category of the middle class, the *labour aristocracy* from the category of the working class, and the *rustic gentry* from the category of the peasantry. These possibilities foretell another role of quality as a measure variable, namely, culture may denote the formation of identical or parallel subgroups in different classified groups: such as, the group labelled intelligentsia, whicy may refer to different social status groups. Thus, the qualitative and quantitative variables may cut across predetermined groupings and evolve, analytically, a matrix of group formations.

These possibilities and probabilities related to the object and the subject of enquiry emerge in the sequence of extending the scope of investigation into the living conditions of the people. They substantiate the all-inclusive notion of the quality of life and indicate that the infinite but enumerable field of concerns with the quality of life cannot be delimited by proceeding with one or another perspective of life and living. On the contrary, as the course of research proceeds in extent and depth, more and more life concerns are brought to account, which may be treated as quality or quantity, behavioural or perceptual, and objective or subjective.

At the same time it is seen that, to begin with, the living conditions of the people is a conceptually valid and operationally feasible proposition in respect of the quality of life research. Therefore, the attempts of some scholars (e.g., Bestuzhev-Lada 1980) toward systemizing the labels employed to depict the conditions of living are commendable, but not of those who would define the notion of the quality of life on the basis of a quality—quantity, perceptual—behavioural, and subjective—objective dichotomy of the manifestations of life. Enforcement of these dichotomies imposes constraints upon the field of enquiry and is, therefore, harmful to the quality of life research.

It is seen in this context that the economists and the planners tend to appraise the quality of life by means of quantitative behavioural variables exclusively, which they regard as objective. The psychologists, on the other hand, tend to be engrossed with the qualitative perceptual variables, which they acknowledge to be subjective. The dichotomies thus supposed and maintained between quantity and quality, behaviour and perception, and objective and subjective, may not be held rigidly by many scholars. However, the contemporary operation of the quality of life research is noticeably directed into two streams of the so-called objective, behavioural, quantitative variations *or* the so-called subjective, perceptual, qualitative variations of the manifestations of life.

Therefore, it is necessary to point out that perception and behaviour are complementary to the quality of life research, and the two kinds of variables—perceptual and behavioural—are laid on two axes of quality to quantity and subjectivity to objectivity. The frame of reference to the quality of life research is defined on this basis. However, the point deserves explication because of the controversy on quantification of quality, the location of the quality of life research between the polar concepts of subjectivism and objectivism, and the procedure of research for empirical observation of the relation between perception and behaviour without subscribing to the doctrine of empiricism.

FRAME OF REFERENCE

The qualitative and quantitative measure variables of the quality of life research, applied for the determination of the object of enquiry and classification of the subject of enquiry, do not inhere an unbridgeable gulf between quality and quantity. In that context, the history of empirical social research has shown a trend from quality to quantity in the formulation of measure variables as knowledge accumulates on the nature and the extent of variability in the subject and the object of enquiry.

A measure variable of the object of enquiry, denoting the absolute presence or absence of one property or a set of properties, draws a *nominal* distinction between two or among several subjects of enquiry. In this case, variation among the subjects is purely by quality which distinguishes them as 'this', 'that', and 'that'. These distinctions, denoted by the object of enquiry, are not measurable because no relation is conceived among the objects and, therefore, among the subjects.

Some common examples in this respect, as obtained from the immediate past and the contemporary topics for social research, are the subject and the object denoted as the civilized and the primitive, the Occidentals and the Orientals, the traditional and the modern, and the West with the rational 'this worldly' ethic vis-à-vis the East with the spiritual 'other worldly' outlook.

The purely qualitative and apparently immeasurable identification of the subjects and objects of enquiry, as explained and illustrated, soon becomes obsolete or inadequate as knowledge begins to accumulate through social research. Then, the discrete series of unrelated subjects, qualified by nominal distinction of their properties, is first transformed into a *qualitative-ordinal* series. This is engineered by the relation drawn between (or among) the objects of enquiry, which replaces the previously conceived insurmountable difference between 'this' or 'that' by the presence of *more* of 'this' property (or a set of properties) and *less* of 'that' property (or a set of properties). In that event, all manner of dichotomies such as the ones illustrated above disappear.

The primitive—civilized dichotomy, dictated by 19th century ideology of colonialism, was replaced by evermore precisely defined properties of change for delineating the course of development of the world society, as explored by Morgan (1964), Engels (1948), Simmel (in Wolf 1950), Tönnies (1955), Malinowski (1944, 1947), Hobhouse (1938), among others. Rudyard Kipling's 'twain'—the Occident and the Orient—did meet and eventually led to the formation of the United Nations. The traditional—modern dichotomy was replaced by specific properties to denote the 'modernity of tradition' (Rudolph and Rudolph 1967), the 'modernization of tradition' (Singh 1973), and so on. Also, in the light of their defined properties, the so-called spiritual 'other worldly' outlook and the rational 'this worldly' ethic have been found more or less in the East and the West or across the East-West boundary.

With further accumulation of knowledge on the properties of the qualities which had denoted a nominal distinction among the subjects of enquiry at the beginning, the ordinal distinction yields a *qualitative-numeral* series of 1, 2, 3, . . ., n, in the light of the *increasing* or *decreasing* presence of the property (or the set of properties) of 'this' and 'that' quality among the subjects of enquiry. In this case, the relations among the objects of enquiry are more precisely delineated for each object than before: but, as yet, the serial distinction of numbers is numeral and not numerical, i.e., the differences between 2 and 1, 3 and 2, and so on, are not of the *same* quantity as of one unit.

On this basis and with reference to the examples cited, the stages of social development are explored in various ways, such as, a scale of tradition to modernity is designed; usually in the light of Rostow's (1962) *The Stages of Economic Growth*. During this course of investigation, rationality attains a value-free empirical definition of optimization of the ends and the means with reference to scarce resources, material and mental, in place of previously value-charged idealistic definition contained in studies like *The Protestant Ethic and the Spirit of Capitalism* (Weber 1958a). Thus, rationality (or the lack of it) in the context of 'this' or 'the other' wordly outlook becomes measurable on an ordinal-numeral scale.

The next and the last step in the trend from quality to quantity is to ascertain unit-interval distinctions in the qualitative-numeral series, so that, the differences between 2 and 1, 3 and 2, and so on, may all be the same and equal to 1. This is possible in case knowledge on the variable presence or absence of the property (or set of properties) of 'this' or 'that' quality attains the level of precision for denoting *how much* more (or less) of the property (or set of properties) with respect to each and all objects and subjects of enquiry. The measure variable will, then, record *unit-interval* distinction from the nominal distinction at the beginning and in course of qualitative-ordinal and qualitative-numeral distinctions.

This attempt is also noticeable in contemporary social research with respect to specific objects of enquiry, such as, rationality, alienation, use of labour-power and the measurement of socially necessary labour in different configurations of the world society; the last being intrinsically associated with the quality of life research. In a broader canvas, the unit-interval distinctions are now universally employed for the construction of indices of social and political developments, along with the indices of economic development.

With reference to researches into the living conditions of the people, the trend from quality to quantity is clearly underlined. For instance, from a nominal or ordinal distinction in food intake, in the form of presence or absence and more or less presence of protein and fat vis-à-vis the carbohydrate intake, the consumption of food is now measured on a unit-interval scale of nutrition. From a nominal distinction of occupations as non-manual or manual, a qualitative-ordinal distinction of high, middle, or low grade occupations (non-manual and/or manual) has been in use for several decades; and from a qualitative-numeral series of occupations for the measurement of social mobility as an attribute of living conditions (e.g., Glass 1954), the possibility is examined for a unit-interval grading of occupations (e.g., Hope 1972; Ridge 1974; Goldthorpe and Hope 1974).

Similarly, the consumption of the products of material culture are now placed on an ordinal-numeral scale; such as, the latest to the more and more antiquated styles of dress, household furniture and fittings and house types. Beyond material culture, the cultural services and amenities like education, leisure, etc., are measured in the light of the nodal points of improvements in the form and content of the facilities to become cultured and use culture. These attempts have attained precision to that extent as to rate quantitatively the quality of hotels marked by 1 to 5 stars in the global context, and, in a similar manner, the universities in some nation-states are graded by the supreme educational authority.

Music, literature, paintings, etc., which are commonly regarded as *the* products of culture appreciable only qualitatively, are also seen to be measurable along the trend from quality to quantity. The common person will appreciate these manifestations of culture by drawing a nominal distinction of good or bad, but the knowledgeable persons will rate them as excellent, good, indifferent, bad, or very bad. A 5-point ordinal-numeral scale, with 'indifferent' denoting the zero point between 2 plus and 2 minus points, is thus used, knowingly or unknowingly.

The point is clearer in regard to the colour-schemes for dresses to wear, paint for the house, and such other cultural appreciation of objects, which is commonly considered as purely qualitative and highly individualistic. For example, even those who very specifically like the colour red for these objects are known to vary in their appreciation of red with an admixture of some other spectral colours in different proportions, e.g., so much of black, that much of yellow, etc. However, knowledge has accumulated to the extent of measuring the admixtures on a unit-interval scale and producing objects on a mass scale for consumption by individuals.

In sum, the trend from a purely qualitative nominal distinction to a quantitative ordinal-numeral distinction is in operation with respect to culture. And, there is no inherent constraint upon the trend reaching the state of full quantification of unit-interval distinction, provided the ever-accumulating knowledge can be systemized to the extent of how much interrelations among the culture elements and attributes. It is on this basis that a unit-interval scale is in use for the beauty contests in the light of somatometric and somatoscopic measurements.

The mode and the way of life, also, can be similarly measured as in the case of material and existential culture, because these labels are concerned additionally with what is broadly designated as the 'spiritual' culture. Therefore, with respect to all varieties of culture, the requirements for measuring the mode and the way of life are: (*a*) enumerating their mutually distinct but analogous (parallel) or homologous (common in origin) attributes, and (*b*) reducing these attributes systematically for a precise and comprehensive understanding of what the concepts imply.

This ongoing trend from quality to quantity, with reference to the all-inclusive notion of the quality of life, follows the basic tenet of science: divide and collect. It supports Lord Kelvin's remark: 'When you can measure what you are speaking about and express it in numbers, you know something about it, but when you cannot measure it, when you cannot express it in numbers, your knowledge is of a meagre and unsatisfacory kind' (quoted in Mahalanobis 1950: 7).

But there is a formidable objection from the holistic point of view to supporting this trend from quality to quantity; namely, the whole is not just the summation of its parts. Therefore, the assertion is that the integral whole cannot be appreciated by mere collection of its components, whether or not these are examined as qualitative and/or quantitative variables. On the contrary, the only way to appreciate the integral whole is synoptically, i.e., by affording a conspectus or general survey, and not analytically.

This viewpoint is endorsed by some scholars with particular reference to the quality of life research on the grounds that quality can be appreciated only as an integral whole. Therefore, they argue, the quantitative variables in general, and the variables quantified from the pristine state of quality in particular, project a false reality because the matrix of interrelations among the parts, which structures the integral whole, cannot be revealed comprehensively by means of analysis.

The argument, however, is falsified by the facts of common experience in everyday life. Any issue is appreciated evermore precisely and comprehensively by a systematic enumeration (division) of its properties and their *systemic* integration (collection) in the light of accumulating knowledge on interrelations among them. Of course, knowledge forms an asymptotic relation with reality which is never realized fully and finally except at the state of *nirvana*, a Buddhist beatitude. But, at that state, knowledge becomes meaningless with the extinction of individuality—the Ego.

Against this limiting condition to the accumulation of knowledge, science endeavours to reduce the gap between reality and its understanding, and it is empirically seen to attain success. For example, the sample of blood taken from the vein of a person does no longer belong to that integral whole—the Ego, but the chemistry of that sample of blood approximates reality to the extent of diagnosing the viability of that integral whole. Many such examples attest to the fact that the trend from quality to quantity is not only a feasible but also a necessary proposition for a precise and comprehensive appraisal of reality, particularly in the context of the quality of life research.

Therefore, while hasty and uncritical quantification of qualitative data would do more harm than no quantification at all, a point endorsed by the rigorous quantifiers themselves (e.g., McGranahan et al. 1985: 2–3), there is no reason to doubt the usefulness of pursuing the trend from quality to quantity. This potential of the quality of life research is obscured by the so-called holistic approach and constrained by the imposition of a quality—quantity dichotomy.

The same would be the outcome of a behavioural—perceptual and the corresponding objective—subjective dichotomy in the context of the quality of life research. The two related dichotomies emerge from an *absolute* concept of objectivity and subjectivity applied to the manifest and the latent actions of individuals: the manifest actions are interpreted as objective behaviour and the latent actions as subjective perception.

The manifest actions denote the behaviour of an individual by their repetition for expressing social meanings. In its turn, behaviour is a social characteristic because it exists by being reciprocated by other individuals: in consensus, for upholding society as a product and, in conflict, for changing society as a process. Either way, viability of manifest actions and, thus, of behaviour, depends on their operation beyond Ego. Therefore, behaviour is considered as totally objective.

The latent actions, on the other hand, denote the perception of an individual, because, in accordance with the commonsense understanding, perception is 'action by which the mind refers its sensations to external objects as cause' (*The Oxford Concise Dictionary*). But, for an individual, the latent actions need not be repetitive, nor does their viability depend on reciprocation by other individuals. Therefore, perception is regarded as totally subjective.

Apparently, therfore, behaviour and perception are dichotomous on the basis of objective—subjective dichotomy of the manifest and the latent actions of individuals. But, to begin with, the two kinds of action refer to the Ego and are, therefore, subjective. Behaviour is treated as objective because of commonality of manifest actions in view of the social meanings attached to them in repetition and reciprocation. However, the commonality of manifest actions does not embrace all individuals in society. If and when it does, behaviour loses its significance for research; it becomes a constant like the mere presence of humans themselves—all humans eat, sleep, and excrete. Appositely, it is the differential behaviour of the subjects of enquiry, i.e., different commonalities of behaviour in respect of the objects of enquiry, which makes behaviour objective and an issue for research.

On the other hand, perception may not be repetitive and reciprocal, but if its occurrence were indiscriminate with respect to each and all individuals, then perception would forfeit its empirical relevance to observation and deduction. In that event, by merely chartering a random space, perception would not be amenable to analysis and comprehension. However, because perception does not vary in a random manner, it is structured into perceptual variables for denoting commonality among individuals in a small or large measure.

Thus, the issue is the commonality of the manifest and the latent actions, and not the absolute concept of behaviour being objective and perception being subjective. This means that the similarity and the difference between behaviour and perception should be assessed by the *state of objectivity from subjectivity*, as indicated by the extent and the depth of commonality of the manifest and the latent actions. Therefore, the point in the context of the quality of life research is of the theoretical validity of the state of objectivity of behaviour and perception from subjectivity, and the practical relevance to the course of research of the *relative* state of objectivity of behaviour and perception.

As for validity, the all-inclusive notion of the quality of life is formed by the blending of behaviour and perception. For example, the concept of poverty, an important concern for the appraisal of the quality of life, is translated into 'objective', behavioural, and quantitative variables of per capita income, expenditure, consumption of material goods and services, etc. These measure variables are uniformly applicable to all societies because non-monetized society has virtually disappeared from the world. Yet, poverty has not been, and is not, perceived in the same manner in all configurations of world society—in the contexts of Johnson's and Nixon's USA, Indira Gandhi's India, Sajogyo's (1977) Philippines, and Manghahas's (1983) Southeast Asia and the Pacific. The variations are not just person-oriented, or concerned with the standard of living alone. Pointedly, the variations introduce perceptual variables of the style of living, the mode and the way of life, etc.

These variations indicate that commonality (= objectivity) of poverty may be established at the world level by the behavioural variables, but that will present an incomplete picture of poverty by leaving out variable perceptions of the 'thing'. At the same time, the variations indicate that the perception of poverty is not at random in the world-scale. Its commonality (= objectivity) is attested to or suggested, at any rate, by the cultural distinctions epitomized by various configurations of the world society. Thus, the behavioural objectivity of poverty at the state of universality is blended with the perceptual objectivity of poverty at the state of particularities, but not with singular subjective perceptions of individuals.

The example illustrates that the notion of quality of life rests upon what one has selectively inherited from the past, which is internalized as culture, and what one encounters externally in view of the contemporaneous social forces. The point is endorsed by contemporary definition of culture, which does not revise Tylor's classic definition but underlines perception along with the usual practice of interpreting culture by the behavioural variables of culture products—culture presents 'an aggregate of values and traditions which is deeply linked to the everyday life of the people, and in that sense, it is a matrix of perception which allows one to apprehend the world' (International Centre for Development 1979).

Thus, culture and society determine the quality of life of an individual and establish commonality among individuals by group formation. The groups enlarge by commonality of behaviour and/or perception, as apposite cultural and contemporaneous social forces cut across the existing place, time, and people dimensions of variation in human society and register the state of objectivity from subjectivity in ever-greater extent and depth. However, the underlying point is that the state of objectivity of perception and behaviour may or may not be on par.

For example, the desire for world peace is perceived universally today, but the corresponding behaviour is not worldwide, that is, perception is at a higher state of objectivity than behaviour. Alternatively, the perception of one world may not yet be universal, although it has been advocated for a long time, but, behaviourally, the world societies are coming closer and closer; that is, behaviour is at a higher state of objectivity than perception. On the other hand, the perception and behaviour may attain the same and a formidable state of objectivity, as in the case of the contemporary Black Movement in South Africa, the upheaval against the Raj in the Indian subcontinent after the Second World War, etc. In such events, there is no doubt that perception is as objective as behaviour.

This point of perception and behaviour is readily accepted in every-day life. For example, the colour red is not *invariably* seen as red: one in thousand(s) of individuals (say), will see it as green because of their being diagnosed as 'colour blind'. Even so, in any society, the state of objectivity (commonality) in perceiving red as red is so high that it can be unquestionably associated with the state of objectivity (commonality) in urban behaviour in order to stop people from crossing the street when the traffic signal is red and not green. Similar is the perception and behaviour with respect to touching fire.

In sum, the theoretical validity of the state of objectivity from subjectivity is not a matter for doubt in the case of both perception and behaviour. On the contrary, the quality of life research would forfeit its validity in case the Ego-distinction in perception and be-haviour, purely subjective at that state, would form a random space for the individuals. The random space would posit the *null* point of absolute subjectivity, at which all individuals would theoretically vary in their perception and behaviour. This means that if the *null* point is held in reality, any course of empirical research becomes useless. Therefore, the validity of the quality of life research is established by the transcendence of subjectivity in the perception and behaviour of all individuals.

The theoretical validity of the state of objectivity of perception and behaviour is noticeably relevant to the operation of the quality of life research in the context of the non-dichotomous, complementary, and the *relative* state of objectivity of the latent and the manifest actions. The course of research is concerned with a 'better' quality of life which, first, cannot be perceived without perceiving the contempor-aneous quality as bad or not good enough and which therefore should be improved in the future. The two evaluations of the quality of life, contemporaneous and in the future, are thus matters of perception at two time-points of the immanent reality and its appraisal as good or bad, desirable or undesirable, needed or to be discarded, wanted to have or to be removed. At the same time, a better quality of life implies manifest actions and their resultants. Therefore, in addition to two sets of perceptual variations in quality and quantity of what the quality of life *is* and *should be*, the quality of life research is concerned with the behavioural variables for establishing the better quality of life.

Thus, the quality of life research pursues the axis of perception—behaviour—perception syndrome of individuals, which registers complementarity of the two kinds of manifest and latent actions. At the same time, perception and behaviour do not operate in an insular and dichotomous manner because the relative state of objectivity of perception and behaviour forms the base for the quality of life research. As illustrated, a better quality of life is attained when both perception and behaviour are at a high and formidable state of objectivity, and one does not lag behind the other.

The syndrome of perception—behaviour—perception and the relative state of objectivity of perception and behaviour can be precisely and comprehensively examined because both perception and behaviour refer to 'external objects', the material and the mental attributes of life products and processes—which exist objectively. In other words, the quality of life research is not concerned with what is stated as the metaphysical reality and which is propagated by the idealist philosophers, the fundamentalists, the transcendentalists, etc., by subscribing to the doctrine that knowledge is subjective and therefore there is no external or objective test of truth.

On the other hand, while being concerned with the social reality (i.e., the physical reality viewed in the context of society and culture), the quality of life research cannot subscribe to objectivism, i.e., the doctrine which proclaims knowledge as superior to Ego. The course of research is concerned with the perception—behaviour—perception syndrome and is thus structured on the meanings attributed by individuals to society and culture in respect of one's own quality of life and of those beyond Ego. Therefore, knowledge in the context of the quality of life research is Ego-based.

In its turn, the Ego-based knowledge of society and culture cannot be devoid of apriori knowledge which would be consolidated into theories, however crude or fine and personalized or generalized the theories may be with respect to one or another individual. Therefore, while being concerned with empirical investigations into matter and mind on the basis of observation and experiment, the quality of life research cannot also subscribe to empiricism, i.e., observation and experiment devoid of theory.

Now, in the light of the foregoing explanations, the frame of reference to the quality of life research may be outlined as:

1. By conceiving it as an all-inclusive notion, the quality of life is to be treated as a 'phenomenon' which, by its commonly accepted meaning, stands for something of which the constitution and the cause are knowable and partly known but not yet completely.

2. The quality of life should therefore be viewed with reference to a field of infinite but enumerable 'things' which constitute the subject and the object of enquiry: a thing defined as 'whatever is or may be an object of thought, including or opposed to person' (*The Oxford Concise Dictionary*).

3. The quality of life research is not concerned with subjectivism, defined as without external or objective test of truth, because the 'things' constituting the phenomenon of quality of life, and therefore the phenomenon itself, would refer to the material and the mental attributes of life products and processes, and not to the metaphysical reality.

4. The quality of life research does not subscribe to objectivism, defined as knowledge superior to Ego, because it is concerned with the appraisal of social reality for attaining a better quality of life and, therefore, explores the perception—behaviour—perception syndrome of individuals.

5. The quality of life research will also not subscribe to empiricism, defined as observations and experiments devoid of theory, but will be concerned with the empirically understandable reality, because the perception—behaviour—perception syndrome of individuals involves their prior knowledge consolidated in various ways and built into personalized or generalized theories.

6. The quality of life research acquires validity by (*a*) removing the false dichotomy of perception being subjective and behaviour being objective, and (*b*) treating both in accordance with the state of objectivity (commonality) attained from absolute subjectivity of Ego-wise perception and behaviour chartering a random space in theory.

7. The quality of life research becomes relevant to sciencing by ascertaining the relative state of objectivity of perception and

behaviour for achieving a better quality of life, namely, whether perception is at a lower or higher state of objectivity than behaviour, or both are equally insignificant or formidable.

8. The quality of life research is necessary to elicit the objectivity (commonality) of aspirations, expectations, and achievements of individuals to attain a better quality of life than contemporaneously, in terms of apposite perceptual and behavioural variables employed as the object of enquiry to the initially identified groups of individuals as the subject of enquiry, and recasting the individuals into analytically evolved groups according to the valuations of the quality of life they register from the analysis of the perceptual and behavioural variables.

9. The quality of life research will be even more efficient if, in place of treating quality and quantity and subjectivity and objectivity in binary opposition, the ever-accumulating knowledge on the two trends from quality to quantity and from subjectivity to objectivity are captured by the perceptual and behavioural variables representing the properties of the 'things' constituting the phenomenon of quality of life.

The aim of this study is to develop the outlined frame of reference, which charters the task of ascertaining the state of objectivity (commonality) in the perception—behaviour—perception syndrome of individuals attaining a better quality of life. The submission is that by conforming to this frame of reference, the quality of life research should be able to unfold the all-inclusive notion of the phenomenon more and more comprehensively and reveal the path toward a better quality of life more precisely.

TERMS OF REFERENCE

While the frame of reference to the quality of life research does not entertain a conceptual dichotomy in quantity and quality, behaviour and perception, and objective and subjective manifestations of life and the life processes, these dichotomies are found employed for the quality of life research. Restrictive and fallacious as they are, these dichotomies point to the reflective minds of the researchers and thus suggest the terms of reference to the quality of life research.

Economists and planners, as mentioned, are almost exclusively concerned with behavioural research on the basis of quantitative variables in order to perceive reality 'objectively' to improve the quality of life of the people. In that context, they ignore qualitative variations in the appraisal of a better quality of life or treat these variations as introducing a classificatory (and not a measurable) distinction in the field of enquiry. They also equate the individual-wise subjective perception of reality to a group-wise 'objective' perception by experts. Their appraisal of social reality in this manner leads them to formulate what the people *need* in order to improve their quality of life. The approach may be narrowed down to the basic needs of the people anywhere or it may enumerate in detail the needs of the people in a nation-state or in the global context.

This manner of conducting the quality of life research treats the *level of comprehension* as fairly constant, because of the assumed objectivity and unanimity of 'experts' on what the people need. The *level of analysis* is also held constant by conceiving the needs of predetermined social groups, i.e., of groups already identified and not evolved from analysis, such as, a community of individuals within a nation-state or across several nation-states, or, all the citizens of a nation-state. Variations are, therefore, at the *level of reduction of data*, with reference to the experts' variable assertion of efficiency of one or another statistical technique for reducing the need data, and at the *level of enumeration of data* in consideration of what the people need—concisely, primarily, or exhaustively—in a nation-state or in the global context.

The concept of basic human needs seems to fulfil all the above conditions. While the field of enquiry is for behavioural research on an 'objective' perception of social reality by attending to appropriate sets of quantitative variables, the needs of the people are believed to be comprehended by the 'experts', precisely and comprehensively, under the headings of food, clothing, housing, health, education, leisure, security, etc. The experts may differ on the enumeration of need items under these levels, and on the manner of statistical reduction of need data. However, at the levels of analysis and comprehension, they are united on what the people need basically. But fallacies emerge because, first, the qualitative variables at the levels of data enumeration and reduction are ignored and, second, the non-expert perception of basic needs at the levels of analysis and comprehension.

All the need items, basic or otherwise, are culture bound. Even in the case of food, any standardized quantitative measure of nutrition cannot override the determining role of culture-specific food intake, which is no less marked in the USA, USSR, France, and China than in Japan, India, Iran, and Nigeria, for example. The input of culture for the formulation of the basic needs of the people is perhaps more pronounced with respect to clothing, housing, health, education, leisure, security, etc., as suggested by the 'poverty studies'. This variability in quality, registered within and across different configurations of human society, cannot be ignored at the levels of enumeration and reduction of need data.

It is also seen that the gamut of qualitative variations allot differential priorities to even those need items which are conceived by the experts as basic. The point would be ignored at the peril of jeopardizing the usefulness of the concept of basic human needs. Therefore, the 'experts' have come to realize that neither can the qualitative variables be ignored nor can the individual-wise subjective perception of the basic needs be neglected (Cole and Lucas 1979: 43):

·The unequivocal answer is that the people themselves should decide on the scope, content and priority of their own basic needs (Ghai, D.; Alfthan, T., 'Methodology of basic needs', ILO Working Paper, Geneva, 1977)

A basic needs strategy includes mass participation of the people, both in defining basic needs and in the decisions taken to meet basic needs (Hopkins, M. J. D., 'Basic needs approach to development planning', ILO Working Paper, Geneva, 1977)

There must be a mechanism introduced into the planning process through which representatives of organized groups choose basic needs (ILO Meeting. *Basic Needs: Strategies for Eradicating Rural Poverty and Unemployment*. Geneva, ILO, 1977).

Thus, the concept of basic human needs fails to limit the scope of appraisal of social reality for a better quality of life to 'objective' behavioural research on the basis of quantitative variables only. It also does not hold the levels of analysis and comprehension of a better quality of life constant in the light of assumed objectivity and unanimity of the experts. The 'mass participation of the people' for perceiving their basic needs and acting for their realization, along with the perception and action roles of the experts who represent the elites of society, introduces variability at all the four levels of data enumeration and reduction, and analysis and comprehension, of the qualitative and quantitative, behavioural and perceptual, and the 'objective' and 'subjective' variables.

Even so, there are attempts to design the quality of life research on the 'objective' behavioural base and with reference to quantitative variables only, by pointing out that (*a*) a blending of quality and quantity is an 'impossible' task, and (*b*) the course of research can be so organized that the quantitative behavioural variables may 'not cover all human needs, but it does cover the most essential of them.' One of the most articulated attempts of this kind explains the standpoint by the following arguments (Drewnowski 1974: 34–38):

1. [A social phenomenon is] a product of conceptual organization of separate facts [because] social phenomenon studied by social scientists are mainly complexes of correlated facts and can be expected as a rule to have more than one measurable aspect.
2. As long as no quantification is attempted, that aggregation is mainly an intuitive operation and no clear-cut rules for its performance can be established.
3. [However], the aggregation procedure must be performed *for each aspect separately* (keeping in mind that the integration of aspects is impossible).
4. The concept of 'measurable welfare' which is being introduced here is supposed to provide a quantitative expression for the level of satisfaction of human needs which would be free from the difficulties connected with the application of the concept of 'social utility' in welfare economics.
5. Its independent variables are limited in number and their selection is based on *an agreement of experts about what are the essential components of human needs* [emphasis added]. Then those variables are expressed in terms of *specially selected measurable indicators* [emphasis added].
6. Such a 'measurable welfare' function evidently does not cover all human needs, but it does cover the most essential of them.

Drewnowski's insistence on purely quantitative research, because 'the integration of aspects is impossible', characterizes reality as of known and *unknown* (= impossibility of knowing) properties, in place of known and *knowable* properties. The procedure seems to uphold the pristine purity of objective research but, in fact, allows for meta-physical speculations on the 'unknown' as 'God playing dice' (Einstein, quoted in Born 1956: 90). In any case, the neglect of knowable properties of reality, which are qualitative and subjective to begin with, keeps covered the scope of the quality of life research.

Significantly, Drewnowski also begins with a subjective and selective perception of human needs, but sanctifies its objectivity by 'an agreement of experts'. Thus emerging from his own and expert-wise subjective perception of human needs, his declaration of covering 'the most essential' of 'all human needs' becomes just a bold assertion. In sum, Drewnowski's meticulous attempt is not free from the fallacy noted in the context of the experts' exploration of basic human needs.

The point of blending quality and quantity, combining behaviour and perception, and increasing objectivity of quality of life research has been noted or implied by some powerful advocates of human needs (e.g., Galtung and Wirak 1977; Miles 1986). But the mainstream economists and planners remain concerned with a quantitative, behavioural, and the so-called objective appraisal of social reality in order to define the needs of the people for a better quality of life. Even so, this line of quality of life research should not be ignored for two main reasons.

First, the experts may differ among themselves in defining and projecting the needs of the people, but they assume a group character in appraising social reality for a better quality of life. Thus, in analogous or homologous group formations, the experts register commonality in their evaluation of the quality of life, i.e., they denote nodal points on the axis of subjectivity to objectivity for the exploration of life quality. Therefore, although the need-based quality of life research is not objective per se, and is partial in content as a result of excluding the qualitative variables and neglecting the non-expert perceptions, this line of enquiry embodies a distinctive perspective for the appraisal of a better quality of life.

Second, this perspective is directly enforced by the elites in a nation-state or in the global context. They view the concerned social space from the top, as it were, and wish to learn what the people need in order to attain a better quality of life. Therefore, they induce, or make use of, the experts to provide the necessary knowledge: obviously, the experts do not operate in a social vacuum. Thus, the elitist concern with the need-based research provides it with a distinctive significance toward formulating a comprehensive course of quality of life research.

There are other expert-elite attempts to appraise the quality of life, which appear to be different from the conventional need-based research but, in essence, carry on the same line of research. For example, the attempt of Gillingham and Reece (1980) to resolve the 'Analytical problems in the measuring of the quality of life' in the light of 'utility maximisation', suffers from the same fallacy and inadequacy as pointed out in the context of Drewnowski's (1974) monograph.

Some of these attempts may also be inconsequential because the proposed quality of life (QOL) indicator may not indicate characteristics beyond those that its constituents express directly; that is, it serves as an index of its inherent properties but fails to *indicate* properties beyond its construction. A case in point is employing per capita GNP to denote the quality of life, which seemingly registers the crucial need of the people as denoted by its construction, i.e., an individual has, on an average, so much spending power in society.

As a QOL indicator, GNP per capita should indicate that the large majority of individuals in the society are in a position to spend the presumed power in order to meet their wants. But in the light of acute inequality in the distribution of GNP in many nation-states, per capita GNP may conceal the fact that the spending power of the masses is usurped by a tiny minority. Because of this built-in limitation, among others, per capita GNP is an inconsequential indicator of the quality of life. Even so, Inkeles and Diamond (1980: 75) would employ it while admitting that the measure is 'inadequate, debatable, troublesome, static, and confining.'

Another attempt in this vein is of some consequence to indicate the quality of life, but inadequately. A case in point is the concept of Physical Quality of Life (PQL). The concept was mooted in the USA in the context of the *World Development Agenda* to indicate the state of well-being of nation-states by a set of indices (PQLI) like the literacy rate, infant mortality, and life expectancy at birth (Morris 1977: 147–54). The indicator PQLI may serve as a rough and ready reckoner to a donor country like the USA in the context of providing aid selectively to Third World countries. But any claim that it may systematically and comprehensively indicate the quality of life would be hazardous.

PQLI has been imputed to reflect merely the indicative potential of per capita GNP (Mukherjee et al. 1979), but the findings are disputed or contexted (Vidwans 1985; De 1984). However, the point is that PQLI may register a correlation of some *most minimal* needs of the people, which have an overt manifestation in the indices chosen. For this reason PQLI may equate with per capita GNP of those countries where the latter index possibly operates as a more or less valid (but not an efficient) indicator, because of less pronounced inequality in GNP distribution. However, besides its dubious meaning, the limited scope of researches into the Physical Quality of Life of the people is admitted by the sponsor of the concept (Morris 1977: 147):

The PQLI does not attempt to measure the many other social and psychological characteristics suggested by the term 'quality of life'—justice, political freedom, or a sense of participation. It is based on the assumption that the needs and desires of individuals initially and at the most basic level are for larger life expectancy, reduced illness, and greater opportunity. The index does not measure the amount or the type of effort put into achieving these goals, but the extent to which they are being met—that is, it measures *results*.

A more comprehensive attempt in the field of need-based quality of life research than even the conventional kind discussed with reference to basic human needs and Drewnowski's endeavour to include all varieties of need, is of constructing a hierarchy of needs to meet the wants of the people successively and systematically. There is sound logic behind the formulation that: (*a*) after the 'right to work' for survival, one may assert the 'right to choose occupation'; (*b*) after attaining security 'against attack, war', one may demand the 'right to travel and be travelled to'; and (*c*) after the realization of noticeable prosperity in the form of 'well-being, happiness, joy', one may aspire for progress in the form of expressing one's 'potentials syn- and diachronically' (Galtung and Wirak 1977: 22–23). But illustratively useful as the formulation is, it cannot be translated into a design of research within the confines of 'human needs' felt by the experts themselves.

On the contrary, the formulation indicates the necessity of correlating the elites' concept of need with the masses' concept of want. The relationship cannot be established by a purely conceptual construct, however skilfully designed. It would posit an alternative appraisal of the need-based quality of life, among others (e.g., Miles 1986). This point and the perspectives of need and want are implicit to an interesting discussion on the concept of well-being (Sen 1986).

However, the gap between any formulation of needs and the reality has been noted in the context of Maslow's (1971) intensive efforts to meet the gap (Michalos 1974: 125):

> The existence of a great gap between Maslow-type needs and specific items of actions in the world is one reason why the attempt to develop indicators from needs does not seem worthwhile . . . Indeed, contrary to those who think we might be able to construct a theory of value based on needs. I am sure that the logic of the

situation is just the reverse. Values are *prior* to needs and required for their definition. To see that this is so, consider what one means to say about something when one says that it is needed. At the very least it is assumed that if someone needs something, that person would suffer from some form of *deterioration* in its absence.

Michalos' argument against the need-based quality of life research focuses on a complementary aspect of reality. It refers to what the people want, in conformity with or in contradistinction to the assumed positive focus on what the people need. A want-based quality of life research has thus emerged, mainly advocated by the psychologists as mentioned before.

The want-based quality of life research questions the adequacy of the need-based research and, therefore, deals with the perception of the masses for a better quality of life, i.e., their aspirations, expectations, and achievement orientation in that context. Qualitative variables are taken into account along with the quantitative variables, although quality may be stressed more than quantity. Also, action in the perception—behaviour—perception syndrome of individuals is mostly implied by the presence or absence of their achievement orientation, in place of examining their actual behaviour in the context. However, in search of commonality in the perception of individuals, the course of research attends to the trend from subjectivity to objectivity.

The level of comprehension of a better quality of life includes diverse possibilities from the side of the people: they may perceive a better quality of life in material or spiritual gains, in the organization of a harmonious social existence, or in rousing the social consciousness of the milieu. The level of analysis may refer to the predetermined groups of individuals, for which the want data are collected as for the need data, or to the groups evolved in the light of commonality of wants of the people. The levels of data enumeration and reduction would of course vary as in the case of need-based research.

Thus, theoretically, the want-based quality of life research is unconstrained by the elitist perspective, unlike in the case of the need-based research. Also, it claims to comprehend the all-inclusive notion of the quality of life in a systematic and perhaps better manner than the need-based research:

I am not arguing that needs are unimportant or that they should be ignored. I am merely arguing that those who think that they can reduce information overload in social reports by excluding wants with all their troublesome evaluations, will find exactly the same sort of troublesome evaluations in the area of needs (Michalos 1974: 125).

The controversy on human needs and wants has underlined the fact that although needs and wants are but two sides of the same coin, the manner in which they are posited expresses two complementary aspects of the quality of life research:

1. The experts on formulating the needs of the people have the privilege of a systematic consolidation of knowledge by means of education and academic assignment. The elites, who are advised by these experts, hold power over society. Therefore, the need-based quality of life research amounts to what the elites conceive as the needs of the people and *induce* change in society in order to meet the needs and thus improve the quality of life of the masses.
2. The masses are not privileged to have a systematic consolidation of knowledge by means of requisite education and assignment, but realities provide them with the panorama of knowledge. They do not also hold power over society, but their power is felt immanently. Because of this latency in knowledge and power, the masses accept from the elites what they wish to, and also act on their own, in order to *infuse* change in society to improve their quality of life. Therefore, the want-based quality of life research is concerned with eliciting what the people want and how they realize their wants.

Thus, in the context of a better quality of life, the elites behave as change *promoters* and the masses as change *recipients* and *actors*. They may thus register two distinctive ways of evaluating social reality for a better quality of life: the change promoters viewing society from the top, as it were, and the change recipient-actors concerned with the society from the bottom, as it were. Therefore, while all individuals in a society may vary with reference to the perception—behaviour—perception syndrome of the quality of life, a distinction of the syndrome from the sides of the elites and the masses, respectively, would be usefully introduced into the course of research.

The elite-mass distinction has a crucial bearing on the quality of life research because, isolatedly, neither the elites nor the masses can be effective in attaining their common objective of a better quality of life, while the distinction is a reality in all societies. The masses may be action-oriented but may not meet their wants because the exogenous forces have a determining role. On the other side, the exogenous forces, emerging from the seats of power (one of which may define the Establishment), have a determining role for the fulfilment of the needs of the masses, but not a decisive one. It may appear to be decisive when an established power assumes a dictatorial stance but, as history testifies, it cannot be durable.

Contrariwise, the joint performance of the wills of the elites as change promoters and of the masses as change recipients and actors cannot but induce and infuse change in the social processes and yield a better quality of life. This is noticeable all the time and is clearly revealed at the time of a cataclysmic change, e.g., a revolution, which denotes that the will of the majority of the masses has coincided with the will of a formidable section of the elites.

The populist minded scholars may find an 'elitist' bias in this approach but, in fact, the bias is on their side. These scholars may justifiably quote the eleventh thesis of Marx on Feuerbach in the context of a revolutionary change in society: 'The philosophers have only *interpreted* the world differently, the point is, to *change* it.' However, for changing the world, it is essential to bear in mind the third thesis of Marx on Feuerbach: 'The coincidence of the changing of circumstances and of human activity or self-changing can only be comprehended and rationally understood as *revolutionary practice*' (Marx 1942: 198–99).

In any case, whether a scholar is Marxist, non-Marxist, or anti-Marxist in ideology, the practice of the quality of life research would be facilitated by designing it under two complementary terms of reference to the elites and the masses. This means developing the need-based and the want-based research as mutually distinct but inter-related components of the complex whole, the quality of life.

DEVIATIONS

The history of the quality of life research shows that its two terms of reference to the elites and the masses have not been treated in a systematic or unconstrained manner from the level of data enumeration to the level of comprehension of a better quality of life. The elites' viewpoint of needs of the people has either become the monopoly of the power *in situ* or the experts have been given a free play to enumerate the needs, but the need-based research has been designed and the results comprehended in the light of the valuation of the Establishment of what the people need in order to attain a better quality of life. The viewpoint of the masses regarding what they want for a better quality of life has been treated as auxiliary to what the power-wielding elites have decided about what they need.

Thus, a unilaterally imposed value preference of the power-wielding elites has put a constraint upon variable appraisals by all elites of what the people need for a better quality of life. In that context, an omnibus and indiscriminate collation of need data have become fruitless and virtually meaningless. On the other side, the subservience of want-based research to the official elites' version of the need-based research has put restrictions on the enumeration of want data and, sequentially, on the levels of data reduction, analysis, and comprehension of the want-based research. As a result, variability in the appraisal of a better quality of life by the masses has been confined.

The false distinction of the need-based research being objective (as dealing with quantitative behavioural variables) and the want-based research being subjective (as dealing with qualitative perceptual variables) has come in aid of these deviations from a systematic and comprehensive treatment of the two terms of reference to the quality of life research. It has also put constraints upon the level of analysis of the want-based research, in so far as analytically evolving groups of individuals by their state of objectivity (commonality) in perceiving what they want, in place of remaining restricted to the predetermined groups as the subjects of enquiry.

These deviations are largely due to policy implications of the quality of life research, although they may appear as the results of the experts' endeavour to make the course of research value-free, value-accommodating, or precisely distinguished by objective and subjective valuations. However, the policy implications in the context of the quality of life research should be distinguished from the perennial human concern with the appraisal of social reality to achieve an ever-better quality of life.

History testifies to the fact that humankind has always observed and experimented with itself for (*i*) the survival of the species, (*ii*) security in the life span of individuals, (*iii*) material prosperity for well-being, and (*iv*) mental progress to unfold the potentials of individuals. Failure in the process of realizing these four *cardinal* valuations for the human species has led to the disappearance of some societies from the world scene. Some other societies have revised their structure and function in accordance with the process, while retaining their identities. Also, new societies have appeared on the social scene.

However, the policies evolved in the context of this perennial human concern refer to an endemic *search* in society for a better quality of life, and not to an organized, purposeful, and institutional undertaking as the quality of life *research*. This has emerged as a social necessity at a particular point in human history, namely, after World War II, when the realities of life and living became less obscure to the masses than ever before, and the elites' continual efforts for a systematic consolidation of knowledge on society, people, and their culture reached a critical phase of accumulation.

World War II brought the world societies nearer one another, and investigations into the life of the people, within and beyond one's own society, gathered an unprecedented momentum from the 1950s. The 1960s witnessed an information explosion on the societies, the people, and their culture. The items of social information could no longer be assimilated separately, nor could they be effectively summarized by the construction of indices out of two or few more items at a time. The indices had also become numerous. Therefore, the social scientists became concerned about the formulation of *master indices* which would denote the findings of a set of correlated indices.

The concept of social indicators was mooted to present these master indices. They will indicate properties beyond their own constituted findings, as explained in the context of employing per capita GNP as a social indicator or a quality of life indicator. But, purely on technical ground, so many indicators could thus be prepared that they would form a mass of what has been labelled 'good statistics'. Therefore, the problem emerged of 'so much information that much of it becomes not only useless but self-defeating' (Michalos 1974: 114). Evidently, the resolution of the issue is not in the methodology of *how* the social indicators can be formulated more and more efficiently, but in the conceptualization of *why* they should be formulated.

The issue is germane to the fact that human society exists and changes as an organic entity, and so does a configuration of the world society. Therefore, as the space of social information is explored more and more extensively and deeply, sets of correlated indices are revealed in rapidly increasing number. This means that the master indices or the social indicators also accumulate on a massive scale and, correspondingly, their usefulness in encapsulating information diminishes (as of the previously useful indices) unless they are purposefully selected out of all their possible formulations on valid, relevant, and necessary ground.

Basically, the ground is understanding social reality for the appraisal of a better quality of life of the people. Both understanding and appraisal are variable proposals for the elites and the masses. Of the masses, the variations are conceded up to an extent. But, from the beginning of the social indicators research, which in fact presented the need-based quality of life research, the ground has been unilaterally value-loaded by the perception—behaviour—perception syndrome of the power-wielding elites in society. The project of social indicators research was first launched in the USA, and Sheldon and Moore (1968: 4) identified the sponsoring and the conducting groups as comprising 'those who have undertaken responsibility for bringing about publicly approved changes.'

The qualification 'publicly approved changes' is democratic enough to suggest that the value-load of the social indicators research is uniform for the knowledgeable elites at any rate; but the suggestion is of dubious worth. In any configuration of human society there are elite groups which do not hold power and do not approve of the value premises of the elite group in the Establishment, but are willing to undertake the responsibility for changing society. These groups are located in the 'Opposition' bench of many nation-states and in all nation-states they constitute the heretic bodies proclaiming the fundamental or extremely radical views. Naturally, therefore, controversies soon emerged in the USA regarding the definition of social indicators and its utility (Land 1978: 13–14).

In course of time, sharp comments were made against the government-sponsored social indicators research. For example, with reference to *Science Indicators 1976*, it was stated that:

SI/76 is not a good model of science. More properly, the model that it provides is inadequate in respects that are crucial both to a scholarly understanding of science and to its wise management. . . . Some of these shortcomings, as I judge them to be, may be ironic results of the fact that SI/76 and its predecessors are political documents (McGinnis 1979: 171).

Miller (1974: 56) had suggested broadening the value base of social indicators research and had proposed that: 'Government efforts with social indicators and analyses should be offset by parallel efforts outside government which criticize official efforts and prevent the monopolization of knowledge.' Concretely, he proposed that 'It would be wise to encourage counter-indicators and counter-analyses.' But the US Government upheld its monopoly and pursued the definition of social indicator as a 'statistic of *direct normative interest* [emphasis added] which facilitates concise, comprehensive and balanced judgements about the conditions of major aspects of a society' (United States Department of Health, Education, and Welfare 1969: 97).

The assumed 'normative interest' has been argued to accommodate the elites' differential appraisal of social reality for a better quality of life under the following premises:

1. A careful reading of the definitions leads one to the following generic definition: social indicators are statistics which measure social conditions and change therein over time for various segments of a population.
2. Its generality derives from the fact that it allows almost any index of social activity (social statistics) to be classified as a social indicator provided that index can be constructed as reflecting a social condition of some population.
3. If one surveys the definitions, one finds very little consensus on the criteria which would be applied to sort out the social conditions that should be measured. They all indicate in one way or another that social indicators should index 'socially important' conditions, and that social importance must be assessed relative to the values, goals, and norms of the society.
4. [The] most general conception of social indicators requires only that they may be indices of social conditions. If, in addition, we add the external validity criterion that such indices must be arguments in a social welfare function, then we get those social indicators known as goal output indicators.
5. Certainly, it is not necessary that the two sets of social indicators be identical. Social scientists will be called upon to provide different indicators as components of the welfare function.
6. In this way, social scientists can serve an 'analysis' function in social indicators which is distinct from the 'design' or 'planning' function associated with social policy.
7. This distinction helps to clarify when 'normative' considerations

enter into social indicator activities. Clearly, the values of the social scientists are always present. Social indicators research can never be free from this influence of values, but its impact can be minimized by ensuring that a diversity of orientations are represented (Land 1978: 14–16, 21).

Land's arguments do not support value-free social indicators research. He is, thus, against the contention that the valuations of the needs of the people can be made uniform for all expert-elites, which has been the attempt of several scholars either conceptually (e.g., Seers 1972: 28) or methodologically (e.g., Hellwig 1974; Ivanovic 1974). Also, while his formulation of 'social conditions' is in line with Drewnowski's quantitative, behavioural, and objective investigation into the needs of the pople, Land, unlike Drewnowski, disclaims an agreement of experts'. Thus, he accepts the obvious truth that understanding reality by means of social indicators cannot avoid the issue of the variable value preferences of the elites in determining the needs of the people to attain a better quality of life.

In this respect, a shift is noticed from the 'publicly approved' approach, which is implied to keep the elites' valuation of the needs of the people uniform and thus make it operationally value-free, to a value-accommodation approach which takes into account 'the values of the social scientists' with reference to the 'normative considerations'. But, Land's arguments do not override the governing policy implications of social indicators research in 'design or planning function', with respect to which the social scientists are allotted an 'analysis function'. Evidently, the 'normative considerations' do not eliminate, and can hardly 'minimize', the control of the power-wielding elites on the social indicators research.

Therefore, although Land's arguments in support of the official policy seem to endorse Miller's proposal to take note of variable appraisals of the needs of the poeple, the two are very different. In place of merely 'ensuring that a diversity of orientations are represented', as Land has argued for, Miller's proposal for 'parallel efforts outside government' and for 'counter-indicators and counter-analysis' would have led to the formulation of different sets of indicators in accordance with different appraisals of social reality for a better quality of life. There would then be scope to examine the *relative* efficiency of respective sets of indicators and reject all but the most efficient set to induce the necessary changes in society.

By thus following the course of rejection of extraneous variations to the given context and thereby consolidating knowledge systematically, the social indicators research would have met the objective of sciencing; namely, ascertaining the validity, relevance, necessity, and efficiency of sets of indicators for a precise and comprehensive understanding of social reality and the corresponding appraisal of a better quality of life of the people. For this purpose, an accommodation of different valuations of social reality and the quality of life is a theoretical and methodological imperative to place them on the *null* base of no valuation at all, in order that the relative efficiency of all these valuations be duly tested. Shifting the *null* base to the positive base of the official elites' valuation of social reality and the quality of life jeopardizes this very purpose of value accommodation.

In that event, the non-governmental valuations merely float around the governmental valuations, and may be favoured by fragmentary and discriminatory inclusion in the pre-empted body of need data, provided the allotted 'analysis' function is conciliatory to the 'design or planning function associated with the social policy'. Therefore, in essence, the universe of elites' valuations of social reality and the quality of life for the need-based quality of life research would remain an omnibus and indiscriminate mass, and the shift from the value-free 'publicly approved' approach to the value-accommodation approach under 'normative considerations' would be capable of producing only a plethora of social indicators of dubious usefulness.

This, in fact, is what happened in practice, while in the 1970s, the social indicators research spread beyond the United States and many nation-states joined what was described as 'The Social Indicators Movement' (Duncan 1969: 1; von Dusen 1974). In all these nation-states the formulation of social indicators by the not-established power blocs was accepted, although not so many in number, form, and content as from the currently established power bloc. This is clearly noticed in the context of developmental planning (or policy for development without mentioning planning) in the Third World nation-states, and with respect to policy formulation in those nation-states which categorically subscribe to the ideology of a 'free market' (Rossi and Wright 1979: 3).

The result was not unexpected: the 1970s saw great enthusiasm for social indicators denoting the needs of the people and monitoring the supply of these needs for a better quality of their life; 1980 is the decade of dwindling expectations. The UNESCO, which wholeheartedly supported the social indicators research, also sounded a warning note:

With the wide interest expressed in social indicators growing into what has been called 'The Social Indicators Movement', there has been a great laxity in the use of the term to the extent that most of the social statistics which are usually collected for administrative purposes are being rebaptized 'social indicators' (Fanchette 1974: 8).

But, virtually no notice was taken of this sort of warning. On the contrary, the definition of social indicators was clearly delinked from the rationale for their construction and, therefore, the social indicators reverted to the *status quo ante* of being mere indices or 'good statistics'. A well-known definition of social indicators, largely accepted by the 'Social Indicators Movement', is that by Land:

> I propose that the term *social indicators* refer to social statistics that (1) are components in a social system model (including socio-psychological, economic, demographic, and ecological) or of some particular segment or process thereof, (2) can be collected and analyzed at various times and accumulated into a time-series, and (3) can be aggregated or disaggregated to levels appropriate to the specifications of the model (1971: 323).

Even the Soviet scholars, who are commonly regarded as acceptors of one particular valuation of social reality and are, therefore, assumed to disregard its variable appraisals, supported the *raisón d'etre* of the social indicators research for registering the efficiency of evaluating the needs of the people: 'The dynamic rows of social indicators must reflect the "actual march" of social processes' (Ossipov and Kolbanovsky 1974: 3). However, the unilateral value-load of the social indicators research from the side of the Establishment was held fast while reversing the role of social indicators to 'social statistics' serving as 'components in a social system model'.

The manoeuvre merely promoted the enumeration of the needs of the people by the elites appraising social reality in various ways, because the omnibus enumeration was of little consequence to the need-based quality of life (= the social indicators) research. This is evident from the fact that the 'specifications of the model', according to which the enumerated needs are 'aggregated or disaggregated', rest upon the issue of 'policy relevance' and lead to the formulation of 'predetermined variables' in the light of the power-wielding elites' appraisal of social reality for a better quality of life of the people. The point is underscored in a review of 'Social-indicator model building: A multiple-indicator design' (Warren et al. 1980: 277–78):

> The recent work of James G. Anderson (1972; 1973a; 1973b; 1974; 1976) is one of the best known applications of a social-system orientation in social-indicator modelling. The general background for Anderson's models seems to be largely drawn from the work of Gross (1966), Land (1968; 1975), Feldstein (1967), and Duncan (1966). Gross (1966) was one of the first in the field to suggest that social-indicator models should incorporate important social and economic variables needed for exploring the structure and performance of social systems. Land (1975) had developed a general framework for social-indicator modelling that is policy-relevant and social systems in orientation . . . . [Anderson's] model includes *predetermined* and *endogenous* variables. Exogenous variables and lagged variables are classified as different types of predetermined variables.

The upshot is that virtually any social statistic is now labelled an indicator and the production of social indicators continues *ad infinitum*, without testing their efficiency in an appropriate manner, as suggested by Miller for example. Critical scholars have therefore suggested a family planning of enumerated needs of the people. A. C. Michalos (1974: 107–31), the editor of the reputed journal, *Social Indicators Research* with the subtitle 'Quality-of-Life Measurement', pointed to this issue while proposing 'strategies for reducing information overload in social reports' and advocated the want-based quality of life research in place of the need-based research.

But the want-based research, which is conventionally known as the quality of life research, like the social indicator research representing the need-based research, did not have an unconstrained field of operation and comprehension. Its auxiliary status to the need-based research was accepted from the beginning, as Bharadwaj and Wilkening describe (1980: 337):

> The recognition that the economic health of a nation is not synonymous with individual satisfaction and well-being had led to the development of social indicators to assess individual quality of life. . . . The new emphasis is on the monitoring of change in goals, values, attitudes and satisfaction that affect individual lives and

nations. The overall thrust appears to be 'the development of a set of "dependent variables".'

As 'dependent variables', the want data are circumscribed in their enumeration by the 'independently' enumerated need data. Therefore, the subservience of the want-based research to the need-based research cannot but offset a full coverage of the appraisal by the masses of what they want for a better quality of life. The restriction also has a deleterious effect on the possibilities of the want-based quality of life research.

The imposed constraint at the level of enumeration of want data is naturally extended to the level of data reduction. The allotted task is merely to ascertain the nature and extent of agreement of the pre-determined groups of individuals, the subjects of enquiry, to the imposed 'independent' valuation of what they need. As a result, the want-based research is reduced to attitudinal studies of the imposed need-data items on a *n*-point scale of agreement and disagreement, and is made to 'function as pseudo-plebiscites' as Johansson (1973) caustically remarked.

Pursued in an auxiliary capacity to the need-based research, the want-based research also fails to realize its potentials at the level of analysis. As discussed, any course of social research begins with pre-determined groups of individuals at the levels of data collection and reduction. At the level of analysis, these groups are also the *units of analysis* for administrative and policy research because researches of this kind are concerned with monitoring the effects of an administrative measure or a policy applied to a group of people. Therefore, when the change promoters in the Establishment sponsor the quality of life research in order to further their policy measures, the components at the level of analysis of the want-based research are the groups of individuals identified at the level of data collection—the citizens of the United States (Young and Maccannell 1979) or of an African state (Oyebanji 1982), the inhabitants of a particular settlement (Tunstall 1979; Golant and McCutcheon 1980), the peoples of a set of ter-ritories (Sheer 1980), and so on.

These predetermined groups may be subdivided by classificatory attributes relevant to, and necessary for, administrative or policy research; ethnicity, occupation, income groupings, rural-urban dis-tinction, etc. But, since the needs of the people are valued uniformly and unilaterally by the Establishment, it is irrelevant and unnecessary for the course of want-based research to recast the individuals into analytically evolved groups by ascertaining commonality in their perceptions of the quality of life.

On the contrary, group formation by commonality of individual perceptions of the quality of life, which would cut across the predetermined groups for the want-based research, is relevant to different appraisals of the need-based quality of life research. In terms of different sets of needs or differential priorities allotted to the same set of needs, these appraisals define various valuations of a better quality of life, i.e., different value groupings. Correspondingly, the want-based quality of life research should reveal, at the level of analysis, which value groups are formed for a better quality of life by cutting across the subjects of enquiry, i.e., the predetermined groups. In this respect, the want-based quality of life research holds the potential of variable perceptions of individuals acquiring a classificatory role with reference to the subjects of enquiry, besides its determining role as objects of enquiry.

Group formation by self-assessment of the quality of life is also necessary to realize the inherent pontentials of want-based research. More precisely than with reference to the predetermined groups, these analytically evolved groups would denote the *units of analysis* to ascertain the causality and the processes to attain a better quality of life by the masses. The level of comprehension of the want-based quality of life research would then be enriched by ascertaining the state of objectivity (commonality) of the masses of the people in perceiving a better quality of life.

On the other side, once the want-based research is geared to an unilaterally value-loaded need-based research, the level of comprehension may not be concerned with any variability in want data. The constraint imposed at the level of data enumeration may thus logically constrain the levels of analysis and comprehension, and limit the level of data reduction to finding agreement or disagreement with the imposed value load. An extreme example in this respect is the standpoint of two researchers on the want-based quality of life (Markides and Martin 1979: 92):

> In our analysis . . . we avoided the examination of variables which themselves are measures of satisfaction with certain facets of life, since we believe that knowledge that persons who are satisfied with certain aspects of their life tend to be more satisfied with their life as a whole does not lead to better theory.

A holistic appraisal of social reality for a better quality of life is suggested by this approach. In practice, it advocates a synoptic valuation of the ordained appraisal of the quality of life against any analytic valuation of the want data, however circumscribed their field of enumeration might be because of the imposed value-load.

However, strong arguments have been put forward in support of analytic valuation for the want-based quality of life research, and against a synoptic valuation:

> From the point of view of explaining (global) satisfaction with life as a whole by analysis of its constituent elements (domain satisfaction with family relations, with finances, housing, etc.), there is no more direct route to 'better theory' . . . . If there is going to be any analysis of satisfaction with life as a whole, it must be in (other evaluative) terms of satisfaction with particular domains of life (Michalos 1982: 3).

Also, empirical investigations have substantiated the necessity of analyzing the want data. The ultimate evaluation of the quality of life is commonly regarded by the quality of life researchers as 'satisfaction with life' or happiness. Milbrath (1978: 36) stated: 'I have come to the conclusion that the only defensible definition of quality of life is a general feeling of happiness.' 'Satisfaction' and 'happiness', the two ultimate evaluations, are considered the same by some scholars while a relation is drawn between the two by some others (Michalos 1980). However, the ultimate evaluation is regarded by many scholars as a variable to be examined with reference to individuals' perceptions of a better quality of life at the level of comprehension of the want-based research.

These scholars, who also plan their enquiries with reference to 'satisfaction' as the ultimate evaluation of the quality of life, find it useful to distinguish between the levels of analysis and comprehension. For example, Andrews and McKennel (1980: 129) have pointed out that 'different question wordings (e.g., asking about 'happiness' versus 'satisfaction') would result in measures with different orientations.' Therefore, the concept of 'domain satisfaction' was mooted with reference to 'numerous specific life concerns' of the people (ibid.), and 'satisfaction' has been conceived as the terminal point of a course of aspirations and expectations (e.g., Hankiss 1978: 84).

These attempts tend to transform the convential quality of life research into a systematic and comprehensive course of the want-based research. In place of routine analysis of attitudinal data on an *n*-point scale of agreement—disagreement to the imposed valuation of a better quality of life, 'causal factors of substantive interest' are distinguished from 'problems of measurement' (Moum 1981). Also, the ongoing application of *Multiple Discrepancies Theory* (Michalos 1985) shows promise.

However, the attempts toward a systematic and comprehensive formulation of the want-based research do not seem to question any enforced unilateral valuation of the need-based research. On the other side, those protagonists of the need-based research who stand against a unilateral valuation of the quality of life do not appear concerned with the want-based research. Under the circumstances, the dominant trend of the want-based research is the production of 'dependent variables' in the context of the 'independent' need variables enumerated predominantly, or exclusively, by the power-wielding elites in society.

It follows logically from this manner of conceiving and organizing the quality of life research that it is conditioned by the quantity—quality and the objective—subjective dichotomies, although the artificial distinction drawn between what is objective and what is subjective has not escaped the notice of some critical scholars (e.g., Andrews and Withey 1976: 5). The result is that the programme of quality of life research is not built upon the state of objectivity of the behavioural and perceptual variables which follow the trend from quality to quantity.

As it is, the 'subjective' quality of life indicators refer to the masses as change recipients, and the 'objective' quality of life indicators to the elites in the Establishment. The not-established elites have little to say in this organized, purposeful and institutional undertaking, while the masses as actors in the change processes are not in the picture. This is the formulation of the quality of life research (need and want based) that has been voiced by Sheldon and Land (1972) in the context of the USA. The United Nations (1975: 27) experts have assured its general validity:

Without a precise definition of the term we can say that social indicators are constructs, based on observations and usually quantitative, which tell us something about an aspect of social life in which we are interested or about changes that are taking place in it. Such information may be objective in the sense that it purports to show what the position is or how it is changing; or it may be subjective in the sense that it purports to show how the objective position, or changes in it, are regarded by the community in general or by different constituent groups.

PROBLEMATIC

The deviations examined in respect of the two terms of reference to the quality of life research, which have met with dissent and protest from the social science community, highlight the problematic the quality of life research encounters presently. The problematic arises from the stipulation that variable appraisals of social reality for a better quality of life, which are to be explored from the sides of the elites and the masses, respectively, should be treated on an equal footing and as mutually distinct but interrelated.

The importance of this stipulation was noted by the reputed sociologist Ogburn as early as in 1953 (see Blumer 1983). It has also been felt by some scholars engaged in the quality of life research (e.g., Seashore 1978). However, the problem cannot be resolved on the basis of any integrating principle formulated by a researcher for the evaluation of variable appriasals of the quality of life, such as, 'An integral indicator of the quality of work and quality of life' (Kiurnov 1980), unless that principle is universally acceptable and thus attains the status of *cardinal* valuation. Otherwise, any such attempt will yield another *ordinal* valuation of the quality of life in the series of all ordinal valuations made by the elites and the masses.

In other words, there must be a *null* point for the evaluation of variable appraisals of a better quality of life, like the zero point on a scale of measurement. But this *null* valuation must be beyond Ego applicable to all humans, and, at the same time, commensurate with the experiences and expectations of the humans. Therefore, as explained earlier, subjectivism, objectivism, and empiricism per se are ruled out of the province of the quality of life research. On the other hand, the *null* valuation must represent the goal of the quality of life, and the purpose of the quality of life research should be to posit the most efficient manner of reaching toward that goal from empirical considerations.

A holistic appraisal of the quality of life is thus indicated along with the consolidation of knowledge from empirical observations of variable appraisals of a better quality of life. But, holism must not mean a subjective, pragmatic, or non-empirical formulation of the cardinal valuation for humankind. An apposite cardinal valuation in this respect has been posed by the non-idealist philosophers for hundreds of years, in the East and the West, and has been pursued by social scientists who are not subjectively idealist or vulgar materialists. As noted, this cardinal valuation comprises four empirically validated attributes specific to humankind: (*i*) survival of the species, (*ii*) security in the life span of humans, (*iii*) material prosperity for well-being, and (*iv*) mental progress to unfold the potentials of all individuals belonging to the species.

In the light of these four attributes of cardinal valuation, the purpose of the quality of life research is to ascertain the relative efficiency of all available and possible appraisals, i.e., the ordinal valuations, of a better quality of life. Therefore, the quality of life research is involved with the following four tasks in successive order: (*i*) analyzing each one of the available appraisals of social reality for a better quality of life, (*ii*) interrelating the appraisals from the respective sides of the elites and the masses, (*iii*) synchronizing the two series of interrelated appraisals in the light of their agreement or disagreement, and (*iv*) examining the synchronized series of ordinal valuations against the aforementioned cardinal valuation of the goal of humankind.

A pair of ordinal valuations from the sides of the elites and the masses, respectively, may agree with any one, several, or all the four attributes of the cardinal valuation, or with none. In the light of an overall agreement or disagreement with the four attributes, the pair will register one of four possibilities: (*i*) agreement with both the elite and the mass valuations, (*ii*) agreement with the elite but disagreement with the mass valuation, (*iii*) disagreement with the elite but agreement with the mass valuation, and (*iv*) disagreement with both the elite and the mass valuations. These possibilities are worth noting because history testifies to distinctive changes with respect to a better quality of life of humankind at these broad levels of agreement and disagreement of the predominant ordinal valuations of the elites and the masses to the cardinal valuation.

As mentioned, the first signifies a revolutionary improvement; the fourth a degradation of humanity as witnessed in Nazi Germany, Fascist Italy, and Tojo's Japan. The second signifies a conflict in society, intervening against improvements in the quality of life of the people, which happens, for instance, when the obscurantists and the traditionalists oppose measures for social development. The third portends a civil war for a better society and a better quality of life, as happened in the USA, for instance.

Therefore, the quality of life research may examine the overall or the detailed possibilities of agreement—disagreement of the paired valuations from the sides of the elites and the masses with the combinations of the four attributes of cardinal valuation. Research, however, can only proceed to this extent in the context of the perception—behaviour—perception syndrome of a better quality of life. It cannot achieve results in actually improving the quality of life.

This means that the efficiency of any course of change induced by the elites or infused by the masses is ultimately established by its resultant in society. Realities of nature and society are thus appreciated by means of *observations* at the proximal time point t_i and the distal time point t_j. Sciencing as an organized and purposeful endeavour in this context is concerned with observations and experiments intervening into realities. The human society is not exempted from these experiments despite the common value judgement against experimentation with human beings.

From the time of its evolution, human society has experimented with itself and the natural and the man-made environment, while, at the same time, keeping in harmony with nature. Because of these experiments, or lack of them in a relatively inert society, configurations of human society have disappeared and new configurations have emerged, or the old ones have been revised. The concept of tradition to modernity acquires a meaning in this context only, and bears out the elite-mass distinction and conjuncture in the course of experimentation; the leaders' attempts fail without the support of the masses, and the masses fail to conduct an experiment without appropriate leadership to mobilize themselves.

But, experiments with human beings are not carried out in isolation in any place, time, and people-bound configuration of human society. Several experiments are conducted simultaneously because of different ideologies, various strategic formulations of these ideologies, and translating the strategies into priorities in a complementary or contradictory manner. Therefore, testing the efficiency of variable appraisals of social reality for a better quality of life is not a matter of deduction in sciencing, unlike in the case of physical and biological research.

The physical reality can be deduced by experimentation under insular conditions. Similarly, in the case of biological research, a batch of drugs is tested in a laboratory in order to deduce the efficiency of particular ingredients and specific proportions of the ingredients, and to thus produce an efficient drug to cure an ailment. But, except under transitory dictatorial domination, sciencing social change is a matter of inference to be drawn on a probability basis from the operation of various ideologies in practice.

It is in this context of probability of inference that the concept of relative efficiency of different appraisals of a better quality of life is applicable—which appraisal in a given society and culture is likely to be the most effective in bringing about a better quality of life, which one less effective, and so on, to, which one is likely to be the least effective in view of the cardinal valuations for humankind.

It also follows that probability inference on the relative efficiency of all available and possible appraisals of a better quality of life cannot be drawn unless all these appraisals are treated on an equal footing as mutually distinct but interrelated, and the course of research undertakes the task of analyzing them systematically and interrelating and synchronizing them *systemically* as components of a complex whole.

These two conceptual and methodological requisites of the quality of life research pose the problematic to the research project. In the same or different manner for the need-based and the want-based research, the problematic emerges at the levels of data enumeration, reduction, analysis, and comprehension. The forms the problematic takes are associated with the issue of validity, relevance, and necessity of the appraisals of a better quality of life. Therefore, these issues require examination before any inference may be drawn on the relative efficiency of variable appraisals.

The appraisals from the side of the elites would be valid so long as they formulate the needs of the people from rigorous exploration of the information space on social reality with particular reference to the phenomenon of quality of life. The condition is met by the close association between the experts and the elites interested in improving the quality of life of the people. Therefore, the validity of the need-based quality of life research may not be doubted.

The want-based research does not bear the condition of automatic validation. In this case, the appraisals from the side of the masses will be validated by undertaking field investigations in a manner that would give the individuals the scope for unconstrained exploration of the information space on social reality with particular reference to what they perceive as the quality of life and what they want in order to better it. Therefore, the want-based research encounters several issues to be resolved at the level of data enumeration, unlike in the case of need-based research.

The relevance of valid appraisals of the quality of life will depend on the nature and extent of conjuncture of these appraisals from the sides of the elites and the masses. As noted, an appraisal of a better quality of life will not be relevant unless it is reciprocated by both the elites and the masses, and with appreciable intensity. This condition raises several problems to be resolved at the levels of data reduction, analysis, and comprehension, for both the need-based and the want-based research.

The variable appraisals of the elites should be systematically ordered into mutually distinct components at the level of data reduction; and these components should be systemically related at the level of analysis to represent the complex whole of all available and possible appraisals which the need-based research can yield. The variable appraisals of the masses should also be systematized and systemized. However, the want-based research is involved with the additional analytic problem of group formation by these appraisals; a point which is not relevant to the need-based research because needs can be formulated only with reference to the groups identified at the level of data collection.

Thus, the need-based research will refer to predetermined groups of individuals but will yield distinctive value groups by different appraisals of a better quality of life, and these value groups will be arranged in an interrelated series. Correspondingly, the want-based research will yield different value groups by recasting the predetermined groups of individuals according to differential valuations of a better quality of life. Therefore, at the level of comprehension, the structure of valuations from the side of the masses will reflect which valuations from the side of the elites they reciprocate and the extent to which they reciprocate these valuations.

Analyzed, interrelated, and synchronized in this manner, the *relative* relevance of all appraisals of a better quality of life will be ascertained by interfacing the elites' and the masses' structures of valuation. It will be seen whether the two sets of valuation are totally different from one another or, if some of the elites' valuations are reciprocated by the masses, which one has the largest support, and so on, to the valuation claiming the least support. Thus determined, the relative relevance will denote one aspect for drawing an inference on the relative efficiency of all appraisals. The other and the decisive aspect is given by the necessity of the ordinal valuations.

The necessity of the ordinal valuations will be judged by their proximity to the aforementioned four attributes of the cardinal valuation for humankind, namely, survival, security, prosperity and progress. In that context, an ordinal valuation may be found largely relevant (e.g., in Hitler's Germany), but it may not be necessary to improve the quality of life of the humans. Contrariwise, an appraisal isolatedly sponsored by the elites or the masses may be found necessary in the context of the cardinal valuation.

Between two such extreme possibilities, there are likely to be other ordinal valuations which are more and more necessary and, more and more relevant. Therefore, on the joint consideration of relevance *and* necessity, it should be possible and permissible to draw a probabilistic inference on the relative efficiency of variable appraisals of social reality for a better quality of life.

Defined in this manner, the approach to a comprehensive course of quality of life research would require specific examination of the need-based and the want-based research. These two bases will present the perspectives of the elites and the masses, respectively. Therefore, ultimately, the two perspectives should be interfaced and synchronized in order to ascertain the relative efficiency of various appraisals of social reality for a better quality of life.

Pursuant to this approach, the following chapters will deal with some major points in undertaking a comprehensive course of quality of life research. Chapter 2 is concerned with the need-based research and deals with the Elite Perspective. Chapter 3 is concerned with the want-based research and thus deals with the Mass Perspective. Finally, Chapter 4 is concerned with the elite and the mass perspectives of needs and wants of the people and, thus, presents the totality of the quality of life research.

• 2 •

• Elite Perspective: What Do People Need? •

DATA

The need-based quality of life research is usually equated with social indicators research, as discussed in Chapter 1. Concerned with what the people need to attain a better quality of life, the social indicators research enumerates need data, reduces the data, and formulates the need indicators—labelled social indicators. The validity of need data, enumerated in this manner, should not be doubted because, as mentioned, the experts rigorously explore the information space of society which may be the human society at large or one of its configurations such as a nation-state. In course of this exploration, they attribute the *meaning* of quality of life, i.e., a *datum*, to particular items of information and thus formulate the need indicators on a valid data base.

The problem emerges with the enumeration of too many need data and the resulting plethora of social indicators, as pointed out in Chapter 1. In order to resolve the problem, the relevance, necessity, and efficiency of need data are examined at the level of reduction of data. The objective is the construction of a small number of effective indicators which, as master indices, will each represent a cluster of indices. In this context, the social scientists have begun asking such critical questions as:

1. Although valid, is per capita GNP relevant data to indicate the quality of life in the global context, and not in the context of particular nation-states only?
2. Is the 'poverty line' a relevant indicator of the quality of life in the Third World in view of its conceptualization and construction?

3. Although valid and relevant, is the time-budget on leisure necessary data for the indication of the quality of life in the Third World?
4. Would organic food production be a necessary indicator of the quality of life in the USA because of the nature of food processing?
5. Although valid, relevant, and necessary, are the 'basic needs' data efficient for a comprehensive appraisal of the quality of life in the global or any nation-state context?
6. Do the need data considered for the formulation of the Physical Quality of Life Indicators (PQLI) form an efficient set to depict the quality of life?

In response to these and similar questions, the social indicators research will become more and more useful to the need-based quality of life research. However, besides the aspect of need-based quality of life research which is equated with the social indicators research, there is another which has been rather neglected although it is of deeper significance; namely, the formulation of need indicators after enumerating need data from a more basic source than that provided by the social indicators experts. This basic source is the appraisal of social reality for a better quality of life by the diverse elites in any configuration of human society and in the world at large.

The source materials for this task are the published literature in the global, sectoral (e.g., the Third World), or nation-state contexts, or with respect to any community of people (e.g., an ethnic group). A contemporary example in the global context is some scholars' appraisal of the future of humankind and a better world society (Cole, S. et al. 1978). In the context of the nation-state, the published views of the political parties are of significant interest because they thus proclaim their goal, strategy, and priorities for inducing a better quality of life of the people with whom they are concerned. These points are implicit, and sometimes explicit, to the studies of particular communities of people.

All these documents register a careful exploration of the information space for the enumeration of need data. Therefore, they contain valid data which can be enumerated by following the method of content analysis. The efficiency of content analysis is, of course, of crucial importance in this context.

The relevance, necessity, and efficiency of the data obtained by content analysis are liable to the same scrutiny as pointed out in the context of the experts' formulation and construction of social indicators. Obviously, when the relevance of per capita GNP or the 'poverty line' to indicate the quality of life is questioned, it refers to a valuation contrary to that which uses the data items or the need indicators. The same is true for those need data and need indicators of which the necessity or efficiency is challenged. Similarly, the elites' different appraisals of social reality for a better quality of life generate polemics on which valuation is the most appropriate.

Polemics generate heat but also shed light on different value bases of the controversy. Therefore, as for sets of need indicators obtained from the experts, the point is to ascertain which one of the elites' valuations is the most relevant, necessary, and efficient for the realization of a better quality of life of the people concerned. The point should be examined at the level of comprehension of the results of complementary need-based and want-based research, as explained in Chapter 1. Meanwhile, at the level of data reduction, the task is to assemble the need data proposed by each elite (expert) group, and arrange the assembled data sets for all these groups systematically, i.e., into ordered series of components.

Conventionally, the need data are systematized by the aspects of social reality to which they refer. This is useful and possible for assembling all data sets because the identity mechanism of social reality is usually the same among the appraisers of a better quality of life.

Some of the appraisers may examine new aspects of social reality which the others have not. Also, the others may explore the same aspects but, more or less extensively or deeply. Nevertheless, in the global, sectoral, nation-state, or particular community context, the appraisers hardly ever adopt variable identity mechanisms. This is seen from the programme and manifestos of the political parties in and across nation-states, despite their sharp differences in ideology and practice, and from the summary of aforementioned scholars' variable appraisals of the future of humankind (UNESCO n.d.: 8–9).

However, whether or not arranged conventionally, the need data enumerated with respect to different appraisers can be so arranged as to register their primary and secondary valuations of a better quality of life. The primary valuations will denote the holistic assumptions made and the corresponding deductions and inferences drawn by respective appraisers. The secondary valuations will be concerned with the logistics of realizing the primary valuations. The data obtained by content

analysis of basic source materials can invariably be systematized under
these two categories for each and all elite (expert) appraisers, because
the documents they produce contain, besides logistic details, an introductory overview of contemporary conditions of life and a conclusion
on what the new conditions should be, how they can be enforced, and
why.

The goals and strategies of the political parties in a nation-state
register their primary valuations while the priorities detailed under
respective aspects of social reality would register their secondary
valuations. The literature concerning communities of people or humankind can be similarly treated. In the global context, for example, the
aforementioned summary of the scholars' appraisal of the future of
humankind and the world society registers their primary valuations
under the two categories labelled 'global forecasts and diagnoses' and
'economic and institutional changes'. Their secondary valuations are
recorded under the headings food, materials, energy, environment,
technology, and population.

The variable value content of the data items under primary and
secondary valuations of a better quality of life can be seen in Tables 2.1
and 2.2 prepared in the global context. Table 2.3 shows some primary
valuations in a nation-state context, which will be followed by secondary valuations in course of data analysis. Tables 2.1–2.3 illustrate how
the valid need data enumerated by content analysis of appropriate
documents can be reduced and ordered systematically into a series of
components.

The reduction and ordering of need data into a series of components,
as shown in Tables 2.1–2.3, will lead to a systematic formulation of
need indicators. Each component will contain one data item, a
number of homologous data items which (because of their common
origin) can form a homogeneous cluster, or a number of analogous
(parallel) data items. Indicators can now be formulated with reference
to single or multiple data items.

An indicator structured by a number of analogous data items will be
heterogeneous in composition and, therefore, inefficient for a precise
and unequivocal indication of the facet of reality it is meant to indicate.
On the other hand, indicators formulated on the basis of one data item
each may be too many to defeat the purpose of their construction by
reduction of data. However, both these contingencies will be avoided
by the systematic reduction of data, as it will identify homologous and
analogous clusters of data items along with some intrinsically important
single data items.

Table 2.1
Summary of Primary Valuations of Scholars for a Better World Society and a Better Quality of Life

1 Meadows et al. (1972)
1. Global Forecasts and Diagnoses

Limits reached in next 100 years. Only safe way is to slow down. Population growth is greatest impediment to redistribution. Must achieve equilibrium or face overshoot and collapse.

2. Economic and Institutional Changes

Stop industrial and population growth. Create a totally new form of human society in 'equilibrium'. This requires great moral resources.

2 Mesarovic and Pestel (1974)
1. Global Forecasts and Diagnoses

Developing world crises—regional resource catastrophes could spread world wide and paralyse future orderly developments. Survival of world system is in question. Need technological restraint with social institutional and life-style reforms.

2. Economic and Institutional Changes

Organic growth coordinated global economic cooperation. Five per cent investment aid in LDCs. Create a conservationist global ethic and harmony with nature.

3 Herrera et al. (1976)
1. Global Forecasts and Diagnoses

Catastrophe is an everyday reality in LDCs—extreme economic difficulty predicted in Asia and Africa by 2000. Scarcity is not due to physical limits—population growth is not the major factor. Must achieve basic needs in LDCs but without help this will not happen in a reasonable time.

2. Economic and Institutional Changes

New patterns of self-reliant socialist development world wide needed with limited mutual aid. This requires fundamental socio-political reforms and an end to the ideology of growth.

4 Leontief et al. (1977)
1. Global Forecasts and Diagnoses

Second development decade strategy does not provide for the sufficiently rapid closing of income gap between developing and developed countries—gap would not diminish by the year 2000. Significant changes in economic relations between developed and the developing countries—high growth rates in LDCs coupled with slightly lower rates in DCs—are needed.

2. Economic and Institutional Changes

High investment and a brief expansion of international trade—significant changes in world economic order. Far-reaching changes of social, political and institutional character in developing countries are not discussed.

Source: UNESCO, n.d. *Long Term Educational Planning: Module 1. The Context of Long Term Educational Planning*, pp. 8–9. Paris: UNESCO, Division of Educational Policy and Planning.

Table 2.2
Summary of Secondary Valuations of Scholars for a Better World Society and a Better Quality of Life

1 Meadows et al. (1972)

1. *Food*: Physical and social limits force collapse of agriculture in 100 years—'Law of increasing costs'.
2. *Materials*: 250 years supply only—collapse in 50 years through physical shortage and exponential growth.
3. *Energy*: Needs ultimately adequately supplied by nuclear power.
4. *Environment*: Exponential cost of pollution control cannot be met.
5. *Technology*: Optimism about 'cost free' technology is not justified—blocks to technical progress.
6. *Population*: Collapse at about 16 billion population could level off at about 6 billion.

2 Mesarovic and Pestel (1974)

1. *Food*: Possibilities for expansion of production in rich countries but lack of production capacity especially in Asia.
2. *Materials*: Inexhaustibility cannot be taken for granted.
3. *Energy*: Nuclear power is a 'Faustian bargain'. Use solar power.
4. *Environment*: Need to exist harmoniously with nature or nature will react against man.
5. *Technology*: Exponential growth assumed although 'appropriate' technology is called for.
6. *Population*: 8–12 billion by 2100 if an effective population policy is introduced.

3 Herrera et al. (1976)

1. *Food*: Scarcity in LDCs not attributable to physical limits.
2. *Materials*: Minerals can be extracted at decreasing social cost.
3. *Energy*: Fossil fuels depleted in next 100 years. Nuclear and fusion power is 'inexhaustible'.
4. *Environment*: Increasing economy does not necessarily mean increasing pollution.
5. *Technology*: Technology grows faster than consumption. If LDCs had technology production would outstrip population.
6. *Population*: Highest 14 billion in 2050, lowest 10 billion. Size depends on satisfaction of basic needs.

4 Leontief et al. (1977)

1. *Food*: Dramatic developments bring new land into production and double or treble yields.
2. *Materials*: Tremendous growth in consumption (is) not a problem of absolute scarcity. Problem is how to exploit more costly resources.
3. *Energy*: Coal is relatively plentiful even under conservative estimates.
4. *Environment*: Technologically pollution is a manageable problem—economic costs high but not unmanageable.
5. *Technology*: By the year 2000 developed countries other than the US will use the 1970 technologies of North America—other countries will move in this direction.
6. *Population*: Extremely steep rise in population—UN estimates used average about 10 billion.

Source: UNESCO, n.d. *Long Term Educational Planning: Module 1. The Context of Long Term Education Planning*, pp. 8–9. Paris: UNESCO, Division of Educational Policy and Planning.

Table 2.3
Goals and Strategies of Major Political Parties in India at the Threshold of 1970

1. **Bharatiya Jana-Sangh (JS)**

   The outlook . . . accepts the seeming differences among various entities and aspects of life, but seeks at the same time to discover the unity underlying them (1965: 3). The concept of class-conflict cannot give rise to a spirit of spontaneous and permanent co-operation (*ibid*: 10). *Integral Humanism*: The individual occupies a pivotal position in our system . . . who has the potential to share simultaneously innumerous individual and corporate entities (*ibid.*: 12).

2. **Indian National Congress-Indira (Cong I)**

   The congress pledges itself anew to . . . a socialist revolution which is peaceful and democratic and embraces all our people and permeates all spheres of national life . . . The people have the power . . . to reject the reactionaries and communalists of the right and the extremists, who resort to violence and disorder and try to disrupt the forces of progress in the garb of left slogans (1972: 16).

3. **Socialist Party (SP)**

   The socialist party gives a solemn pledge . . . to end social and economic inequalities and march towards a socialist society in which common man's rights and liberties are safeguarded and weaker sections of our society subjected to social oppression and economic exploitation are liberated from the age-old tyranny (1972a: 12). Socialism means the end of class rule and the establishment of an equal and free society . . . . However, all class societies have historically shown a trend towards caste . . . . Caste is fossilised class. In India this development assumed extreme forms and the social order got completely frozen into a system of hierarchically ordered castes. A relentless struggle has to be waged on all fronts to destroy the caste system, to restore mobility to our social arrangements and achieve equality (1972b: 30).

4. **Communist Party of India (CPI)**

   . . . replacement of the Congress or any other form of bourgeois rule by a government composed of anti-imperialist, anti-feudal and anti-monopoly classes and forces capable and determined to carry out revolutionary changes, reversing the present process of development of capitalism . . . . open up for our people a path of development . . . an intervening stage of noncapitalist development [in which] the classes interested in carrying through this programme [are]: *First* and foremost, the working class . . . *Second*, the broad masses of the cultivating peasants, including the rich peasants and the agricultural labourers . . . *Third*, the rising class of urban and rural intelligentsia . . . *Finally*, the national bourgeoisie, excluding its monopoly section, which is objectively interested in the accomplishment of the principal tasks of the anti-imperialist and anti-feudal revolution (1968: 43–44).

5. **Communist Party of India-Marxist (CPI-M)**

   . . . establishment of people's democracy based on the coalition of all genuine anti-feudal and anti-imperialist forces headed by the working class . . . . The immediate objective . . . demands first and foremost the replacement of the present bourgeois-landlord state and government by a state of people's democracy and government led by the working class on the basis of a firm worker-peasant alliance (1972: 34).

The indicators, efficiently formulated in this manner, are now the concern of the level of analysis for the need-based quality of life research. The actual construction of indicators need not be considered here because it has been extensively discussed by those engaged in the social indicators research, including the present writer (Mukherjee 1975: 88–118; 1981a: 183–95). What is necessary is to examine the method of analysis for application to the efficiently formulated indicators.

ANALYSIS

The construction of indicators is concerned with their *constituent* variables and the *contingent* variables they are meant to indicate. However, at the level of analysis, the indicators represent the *context variables* because they provide the contexts to appraise the quality of life. Their role is, therefore, classificatory with respect to one or another appraisal of the quality of life. The classificatory role can have its analytic variability in case several appraisals of the quality of life are examined simultaneously and these appraisals are to be precisely located within a complex whole of all available and possible appraisals.

On the other hand, in case an appraisal of the quality of life is examined in isolation, the context variables will provide a set of fixed classificatory items to measure the degree of fulfilment of the characteristics they contain, respectively. Thus, for a singular appraisal of the quality of life, which is usual, the *content variables* of the indicators attain the sole concern for analysis. Conventionally, therefore, the formulation of indicators immediately proceeds to the construction of operative indicators, and the course of research is concerned with the analytic variability of their content variables.

The content variables may be represented by a series of continuous variates and measured on an interval scale of unit distances. In case the contemporary knowledge on variations in the constituents of an indicator is at the state of qualitative-ordinal distinction of, say, x occurring 'more' than y but not by 'how much', then the variable characteristic(s) will be represented by a quantitative-numeral series of discrete variates in an ascending order 1, 2, 3, . . . , and measured with the proviso that 3 minus 2, 2 minus 1, and so on, may not equal 1. In case the contemporary knowledge on variations in the constituents of an indicator is of nominal distinction only, which is rather infrequent, then the variations will be noted by the mere presence (= 1) or absence (= 0) of the constituents and their degree of fulfilment will be measured dichotomously.

Thus, the content variables of operative indicators are quantified in all possible ways, and analyzed by applying appropriate techniques. This is true with respect to one or more sets of context variables.

Now, with respect to one or more sets of context variables, the content variables will refer to the people whose needs the indicators are meant to indicate. It may do so directly (e.g., in the context of population growth) or indirectly (e.g., in the context of economic growth to benefit the people). The link subsumed in the latter case may or may not be appropriate, as pointed out with reference to per capita GNP, a 'poverty' indicator, PQLI, etc., but that is the concern of formulating and constructing efficient indicators.

The point is that with respect to one or more sets of context variables, the structure and function of the content variables are to provide the common ground for interfacing and synchronizing the need-based and the want-based quality of life research at the level of comprehension of their respective and relative efficiency with reference to the cardinal valuations for humankind. Meanwhile, at the level of analysis, the scope of quality of life research would be obscured by treating the appraisals of quality of life in isolation.

Firstly, a single appraisal cannot reveal the possibility of bidirectional valuation of any phenomenon, such as the quality of life, by providing facilities for each indicator to be valued positively as desirable, good, etc., *or*, negatively as detestable, bad, etc. Until recently, the negative valuation of an indicator was seldom considered because the appraisal of a better quality of life was positively prescriptive. Negative valuation has now entered the field of enquiry, but as 'disvalues'. These are listed along with the other (positive) values posed by an appraiser. Obviously, for bidirectional valuation of an indicator, at least two appraisers are required, one of whom will have the chance to value the indicator negatively if the other has valued it positively, and vice versa.

Second, as an appraiser will formulate indicators according to his/her perception of social reality for representing the quality of life, all the indicators thus formulated will be in one perspective, i.e., in one dimension as far as the appraiser is concerned. A second appraiser may not consider some or all indicators formulated by the first appraiser, i.e., reject these indicators because he/she perceives social reality in a partly or totally different dimension for representing the quality of life. In pursuance of this facility for dimensional distinction between two appraisers, there will be the possibility for a multidimensional valuation of indicators if field research covers multiple appraisers and a multiplicity of indicators.

Third, the valuation of an indicator by a single appraiser is always unilateral, including the contingency of rejecting an indicator and thus attributing to it the neutral or zero valuation. At least two appraisers are necessary to reveal the possibility of evaluating an indicator bilaterally as positive-neutral, negative-neutral, or positive-negative, while the pair could also value the indicator unilaterally as positive, neutral, or negative. The possibility of multilateral valuation of the indicator will emerge with more than two appraisers disagreeing on its valuation as positive by one, neutral by another, and negative by still another.

The necessity of considering the above three points is dictated by the fact that a singular appraisal of the quality of life would only forcibly be assumed to be an efficient valuation of the people's needs, or even a relevant valuation. As discussed in Chapter 1, the issue of relevance, necessity, and efficiency of need indicators (and, thus, of different appraisals of the quality of life portrayed by clusters of indicators) is resolved at the level of comprehension of identities and differences in the ordinal valuations of what the people need according to the elites and what the people want themselves, against the cardinal valuations for humankind. Therefore, the task at the level of analysis of need-based research, is to arrange variable appraisals of the quality of life in a systematic order of mutually distinct components, and interrelate these components systemically as articulated points of a structure which represents all available and possible valuations of a complex whole—the quality of life.

The task enjoins evolving a course of analysis which will integrate three, theoretically conceived, *infinite but enumerable* spaces of appraisers, indicators, and valuation of indicators by the appraisers. The appraisers should be treated as emerging freely from a space of all possible appraisers, and the indicators should be similarly conceived as emerging freely from a space of all possible indicators. The valuation of indicators by the appraisers, which denotes variable appraisals of the quality of life, will then emerge freely from the space of all possible valuations.

Thus, the course of research should be so designed that the samples of appraisers, indicators, and valuation of the indicators by the appraisers are all comparable over time and space, in order that the need-based quality of life research can proceed in an unconstrained manner and successively cover a larger extent and greater depth. This is possible because the appraisers, the indicators, and the valuation of the indicators by the appraisers are all mutually distinct but also additive in the sense that they may be combined in all possible ways.

The appraisers are additive because they are distinguished from one another while emerging from the universe of all appraisers, but they do not form disparate variables because they are all concerned with the appraisal of social reality for a better quality of life of humankind. The indicators are additive, by themselves and with reference to the appraisers, because they are formulated on the basis of mutually distinct pieces of information to which the datum of quality of life (including the possibility of no datum) has been attributed by the appraisers, and these qualified items of information are treated as single data items or homogeneous clusters of data items. The values attributed to the indicators by the appraisers will be additive, by themselves and with reference to the indicators and their appraisers, because all the indicators can be evaluated by the appraisers on the same bidirectional scale $+...0...-$, which denotes three possible graduation points of positive $(+)$ valuation, neutral or no (0) valuation, and negative $(-)$ valuation.

Bearing upon this flexible relation among the three components of analysis, the appraisers assume the classificatory role and the valuations of the context variables (i.e., of the total number of indicators formulated by the appraisers, respectively or concurrently) assume the analytic role. A pair of appraisers will be distinguished and inter-related by their respective valuations of each and every indicator under consideration. All the appraisers can thus be examined in pairs, so that, the totality of appraiser-pairs registering their paired valuations of all available indicators will provide a precise and comprehensive view of variable valuations of what the people need for a better quality of life in a systematic and systemic manner.

This course of division and summation, which is the essence of analysis, begins with the application of the bidirectional scale to each indicator. The zero point of the scale will operate as the fulcrum for the introduction of all indicators and appraisers involved in the course of analysis, while the valuations of each and all indicators by each and all appraisers will be registered at the three $+$, 0, and $-$ points of the scale.

Obviously, the scale will be of no use if all appraisers value all indicators in one and the same manner as + or 0 or −. In that case, the scope of analysis is forfeited by unidirectional, unidimensional, and unilateral valuation of indicators, as noted for a singular appraisal of the quality of life. In other words, the schema of analysis is applicable to different valuations of the quality of life by two or more appraisers.

An appraiser rejecting an indicator out of the totality of indicators under consideration will, in fact, attribute to it the 0-valuation because the piece of information contained in the indicator is of no concern to the dimension of social reality he/she has explored for the evaluation of the quality of life. This and several other appraisers may thus be located at the neutral (0) point of the scale. Alternatively, by accepting the piece of information contained in the indicator and therefore entering into the course of its valuation through the 0 point, the appraisers may attribute to it their positive (+) or negative (−) valuation.

These possibilities are shown in Figure 2.1, prepared with reference to two appraisers and one indicator. In case of rejection of the

Figure 2.1: Bidirectional, Bidimensional, Bilateral Valuation of an Indicator by Two Appraisers A and B

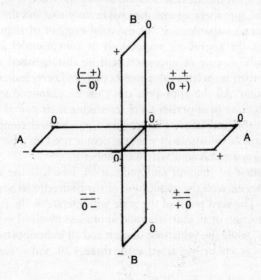

indicator, the +...0...− scale will automatically be transformed into the 0...0...0 scale, and the appraiser will be located at the central 0-point of the scale. Therefore, in case both the appraisers reject the indicator, their paired valuation will be 00. Otherwise, their paired valuations may vary as shown in four quadrants of Figure 2.1, which are formed by two bidirectional value scales of the two appraisers cutting across each other at the focal point 0.

Figure 2.1 shows that two appraisers **A** and **B** can be paired by the three valuations +, 0, and − in nine possible ways as ++, +0, +−, 0+, 0−, 00, −+, −0, and −−. Of these, ++, 00, and −− register the same (i.e., unilateral) valuations, and the remaining six, bilateral valuations. As indicated by the bracketed symbols for alternate pairs of **AB** and **BA**, +0 and 0+, 0− and −0, and +− and −+ denote the same kind of bilateral valuation but indicate different value attribution by the two appraisers **A** and **B**, respectively.

The entry of a third appraiser and additional ones in the schema outlined in Figure 2.1 will be through its focal point 0. With this entry with respect to one indicator, Figure 2.1 will assume a multilateral form while retaining bidirectionality by the value scale +...0...− for the indicator with respect to each appraiser. Thus, three appraisers **A**, **B**, and **C** will register the possibilities of (1) three unilateral valuations of +++, 000, and −−−; (2) 18 bilateral valuations of ++0, ++−, +0+, +00, +−+, +−−, 0++, 0+0, 0−0, 0−−, 00+, 00−, −++, −+−, −00, −0−, −−+, and −−0, with any two of **A**, **B** and **C** agreeing to the same valuation; and (3) six multilateral valuations of **A**, **B**, and **C** disagreeing with one another as +0−, +−0, 0+−, 0−+, −+0, and −0+.

With more and more appraisers evaluating an indicator, the possibilities of multilateral valuations will quickly supersede those of bilateral valuations while for any number of appraisers the possibilities of unilateral valuation will remain constant at three, as, +...+, 0...0, or −...−. This will be realized from the fact that the number of possible bilateral valuations of an indicator is given by the formula $6(2^{a-1}-1)$ and that of possible multilateral valuation by $3(3^{a-1}-2^a+1)$, while the total number of possible unilateral, bilateral, and multilateral valuations is given by 3^a, where **a** stands for the number of appraisers taken into account.

As for more than two appraisers evaluating an indicator, Figure 2.1 indicates that more than one indicator may be brought for evaluation by an appraiser through its focal point 0. The appraiser may then evaluate two indicators unilaterally as ++, 00, or −−; or bilaterally as

$+-$, $-+$, $+0$, $0+$, -0, and $0-$. It will be noticed that the possibility of evaluating two indicators by one appraiser is the same as evaluating one indicator by two appraisers. It will also be noticed that three or more indicators may be evaluated unilaterally, bilaterally, or multi-laterally by an appraiser in the same way as illustrated for one indicator by three appraisers and explained for more than three appraisers. Thus, in accordance with the schema outlined in Figure 2.1, one or more appraisers may appraise a set of indicators unilaterally, bilaterally, or multilaterally.

However, an appraiser will appraise one and all indicators in one dimension by rejecting an indicator with the value symbol 0 or accepting it with the value symbol $+$ or $-$. Two appraisers may evaluate two or more indicators in two dimensions by one of them rejecting one or some indicators which the other evaluates positively or negatively; i.e., by registering the paired symbols $+0$ or -0, irrespective of which of them registers $+$ or 0, or $-$ or 0. Correspondingly, three appraisers may evaluate three or more indicators in three dimensions by Appraiser A accepting an indicator i as $+$ or $-$, and rejecting the indicators j and k as 0; Appraiser B accepting j and rejecting i and k; and Appraiser C accepting k and rejcting i and j. Thus, the possibility opens up for multidimensional valuation of a set of indicators if three or more appraisers evaluate the set simultaneously and the set does not contain less than the number of appraisers.

The possibility and the limiting condition of multidimensional valuation at the minimum of three appraisers and three indicators is shown in Figure 2.2. The inset to the diagram is the bidimensional valuation of Appraisers A and B with respect to the indicators i and j.

Figure 2.2

Multidimensional Valuation of Indicators

(Appraisers $\geqslant 3$,   Indicators $\geqslant 3$)

Appraisers	Indicators				
	i	j	k	l	....
A	+/−	0	0	0	
B	0	+/−	0	0	
C	0	0	+/−	0	
D	0	0	0	+/−	
⋮					

This manner of transforming the bidimensional and bilateral structure of Figure 2.1 into a multidimensional and multilateral complex whole is possible because its focal point **0** serves as the fulcrum for all appraisers and indicators, while the point also denotes bidirectionality of the value scale. It follows that point **0** in Figure 2.1 is the *null* point in the schema of analysis of different appraisals of the quality of life, because at this 'not binding' point, like the zero point in a scale of measurement, the quality of life is not valued at all. Therefore, against this *null* point, it should be possible to systematically evaluate all appraisals of the quality of life as components of a complex whole and interrelate them systemically.

Thus, the schema outlined in Figure 2.1 encompasses all possibilities for an unconstrained and flexible analysis of the quality of life in so far as it is captured by the need-based research. Therefore, several analytic characteristics of the context variables (viz., the indicators) with reference to the appraisers and their valuations, are immediately noticeable.

At the base of the schema, the bidirectional scale and its *null* point reveal two sets of characteristics concerning (*a*) the information content and (*b*) the value content of an indicator in respect of an appraiser. The information content denotes dimensional variability in the appraisal of quality of life, while the value content registers lateral variability in the course of appraisal in the same or different dimensions.

As noted, the piece of information contained in a data item enumerated by one appraiser may not be regarded as datum by another and so the second appraiser may not enumerate the data item. The formulated indicator will then be valued by the first appraiser as positive (+) or negative (−), according to his/her rating of the contained information as desirable or detestable, while to the second appraiser the indicator will be of **0** valuation. Accordingly, the paired valuation +**0** or −**0** of an indicator (irrespective of which one of the two appraisers attributes the + or **0**, or the − or **0** valuation) will register dimensional distinction in the course of appraising social reality for the evaluation of the quality of life, as shown in Figure 2.1.

The dimensional distinction, as noted, may be recorded in another manner when two appraisers as, say, the second and the third, reject the information content of an indicator formulated by the first appraiser. In this case, as shown in Figure 2.2 with reference to Appraisers **B** and **C** and indicator *i*, they will register dimensional unity by the paired value symbol **00** because both of them attribute **0** valuation to the indicator. At the same time, the two appraisers will register joint distinction from other appraisers (e.g., the first appraiser) as a result of exploring social reality in other dimension(s) for the evaluation of the quality of life (viz., with reference to indicators j and k in Figure 2.2).

However, three or more appraisers may not reject the information content of an indicator and, thus, appraise social reality unidimensionally for the evaluation of the quality of life. On the other hand, while rejecting the information content of an indicator, any number of appraisers may not appraise social reality in more than the second dimension with reference to all other indicators. Thus, the value symbols $+0/-0$ (i.e., $+0$ or -0) and 00 for a pair of appraisers occur in an analogous (parallel) manner, and denote the nature and the extent of dimensional variation in the appraisal of quality of life by their incidence with respect to all indicators and all appraisers under consideration.

Therefore, the relative incidence of value symbols $+0/-0$ and 00, with reference to the totality of indicators and with respect to a pair of appraisers and all pairs of appraisers, will elicit the dimensional aspect of appraisal of social reality for the evaluation of the quality of life. Since the total number of indicators and thus the total valuation will be constant for all pairs of appraisers, the percentage incidence of the symbols $+0/-0$ and 00 out of the total valuation will be comparable across pairs of appraisers in a sample and across samples. The underlying possibilities of this course of analysis are indicated in Table 2.4.

Table 2.4
Deductions on Dimensional Variations in Appraisal of Quality of Life From Percentage Incidences of Value Symbols 00 and +0/−0 out of All Valuations (= All Indicators) For Any Pair and All Pairs of Appraisers

Incidence of value symbols		*Deduction*
00	*+0/−0*	
(1)	(2)	(3)
None or negligible	None or negligible	Unidimensional
	Appreciable	Bidimensional
Appreciable	None or negligible	Multidimensional, with the pair exploring a different dimension
	Appreciable	Multidimensional for and across the pairs, and for all pairs

Just as the bidirectional scale reveals dimensional variations by noting the information content of the indicators, so also it registers lateral variations in the appraisal of quality of life by recording the value content of the indicators. As explained, an indicator will register unilateral valuation by all appraisers in case they repeat only one of the three value symbols +, 0, and −. The indicator will register bilateral valuation by the appraisers in case their valuations register two of the three symbols, but not the third, as + and **0**, − and **0**, or + and −. Multilateral valuation will be registered by the indicator when it is valued by at least three appraisers and the valuations by all appraisers present all the three value symbols, in any combination.

Thus, the sensitivity of an indicator with respect to differential appraisal of the quality of life will be indicated by its multilateral valuation and, less intensely, by its bilateral valuation. The set or subset of appraisers with which this form of sensitivity of indicators is associated would be worth analyzing in order to ascertain the nature of lateral variability with reference to the appraisers' primary and secondary valuation of the quality of life and the aspects of life to which the indicators refer. A bivariate distribution of all indicators formulated from the reduction of need data and the +, 0, and − valuation attributed to these data items (and, thus, to the indicators) by all appraisers under examination will set this course of analysis, as illustrated later in Tables 2.5 and 2.6.

The course of analysis may be pursued to register the extent of dimensional and lateral variability in the appraisal of the quality of life. The three graduation points on the bidirectional scale will register the unit distance between any two appraisers with respect to each indicator. In case two appraisers record the same value symbol as ++, **00**, or −−, they would register **0**-distance on the scale with respect to an indicator. Two appraisers will register **1**-unit distance on the scale in case their paired valuation of an indicator is +0 or −0. Lastly, two appraisers will register **2**-unit distance between them in the case of paired value symbol +−, because the contrary valuations will pass on the scale from + to **0** and then to −, and vice versa.

Since the indicators are additive and the paired valuations of any two appraisers is also additive, the total incidence of paired valuations of all indicators as ++, **00**, −−, +0/−0, and +− can be noted with respect to each pair of appraisers and for all pairs of appraisers. From the relative incidence of paired symbols **00** and +0/−0 the nature and extent of dimensional variation among the appraisers can be ascertained. The nature of lateral variability in the valuation of indicators

Table 2.5

Need Indicators Formulated from Primary Valuations of Scholars for a Better Quality of Life, with their Valuations

(Scholars: Meadows et al. = M, Mesarovic and Pestel = MP,
Herrera et al. = H, Leontief et al. = L)

Indicator	M	MP	H	L
(1)	(2)	(3)	(4)	(5)
1. Population-industry growth equilibrium enforced by moral resources	+	−	−	−
2. Conservationist global ethic, with technological restraint	+	+	−	−
3. Organic growth coordinated global economic cooperation	−	+	+	+
4. Self-reliant socialist configuration of world society	0	0	+	0
5. End to the ideology of growth	+	0	+	0
6. Fundamental socio-political reforms in all societies	0	+	+	0
7. Far-reaching social, political, institutional changes in less developed countries	0	+	+	+
8. High growth rates in less developed countries and slightly lower rates in developed countries	−	0	0	+

will be detected from the bivariate distribution of all indicators and their valuations by all appraisers, which is the preliminary exercise to calculate the incidences of the above mentioned paired value symbols. Now, by allotting 1-unit distance to each occurrence of the value symbols +0 or −0 and 2-unit distance to that of +−, the total unit distance can be calculated for each pair of appraisers and for all appraiser-pairs.

The unit distances will precisely distinguish and interrelate different appraisals of what the people need in order to attain a better quality of life. Therefore, the unit distances should be made comparable for any form of categorization and collation of the indicators, appraisers, and their valuations by calculating the percentage incidence of unit distances recorded by appraiser-pairs out of the total unit distance they register in a sample.

Thus, by following the proposed course of analysis, the respective sets of need indicators formulated by all available and possible elite (expert) groups will be placed on a systematically and systemically

Table 2.6
Need Indicators Formulated from Secondary Valuations of Scholars for a Better Quality of Life, with their Valuations

(Scholars: Meadows et al. = M, Mesarovic and Pestel = MP, Herrera et al. = H, Leontief et al. = L)

Indicator	M	MP	H	L
(1)	(2)	(3)	(4)	(5)
1. Zero population growth	+	+	+	+
2. Zero industrial growth	+	−	−	−
3. Absolute cost constraint of pollution control	+	0	−	−
4. Nuclear power for energy generation	+	−	+	0
5. Exploitation of costly resource materials	−	0	+	+
6. Appropriate technological development for less developed and developed countries, respectively	−	+	+	+
7. Rapid agricultural growth in less developed countries	−	+	+	+
8. Maximum use of fossil fuels and solar power for energy generation	0	+	+	+
9. Removal of income gap between less developed and developed countries	0	+	+	+
10. Removal of regional disparity in resource mobilization	0	+	+	+

structured axis of variation. This axis can then be examined against an analogous (parallel) axis structured by the sets of valuation that emerge from the want-based quality of life research. Also, the two axes may be examined against the cardinal valuations of survival, security, prosperity, and progress of humankind in order to establish the relevance, necessity, and efficiency of respective and conjunctured valuations of the quality of life from the sides of the elites and the masses.

The usefulness of this course of analysis with respect to the need-based research is illustrated next in the global and a nation-state context.

EXAMPLE: GLOBAL CONTEXT

An example in the global context is the scholars' appraisal of contemporary social reality mentioned earlier and their recommendations for establishing a better world society which is automatically concerned with a better quality of life of the people. The need data enumerated by content analysis of the documents produced by the scholars and reduced to a series of components would be useful to the present illustration, irrespective of any dispute over a correct representation of the scholars' viewpoints by a content analyst (e.g., UNESCO n.d.: 8–9). Therefore, from the need data reproduced in Tables 2.1 and 2.2, eight and 10 need indicators have been formulated according to the scholars' primary and secondary valuations of a better quality of life. These indicators are shown in Tables 2.5 and 2.6, with the respective sets of scholars' valuations of each indicator as positive (+), neutral (0), or negative (−).

Table 2.5 shows that out of eight indicators formulated according to the scholars' primary valuations of the quality of life, only one (Item 8) registers multilateral valuation. Interestingly, this sensitive indicator refers to the strategy of removing unequal exchange between the developing and the developed societies.

The remaining seven indicators register bilateral valuation, of which four register disagreement on the information content of the indicator by one or more sets of scholars. This indicates that the strategies of the scholar-sets to bring about a better world and a better quality of life of the people rest mainly upon their appraisal of social reality in different dimensions.

Table 2.6 shows that dimensional variability is almost equally noticeable among the scholar-sets with respect to logistics, as in meeting the strategies and attaining the goal of a better world society; i.e., for six indicators out of 10 concerning the logistics and for five out of eight regarding the strategy and the goal. But the variation is now exclusively bidimensional, and the scholars are on the same wavelength in defining their logistics rather than in formulating their strategies and proclaiming their goals. They are now particularly concerned with evaluating an indicator positively or negatively while unanimously attributing a positive valuation to check the growth of population. Moreover, multilateral valuation occurs for 30 per cent of these indicators (for three out of 10) as against 13 per cent (for one out of eight) in the case of primary valuation. Interestingly, the sensitive indicators drawing multilateral valuation are concerned with the use of nuclear power, pollution control, and exploitation of costly resources for the benefit of humankind.

The distinctive characteristics of primary and secondary valuations of the scholar-sets for a better society and quality of life interrelate them in a significant manner. This is seen from Table 2.7 and 2.8

Table 2.7

**Paired Valuations and Unit Distances between Scholar-sets Regarding their Primary
and Secondary Appraisals of a Better Quality of Life**

(Scholars: Meadows et al. = M,   Mesarovic and Pestel = MP,
        Herrera et al. = H,   Leontief et al. = L)

Paired scholar-sets		Paired valuation						Unit distance (+0/−0 = 1 +− = 2)
		++	−−	00	+0/−0	+−	Total	
(1)		(2)	(3)	(4)	(5)	(6)	(7)	(8)

1 Primary Valuation

Paired scholar-sets		++	−−	00	+0/−0	+−	Total	Unit distance
M	– MP	1	–	1	4	2	8	8
	H	1	–	–	4	3	8	10
	L	–	–	2	2	4	8	10
MP	– H	3	1	1	2	1	8	4
	L	2	1	2	2	1	8	4
H	– L	2	2	–	4	–	8	4
Total		9	4	6	18	11	48	40

2 Secondary Valuation

Paired scholar-sets		++	−−	00	+0/−0	+−	Total	Unit distance
M	– MP	1	–	–	5	4	10	13
	H	2	–	–	3	5	10	13
	L	1	–	–	4	5	10	14
MP	– H	6	1	–	2	1	10	4
	L	6	1	–	3	–	10	3
H	– L	7	2	–	1	–	10	1
Total		23	4	–	18	15	60	48

which give, as frequencies and percentages, the paired comparison of
the scholar-sets by their valuation of all eight and 10 indicators of goal
and strategy, and of logistics, and the unit distances they register by
these valuations.

It can be seen from columns 2–4 of Table 2.8 that to an appreciable
extent Leontief and his colleagues register multi-dimensional distinction
from Meadows and his colleagues, and from Mesarovic and Pestel,
with regard to the strategy and goal of a better world society. Otherwise, in about equal proportions, the scholar-sets explore social reality
in one or two dimensions. But when concerned with the logistics of

Table 2.8
Dimensional and Lateral Distinctions among Scholar-sets for Primary and Secondary Appraisal of a Better Quality of Life (as calculated from frequencies in Table 2.7)

(Scholars: Meadows et al. = M,   Mesarovic and Pestel = MP,
Herrera et al. = H,   Leontief et al. = L)

Paired scholar-sets	Dimensional distinction (Percentage of total valuation for each pair of scholar-sets)			Extent of dimensional and lateral distinction (Percentage of total unit distances)
	None $(++/--/+-)$	Partial $(+0/-0)$	Total (00)	
(1)	(2)	(3)	(4)	(5)
1 Primary Valuation (8)				
M – MP	38	50	12	20
H	50	50	0	25
L	50	25	25	25
MP – H	63	25	12	10
L	50	25	25	10
H – L	50	50	0	10
Total	50	38	12	100
2 Secondary Valuation (10)				
M – MP	50	50	0	27
H	70	30	0	27
L	60	40	0	29
MP – H	80	20	0	9
L	70	30	0	6
H – L	90	10	0	2
Total	70	30	0	100

meeting the strategies and attaining the goal, multidimensional distinction disappears and the bidimensional distinction also becomes less marked—particularly between Leontief and Herrera along with their colleagues.

Thus, the first finding is that the perspectives of the scholars differ more in the formulation of their goals and strategies for a better world society, in which case ideology plays a dominant role, than in the formulation of actual measures to be implemented in practice. Even so, there is the second finding that Leontief and Meadows (along with their respective sets of colleagues) tend to appraise a better world society and a better quality of life in a different manner, with Herrera and his colleagues aligning themselves to the Leontief set and Mesarovic and Pestel to the Meadows set.

Column 5 of Table 2.8 shows that irrespective of dimensional distinctions among them, the logistics of meeting their strategies and attaining their goals bring Mesarovic and Pestel (and particularly Herrera and his colleagues) nearer to Leontief and his colleagues than in the context of formulating their goals and strategies. Second, with respect to both primary and secondary valuations of a better world society and quality of life, Meadows and his colleagues stand apart from the other three scholar-sets.

These points can be displayed by plotting the distances among the four scholar-sets in accordance with the percentage-wise unit distances they register among themselves (vide, column 5 of Table 2.8) for the primary and secondary appraisals of a better quality of life. The unit distances incorporate dimensional variations, along with the lateral distinctions, by the paired symbols **00** registering no distinction at all and **+0/−0** registering one unit distance. Broadly, the dimensional and lateral distances are given in three dimensional diagrams in Figure 2.3.

Tables 2.5–2.8 and Figures 2.1–2.3 illustrate how some of the notable concerns during the 1970s for a better world society can be treated for systemizing the antagonistic and allied appraisals of social reality for a better quality of life of humankind. The same method of analysis may be applied to the concerns of the 1980s, as contained in the North-South dialogue, the East-West confrontation, the 'alternatives' proposed by associations of scholars, such as, 'The 1975 Dag Hammarskjold Report' (Nerfin 1975). In all such cases, a content analysis of relevant documents, as illustrated in Tables 2.1 and 2.2, will be followed by the method outlined in Tables 2.5–2.8.

Content analysis will be unnecessary in case the need indicators are already formulated by the scholars, as cited in Chapter 1 with reference to Drewnowski, Galtung, Maslow, McGranahan, and Miles. However, these scholar-wise different sets of indicators may be conceived as emerging unrestrictedly from an infinite but enumerable field of variation in the need indicators, just as the scholars may be conceived as emerging from an infinite but enumerable field of variation in the appraisers of social reality for a better quality of life of the

Figure 2.3: Dimensional and Lateral Distances Among Four Scholar-sets Regarding Primary and Secondary Appraisal of a Better Quality of Life

(Scholar-sets: Meadows et al. =M; Mesarovic and Pestel = MP; Herrera et al. = H; Leontief et al. = L)

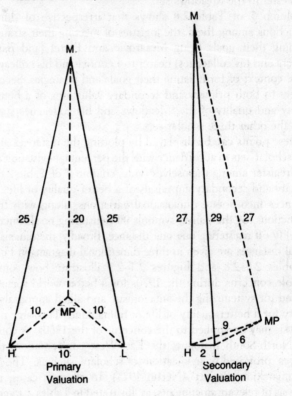

people. In this way, all need indicators and their appraisers may be treated as mutually distinct but interrelated with reference to the betterment of humankind. Therefore, the method outlined in Figures 2.1 and 2.2, and illustrated by Tables 2.5–2.8 and Figure 2.3, may be employed for systemizing the experts' valuations of social reality with respect to what the people need to attain a better quality of life.

Pursued in this manner, the need-based quality of life research would be applicable to the researches of those social scientists who do not live in an ivory tower. Their researches are also concerned with a better world society and better humanity, but their valuations of what is needed to meet the objective may not be geared to the quality of life research while being antagonistic or allied. These valuations are usually treated unilaterally, at the risk of being reduced to doctrines and dogmas. Mere polemics inhere the same risk while somewhat clarifying the valuations in a discrete manner. On the contrary, the relative efficiency of these valuations may be ascertained by following the procedure discussed in Chapter 1, provided the ground is prepared for that purpose by treating the different appraisals of social reality they depict in a systemic manner as being mutually distinct but interrelated. Appropriately, the ground is prepared by the need-based quality of life research because, implicitly or explicitly, these valuations denote what the people need to attain a better quality of life.

Therefore, in the same manner as illustrated, need indicators may be formulated from content analysis of relevant monographs: such as, with reference to Rostow's (1962) 'non-communist manifesto' and the Marxist political economy; Myrdal's (1971) 'modernization ideals' for Third World societies and Frank's (1970) enumeration of attributes of 'development of underdevelopment' in the same place-time-people context; Wallerstein's (1974) conceptualization of the core—semi-periphery—periphery relationships in the 'modern world-system' and the classic Marxist formulation of relations among feudalism, capitalism, and socialism; and so on. The totalities of indicators and their appraisers can then be analyzed in the manner outlined and illustrated, so as to establish a systemic relation among the apparently discrete valuations of contemporary world society, culture, and the people.

Finally, the grand theories of social development can be translated into sets of need indicators as emerging freely from the universe of all possible 'needs' formulated to meet the four cardinal valuations for humankind, namely, survival, security, prosperity, and progress, as discussed in Chapter 1. The grand theories might appear to be disparate, as dealing with the material or the spiritual basis of society, the social existence or the social consciousness of the people. However, on the basis of their human specific appraisals of social reality for a better quality of immanent life, the theories can be translated into 'need' indicators and these indicators can be systematized and systemized by following the proposed course of analysis. The feasibility of this venture is indicated from even brief and cursory extracts of the viewpoints of reputed thinkers and social scientists like, Comte, Engels, Durkheim, Malinowski, Marx, Pareto, Rousseau, Simmel, Spencer, Tönnies, Weber, and others (Mukherjee 1978: 106–20).

The point is that the scope of pursuing the need-based quality of life research is manifold because it may not only systematically arrange all possible valuations of what the people need for a better quality of life, but can also treat all these valuations in a systemic manner for the complex whole of humankind. Therefore, by pursuing the course of analysis briefly illustrated in the foregoing pages, the knowledge on what the people need may be consolidated more and more precisely and comprehensively.

EXAMPLE: NATION-STATE CONTEXT

In the same manner as demonstrated for the global context, need indicators can be formulated in a nation-state context. As mentioned, the content analysis of programmes and election manifestos of the powerful political parties may deserve special attention in this respect because these documents pose their respective valuations of social reality for a better quality of life of the people concerned, and imply inducing change in society to fulfil the enumerated needs.

In the nation-state context as well, the valuations of the elite groups can be distinguished as of primary and secondary relevance. The primary valuations of the political parties would refer to the declaration of their goals and strategies, while their secondary valuations would be concerned with the logistics of meeting these strategies and goals.

India at the threshold of 1970 and in 1977 provides a good example in this context. By the end of the 1960s, the euphoria of Independence had more or less disappeared. The economy began to show signs of crisis from the mid-1960s. In the second half of the decade, the Indian National Congress, which had unquestionably represented the Establishment from 1947, was split up while the left and the right wing oppositions were gaining ground in social polity.

The changes imminent around 1970 were manifest in 1977. By then, the economic crisis had deepened and a political crisis was in the offing. The Indian National Congress did no more represent the Establishment unquestionably. Regional parties had emerged as viable alternatives in the south, and the Communist Party of India-Marxist was posing a formidable opposition in the states of West Bengal and

Tripura in the east. Also, in all states and at the centre (Delhi), the non-Congress and non-communist parties had further gained strength despite, or because of, the Emergency Rule declared by the ruling Congress Party in 1975.

Therefore, the formulation of need indicators from content analysis of the programmes and election manifestos of contemporaneously powerful political parties in India, and the analysis of the need indicators, would be of substantive importance besides demonstrating the usefulness of the proposed course of analysis.

As seen from Table 2.3 which structures need data from primary valuations of the major political parties in India at the threshold of 1970, there were five parties particularly worth noting: Bharatiya Jana-Sangh (JS), Indian National Congress-Indira (INC-R), Socialist Party (SP), Communist Party of India (CPI), and Communist Party of India-Marxist (CPI-M). Of them, CPI and CPI-M did not change their label or identity in 1977; the Indian National Congress-Indira came to be known henceforth as Cong I; and JS and SP merged with the Old Congress (from which Cong I had separated in the 1960s) and with several other parties of smaller stature, in order to form the Janata Party (JP).

The Janata Party of 1977 may be regarded as an amalgam of the SP and JS of 1970, in particular, because these two parties were the moving forces behind its formation and operation, although the historical significance of the Old Congress (Cong O) was not ignored and the first non-Congress Prime Minister of India came from this stock. Also, Cong I may be the label applied to INC-R in 1970 because its identity had not changed by 1977. On this basis, and since new parties of an all-India stature had not emerged by 1977, the noteworthy and comparable political parties in India in 1970 and 1977 would be SP, JS, JP (= SP + JS mainly), Cong I, CPI, and CPI-M.

Now, from the data items enumerated in Table 2.3, eight need indicators can be formulated as representing the primary valuations made by SP, JS, Cong I, CPI, and CPI-M for a better quality of life of the Indian people. These indicators, with the positive, neutral, or negative values attributed to them by respective parties, are shown in Table 2.9.

Table 2.9 and the views contained in Table 2.3 show that the political parties of India visualize their strategy for a better quality of life of the people in the same perspective, but on the goal issue they register bidimensional and multilateral distinctions. JS remains

Table 2.9
Need Indicators Formulated from Primary Valuations (Goals and Strategies) of Five Major Political Parties in India at the Threshold of 1970, with their Valuations

Indicator	JS	Cong I	SP	CPI	CPI-M
(1)	(2)	(3)	(4)	(5)	(6)
1. People's consensus to form a new society because class conflict is harmful	+	+	–	–	–
2. Socialist revolution embracing all people	0	+	–	–	–
3. Overthrow the power of bourgeois-landlord classes	–	–	+	+	+
4. Reject the reactionaries and communalists of the right wing	–	+	+	+	+
5. Reject left wing politics	+	+	–	–	–
6. Destroy the caste system as of *prime* importance	–	–	+	–	–
7. Pursue the non-capitalist path of development by forging alliance of the working class, peasantry (including rich peasants and agricultural labourers), intelligentsia, and national bourgeoisie (excluding the monopoly section)	–	–	–	+	–
8. Establish a state of people's democracy led by the working class on the basis of worker-peasant alliance	–	–	–	–	+

'neutral' to a 'socialist revolution', Cong I wants it to 'embrace all people', SP emphasizes the rights of the 'common man', and CPI and CPI-M aim for socialist revolution by overthrowing 'the power of bourgeois-landlord classes'. Except on this sensitive issue, the major political parties in India at the threshold of 1970 agreed on the information content of the indicators, but they disagreed on their value content by attributing different valuations to them.

The secondary valuations of the political parties, viz., the priorities they allotted to the societal characteristics and thus defined their logistics to meet their strategies and attain their goals, are obtained from a content analysis of the documents mentioned in Table 2.3. Thirty-two indicators could thus be formulated, as shown in Table 2.10.

Table 2.10
Need Indicators Formulated from Secondary Valuations (viz., the logistics of meeting the strategies and the goals) of Five Major Political Parties in India at the Threshold of 1970, with their Valuations

Indicator	JS	Cong I	SP	CPI	CPI-M
(1)	(2)	(3)	(4)	(5)	(6)
Industry and Trade					
1. Liquidation of foreign monopoly capital	−	0	0	+	+
2. Nationalisation of monopolistic industries	−	+	+	+	+
3. Expansion of public (state) sector of economy	−	+	+	+	+
4. Public sector to eventually replace private sector	−	−	+	+	+
5. Public sector to meet gaps in private sector	+	0	−	−	−
6. Production of cheaply-priced essential consumer goods in the public sector and socialization of wholesale trade	−	+	+	+	+
7. Removal of all persons associated with monopolist companies from the public sector	−	0	+	+	+
8. Efficient operation of public sector with workers' participation in management	0	+	+	+	+
9. Labour-intensive consumer industries for creating jobs	+	+	+	0	0
10. All industries labour-intensive for creating jobs	0	+	+	0	0
Agriculture					
11. Rural development to benefit all classes and categories	+	+	−	+	−
12. Land reform to benefit victims of 'semi-feudalism', i.e., sharecroppers and landless peasants	−	−	−	+	+
13. Land reform to benefit landless peasants only	−	−	+	−	−
Education					
14. Definitely secular education	0	+	+	+	+
15. Free and compulsory secondary education	+	+	+	+	+
16. Education linked to the development of a self-generating economy based on advanced science and technology	0	+	+	+	+

17. Adult education in the context of rapid industrialization: Training courses for workers in industrial and commercial organizations	0	0	0	+	+
Language					
18. Regional language for education and administration in each state	+	0	+	+	+
19. English replaced by Hindi as the centre's official language	+	+	+	–	–
20. Sanskrit to be India's national language	+	–	–	–	–
21. Urdu to be declared as a separate language	–	+	+	+	+
Minority Issue					
22. Guaranteed equal rights to all minorities and no discrimination against them	+	+	+	+	+
23. Indian Muslims harbour pro-Pakistan sentiments: needs changing	+	–	–	–	+
24. Special promotion of minority interests	0	+	+	+	+
25. Legal measures against communal (Hindu versus Muslim) propaganda	0	+	+	+	+
Foreign Policy					
26. Regard China and Pakistan as unfriendly	+	–	+	–	–
27. Fight discrimination against Indians in other countries	+	0	0	0	0
28. Propagate the *core* idea of peaceful coexistence	–	+	+	+	+
29. Establish close cooperation with the USSR and other socialist states	–	+	–	+	+
30. Withdraw from British Commonwealth	–	–	+	+	+
31. Build Third World solidarity to fight neocolonialism	–	0	+	+	+
32. Insist on general disarmament, with immediate ban on manufacture and use of nuclear weapons	–	+	+	+	+

Table 2.10 shows that with respect to their secondary valuations of a better quality of life of the Indian people, dimensional variation among the political parties is noticeable for 44 per cent of the total number of indicators (14 out of 32) as against 13 per cent of indicators of primary valuations (one out of eight in Table 2.9). But these

variations are mostly bidimensional while multilateral valuation is recorded for only 13 per cent of the total number of indicators of both secondary valuation (four out of 32) and primary valuation (one out of eight in Table 2.9).

Thus, Tables 2.9 and 2.10 indicate that the Indian political parties at the threshold of 1970 tended to explore different dimensions of social reality to define their logistics, but on a bidimensional base they were more or less on the same wavelength for the appraisal of the quality of life of the people, except with respect to their ideology of goals.

This basic difference is further highlighted by their multilateral valuation of some indicators in Table 2.10, besides their multilateral valuation of the goal issue in Table 2.9 of primary valuation. The multilaterally valued indicators of secondary valuation are: Liquidation of foreign monopoly capital, public sector to meet the gaps in private sector, removal of all persons associated with monopolist companies from the public sector, and building Third World solidarity to fight neocolonialism.

Evidently, the differences among the major political parties in India at the threshold of 1970 were essentially related to political economy, which is also noticeable from Tables 2.5 and 2.6 in the global context but in a rather muted form.

As in the global context, the characteristics of dimensional and lateral variations in the appraisal of quality of life, noticeable from bivariate distribution of indicators and their valuations, are clearly exposed by (*a*) pairing the political parties, (*b*) noting their total paired valuations of all indicators, and (*c*) calculating the unit distances the pairs of political parties register respectively and totally. These variables in the form of frequencies and percentages, as for Tables 2.7 and 2.8, are given in Tables 2.11 and 2.12.

Tables 2.11 and 2.12 show that the primary valuations of a better quality of life of the Indian people are predominantly unidimensional, but JS is distinguished from the remaining four political parties. However, in dimensional and lateral variation, Cong I is nearer to JS and both are almost equally distant from SP, CPI, and CPI-M. These three parties tend to form a cluster against JS and Cong I. It may be worth recalling that while Cong I declared socialism for all as the goal and JS remained neutral on this point, the cluster of SP, CPI, and CPI-M pointed to class contradiction in the path of achieving the goal of socialism.

But the alliance of JS and Cong I is seen to be disrupted in the

Table 2.11

Paired Valuations and Unit Distances among Major Political Parties in India at the Threshold of 1970 Regarding their Primary and Secondary Appraisals of a Better Quality of Life of the Indian People

Paired parties		Paired valuation						Unit distance
		++	--	00	+/0 -0	+-	Total	(+0/-0 = 1 +- = 2)
(1)		(2)	(3)	(4)	(5)	(6)	(7)	(8)
1 Primary Valuation								
JS	– Cong I	2	4	–	1	1	8	3
	SP	–	2	–	1	5	8	11
	CPI	–	2	–	1	5	8	11
	CPI-M	–	2	–	1	5	8	11
Cong I	– SP	1	2	–	–	5	8	10
	CPI	1	2	–	–	5	8	10
	CPI-M	1	2	–	–	5	8	10
SP	– CPI	2	4	–	–	2	8	4
	CPI-M	2	4	–	–	2	8	4
CPI	– CPI-M	2	4	–	–	2	8	4
Total		11	28	–	4	37	80	78
2 Secondary Valuation								
JS	– Cong I	5	4	1	12	10	32	32
	SP	6	2	1	8	15	32	38
	CPI	4	1	1	8	18	32	44
	CPI-M	3	1	1	8	19	32	46
Cong I	– SP	16	3	3	4	6	32	16
	CPI	15	4	1	8	4	32	16
	CPI-M	14	4	1	8	5	32	18
SP	– CPI	18	3	1	4	6	32	16
	CPI-M	18	4	1	4	5	32	14
CPI	– CPI-M	22	6	3	–	1	32	2
Total		121	32	14	64	89	320	242

context of priorities to meet the strategy and attain the goal. With respect to the secondary valuations of the quality of life, Cong I veers towards the cluster of SP, CPI, and CPI-M as regards lateral variation, but explores a different dimension of social reality in order to define

Table 2.12

Dimensional and Lateral Distinctions among Major Political Parties in India at the Threshold of 1970 for Primary and Secondary Appraisal of a Better Quality of Life of the Indian People (as calculated from frequencies in Table 2.11)

Paired Political parties		Dimensional distinction (Percentage of total valuation for each pair of parties)			Extent of dimensional and lateral distinction (Percentage of total unit distances)
		None $(+ +/- -/+ -)$	Partial $(+0/-0)$	Total (00)	
(1)		(2)	(3)	(4)	(5)
1 Primary Valuation (8)					
JS	– Cong I	87	13	0	4
	SP	87	13	0	14
	CPI	87	13	0	14
	CPI-M	87	13	0	14
Cong I	– SP	100	0	0	13
	CPI	100	0	0	13
	CPI-M	100	0	0	13
SP	– CPI	100	0	0	5
	CPI-M	100	0	0	5
CPI	– CPI-M	100	0	0	5
Total		95	5	0	100
2 Secondary Valuation (32)					
JS	– Cong I	59	38	3	13
	SP	72	25	3	16
	CPI	72	25	3	18
	CPI-M	72	25	3	19
Cong I	– SP	78	13	9	7
	CPI	72	25	3	7
	CPI-M	72	25	3	7
SP	– CPI	84	13	3	7
	CPI-M	84	13	3	5
CPI	– CPI-M	91	9	0	1
Total		76	20	4	100

its logistics. In this respect, Cong I registers a measure of multi-dimensional distinction with SP and appreciable bidimensional distinction with CPI and CPI-M.

On the other hand, while the dimensional distinction on secondary valuations is less for the cluster of SP, CPI, and CPI-M, and it is essentially bidimensional, CPI and CPI-M hardly register a lateral distance. Nevertheless, even a small measure of bidimensional distinction between them indicates that these two parties also tend to explore different dimensions of social reality to define their logistics. At the other extreme, JS registers appreciable bidimensional distinction from the four parties, and particularly from Cong I.

Thus, JS is seen to stand apart from the other major political parties in India at the threshold of 1970, just as Meadows (with his colleagues) was found to stand apart from the three other scholar-sets in the global context. Interestingly, as noted in Tables 2.1 and 2.3, Meadows invokes 'moral resources' for limiting growth and JS speaks of 'integral humanism'. On the other side, along with their colleagues, Leontief and Herrera, in particular, and Mesarovic and Pestel, to an extent, point out that global imbalance in material goods and services is hindering the formation of a better world society (Table 2.2). Correspondingly, CPI-M, CPI, and to a certain extent SP, point to class-based exploitation within and beyond Indian society, unlike JS explicitly against this formulation and Cong I somewhat implicitly (Table 2.3).

The ultimate goal of the four parties, as declared in their 1977 programmes or election manifestos, was socialism. However, their strategies to attain the professed goal were not found to have changed substantially from their 1970 stance. In conformity with the standpoint of JS and SP in 1970, the Janata Party (1977: 8) speaks of 'individual initiative' and 'decentralization of economic and political power', but the amalgam does not repeat JS's earlier formulation that class conflict is harmful. Cong I (Indian National Congress 1977) does not speak of 'socialist revolution, embracing all people', but also does not mention class conflict. The CPI (1977) does not speak of the progressive role of the 'national bourgeoisie' in forming a new society, but does not forego its anti-imperialist and anti-feudal stance either. CPI-M (1977: 15) holds on to its stand of overthrowing the power of bourgeois-landlord classes under the hegemony of the working class.

In sum, there is hardly any substantive indication of change in the primary valuations of the major Indian political parties between 1970 and 1977. But, with reference to the logistics of meeting their strategies and the goal, differences among them seem to have been accentuated. This is seen from the formulation of 81 indicators in Table 2.13 in the same manner as for Table 2.10, with the valuations attributed to each

Table 2.13
Need Indicators Formulated from Secondary Valuations (viz., the logistics of meeting the strategies and the goals) of Four Major Political Parties in India in 1977, with their Valuations

Indicator	JP	Cong-I	CPI	CPI-M
(1)	(2)	(3)	(4)	(5)
Industry and Trade				
1. Encourage production of wage (consumer) goods necessary for mass consumption	+	0	+	0
2. Encourage capital-intensive export-oriented growth of industries	−	+	−	−
3. Support decentralization of industries	+	0	0	0
4. Support sick industries	−	+	0	0
5. Support heavy and large-scale industry as a general policy	−	+	+	0
6. Support heavy and large-scale industry 'only when it is not possible to organize such production satisfactorily in the cottage and small sector'	+	−	−	−
7. Take industry and employment to smaller towns and rural areas and create mini industries. Avoid urban conglomeration	+	−	0	0
8. Change from capital-intensive to employment-oriented technologies and industries	+	0	0	0
9. Regard the eradication of unemployment as a basic instrument rather than a distant objective of development and justice	+	−	0	+
10. Current development strategies lead to employment	−	+	−	−
11. Bonus should be regarded as deferred wages	+	0	+	0
12. Workers should participate in management	+	+	+	0
13. Workers should receive proportional benefits from increased productivity	+	0	0	0
14. Encourage higher productivity by creating new capacities and utilizing existing ones	0	+	0	+
15. Invest more in power, transport, and communication	+	+	0	0
16. Take over wholesale trade in foodgrain in the public sector	0	0	+	+
17. Enlarge the public sector with help from friendly foreign countries	0	0	+	0

Table 2.13 *contd.*

Indicator	JP	Cong-I	CPI	CPI-M
(1)	(2)	(3)	(4)	(5)
18. Maximize the scope of private sector	+	+	0	0
19. Enlarge the public sector	0	+	+	0
20. Discourage penetration of multinationals	+	0	+	+
21. Change the policy supporting monopolists and thus encouraging concentration of economic power	+	0	+	+
22. Encourage the Indian and the socialist industrial interests to work together	0	0	+	+
23. Encourage the Indian and the non-socialist industrial interests to work together	+	0	−	−
24. The development pattern should remove the evils of capitalism	+	0	+	+
25. The development pattern should remove the evils of state capitalism	+	0	0	0
26. Avoid capital-intensive, urban-oriented, and centralized path of development in industry as followed in the West	+	−	0	+
Agriculture				
27. The declaration of Emergency went against the abolition of landlordism	+	−	+	+
28. Surplus and reclaimed land should be distributed to the landless only	+	−	0	+
29. Implement a policy of graded land tax according to the size of holding	0	0	0	+
30. Lack of political will is the cause of non-implementation of land reform	+	0	0	0
31. Encourage capital production in rural areas in order to remove poverty	+	+	0	0
32. Present policy aids alienation of the rural people from traditional occupations	+	0	0	0
33. Present policy turns cities into vast camping sites for migrants from rural areas	+	0	0	0
34. Supply inputs for maximum output from land	+	+	0	+
35. Convert forest villages into revenue villages	+	0	0	0
36. Implement a policy of food for work	−	0	0	0
37. Implement favourable terms of trade and higher allocations for the rural sector	+	0	0	0

38. Declare primacy of agriculture, handicrafts, and small industries	+	−	−	0
39. Supply credit to rural areas through banks and other organizations	+	+	0	+
40. Remove maldistribution and hoarding of foodgrain	0	0	0	+
41. Present policy denies remunerative prices to peasants	+	−	+	+
42. Institute parity of prices between peasants' sale of produce and their essential purchases	+	0	+	+
43. Maintain the buffer stock mechanism to ensure remunerative prices to peasants	0	+	0	−
44. Pursue the minimum needs programme	0	+	0	0
45. Decentralize the credit policy	+	−	0	0
46. Decentralize the marketing policy	+	−	0	0
47. Open more markets in rural areas	+	+	+	0
48. Open up backward areas	+	+	+	0

Education and Its Application

49. Compulsory education up to the secondary school level	+	−	0	+
50. Check the catastrophic fall in the standard of college and university education	+	−	0	0
51. Avoid higher and technical education associated with capital-intensive systems	+	−	0	0
52. Encourage application of advanced science and technology to industry and agriculture	+	+	+	0
53. Create a reservoir of technical and scientific manpower for industrialization	+	+	+	0
54. Give more scope to scientists engaged in science and technology	0	+	0	0
55. Give scope to progressive artists and intellectuals	0	0	0	+

Language

56. Faithfully implement the three-language formula (Hindi, English, mother tongue)	+	0	0	0
57. Progressively use mother tongue for higher education	+	0	0	0
58. Give due importance and encouragement to Urdu	+	+	0	0

Population

59. Change the present policy which conducts family planning by coercion and compulsion	+	−	+	+
60. Consider the population problem as the cause and consequence of poverty	+	0	0	0

Table 2.13 *contd.*

Indicator	JP	Cong-I	CPI	CPI-M
(1)	(2)	(3)	(4)	(5)
61. Conduct family planning as an 'integral part of a larger population policy package, comprehending education, health, maternity and child care, family welfare and women's rights, nutrition, employment, and rising living standards'	+	0	0	0
National Policy				
62. The declaration of Emergency was justified against Right Reaction	–	+	+	–
63. Emergency has harmed the social, economic, and political life of India	+	–	+	+
64. Emergency led to the growth of extra-Constitutional power	+	–	+	0
65. The President's Rule benefits the ruling party	+	0	0	0
66. Government policy created political zamindars and encouraged vested interests	+	0	0	0
67. Decentralize economic and political power	+	–	0	+
68. Abolish politicization of banking, ban banking credit for speculative purposes	+	0	+	0
69. Delete the Property Act from the List of Fundamental Rights Chapter of the Constitution, and affirm the right to work	+	–	0	+
70. Reduce the difference between the maximum and minimum income, after tax	+	0	0	0
71. Change the present policy which indirectly supports blackmarketeers, smugglers, tax evaders, and racketeers in foreign exchange	+	–	+	+
72. Ensure fiscal and monetary measures to check inflation	–	+	0	0
73. Break the vicious circle of the rich becoming richer and the poor poorer. Adopt the 'austerity syndrome' to relieve the poor from subserving the goals of elitism, consumerism, and urbanism	+	0	0	0
74. Pay special attention to the urban middle class	0	+	0	0
75. Root out dowry: a prevalent social evil	+	+	0	0
76. Forbid banning of political or social organizations without independent judicial enquiry	+	0	0	0
77. Recall errant legislators, reduce election cost, and lower voting age	+	0	0	0

78. Change through non-violence	+	+	0	0
Foreign Policy				
79. Fight for 'universal and genuine disarmament'	+	0	0	0
80. Expand and deepen India's friendship and political and economic relations with the Soviet Union and the socialist countries	0	0	+	+
81. Organize defence 'with the best possible weaponry and equipments, indigenously produced or procured from varied and dependable sources that will not be cut off in a crisis, with regard to cost-effectiveness'	+	0	0	0

indicator by the parties as desirable (positive +), detestable (negative −), or of no significance (neutral 0).

Table 2.13 does not show those data items on which a unanimous valuation by the four parties had become too well-known. For example, all are in favour of eradication of unemployment, untouchability, illiteracy, and corruption in administration. All of them support the rights of linguistic, ethnic, and religious minorities; the policy of nonalignment with the power blocs in the world; and so on. Negatively, all of them are against imperialism and neocolonialism, family planning by coercion, and anti-social activities like smuggling, black marketing, tax evasion, racketeering in foreign exchange, etc. Interestingly, Cong I had not stressed in its 1972 election manifesto the issue of building Third World solidarity against neocolonialism, although Jawaharlal Nehru was one of the principal architects of the movement.

Because of commonality among the parties in their valuations of certain data items in 1977, the topic of 'minority issue' noted in Table 2.10 is no longer relevant to drawing distinctions among them. Contrariwise, need data are extensively enumerated with reference to other topics, especially industry and trade, and agriculture. Moreover, new topics are seen to have gained importance in 1977 for the appraisal of social reality for a better quality of life; population and national policy, for instance. Therefore, Table 2.13 is prepared with reference to these changed information and valuation contexts between 1970 and 1977.

Table 2.13 shows, first, that many more indicators could be formulated from the logistics of the major political parties in 1977 than at

the threshold of 1970. This is an indication of the heightened seriousness and detail with which all the parties appraised social reality for
the evaluation of a better quality of life of the Indian people.

Second, the table shows that only 11 per cent of the total number of
indicators (nine out of 81) were attributed unidimensional valuation,
as against 56 per cent in 1970. Unidimensional valuation is totally
absent from the topics of foreign policy, education, and language; and
is of a low order for the topics of agriculture, industry and trade, and
national policy. Thus, the indication is that the parties were searching
for new avenues to improve the quality of life in respect of notable
aspects of the people's existence, and, therefore, were exploring different dimensions of social reality as suited to their ideology of the goal
and the related strategy.

Third, the table shows that only 21 per cent of the total indicators
were valued multilaterally, which is of the same order as noted for
1970 in Table 2.10. Also, as in 1970, the multilaterally valued indicators
refer to the economic sector of society (industry and trade, and
agriculture) and foreign policy, with education emerging as a sensitive
issue with 43 per cent of indicators under this topic valued multilaterally. Thus, the indication is that while exploring different dimensions of social reality, the major political parties in India in 1977 did
not change their structures of valuation of the quality of life of the
Indian people.

The above indications are precisely revealed by the dimensional and
lateral distinctions within and across pairs of the four political parties
with reference to their paired valuations of 81 indicators defining their
logistics to improve the quality of life of the Indian people. As before,
Tables 2.14 and 2.15 give the frequencies and percentages of the two
kinds of distinctions, and the unit distances the pairs of parties record
among themselves.

The unit distances among the political parties, given under column 5
of Table 2.15, tend to confirm the impression prevailing in 1977 that
the opposition parties JP, CPI, and CPI-M formed a cluster, CPI and
CPI-M were closely allied, and JP was the spearhead of opposition to
Cong I. But a scrutiny of column 5 and the findings under columns
2–4 of Table 2.15 disturb this impression.

First, it is seen that the distinction of Cong I from CPI and CPI-M is
of the same order as of JP from the two communist parties. Moreover,
the dimensional distinction of JP from CPI and CPI-M is appreciably
larger than that from Cong I, especially with regard to bidimensional

Table 2.14
Paired Valuations and Unit Distances between Major Political Parties in India in 1977, regarding their Secondary Valuation of a Better Quality of Life of the Indian People

Paired political parties		Paired valuation						Unit distance (0/−0 = 1, +− = 2)
		++	−−	00	+0/−0	+−	Total	
(1)		(2)	(3)	(4)	(5)	(6)	(7)	(8)
JP	− Cong I	13	−	7	36	25	81	86
	CPI	18	2	8	48	5	81	58
	CPI-M	17	3	5	54	2	81	58
Cong I	− CPI	8	2	25	38	8	81	54
	CPI-M	3	1	26	36	15	81	66
CPI	− CPI-M	12	4	38	26	1	81	28
Total		71	12	109	238	56	486	350

distinction. Correspondingly, Cong I registers both bidimensional and multidimensional distinctions from CPI and CPI-M in substantial magnitude, while recording very little multidimensional distinction from JP. These points indicate that Cong I and JP were closer together

Table 2.15
Dimensional and Lateral Distinctions among Major Political Parties in India in 1977 for Secondary Valuation of a Better Quality of Life of the Indian People (as calculated from frequencies in Table 2.14)

Paired political parties		Dimensional distinction (Percentage of total valuation for each pair of parties)			Extent of dimensional and lateral distinction (Percentage of total unit distances)
		None (++/−−/+−)	Partial (+0/−0)	Total (00)	
(1)		(2)	(3)	(4)	(5)
JP	− Cong I	47	44	9	24
	CPI	31	59	10	17
	CPI-M	27	67	6	17
Cong I	− CPI	22	47	31	15
	CPI-M	24	44	32	19
CPI	− CPI-M	21	32	47	8
Total		29	49	22	100

for the appraisal of a better quality of life of the Indian people than either was with regard to CPI or CPI-M.

Second, as in 1970, CPI and CPI-M registered the least distance between them than with all other pairs of the four parties, although in greater magnitude in 1977 than in 1970. However, clearly unlike in 1970, the dimensional distinction between CPI and CPI-M in 1977 was very large while unidimensional alliance was of the same order as of either party with Cong I. Moreover, multidimensional distinction, absent in 1970, was now greater than the bidimensional distinction. These points suggest the search of the two communist parties in different dimensions of social reality for the evaluation of a better quality of life of the people, both between themselves and with respect to JP and Cong I as indicated in Table 2.4.

Thus, the underlying realities exposed by the illustrative course of analysis do not support the popular image of 1977 that an anti-Emergency valuation of the quality of life of Indian people had led to a more or less united valuation of the Opposition against that of the Establishment. On the contrary, despite the tactical disappearance of the presumed right wing opposition, the axis of variable valuations of the quality of life did not undergo substantive change between 1970–77 with respect to the major political parties' evaluation of what the people need in order to attain a better quality of life. What happened instead is that subject to the commonality of primary valuations of JP and Cong I on one side, and of CPI and CPI-M on the other, the parties were searching in different dimensions of social reality to translate their ideologies into different streams of practice.

The above points are displayed in Figure 2.4 which broadly outlines in three dimensional diagrams the dimensional and lateral distinctions among the major political parties in India at the threshold of 1970 and in 1977. Figure 2.4 does not present a diagram for the primary valuations of the political parties in 1977 because, as explained, these valuations had not undergone appreciable change between 1970 and 1977.

The 1980s began with the return of Cong I to power and saw an increase in its popularity in 1984. On the other side, the amalgamation of JS and SP proved transitory, with BJP (Bharatiya Janata Party) emerging as a formidable political force. JP splintered in other ways also, while CPI and CPI-M remained united in practice and CPI-M, in particular, gained in popularity. During the decade, the impact of the regional parties of south India, in particular, and also of eastern India,

Figure 2.4: Dimensional and Lateral Distances Among Major Political Parties in India at the Threshold of 1970 and in 1977, Regarding their Primary and Secondary Appraisals of Social Reality for Attaining a Better Quality of Life of the People

(Cong I = Congress Party of India (Indira); CPI = Communist Party of India; CPI-M = Communist Party of India-Marxist; JP = Janata Party; JS = Bharatiya Jana-Sangh; SP = Socialist Party)

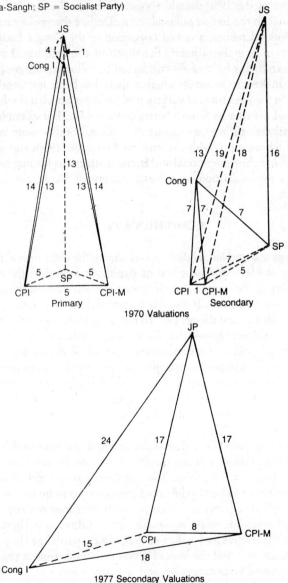

was felt more and more in the all-India context. Do these kaleidoscopic changes protend something more than what is spontaneously visible and assumed, as for 1977?

The close of the 1980 decade appears to be on the threshold of a major change in the Indian political scene. Despite the proliferation of all-India political parties, a united opposition to the Cong I Establishment seems to be in the offing. In this situation, the need-based quality of life research may be usefully conducted by following the proposed course of analysis to ascertain whether there has been any significant alteration in the structures of valuation of the elites on what the Indian people need in order to attain a better quality of life. For example, are the dimensional distinctions among the political bodies more accentuated, which were probably the least marked in the 1950s and less in the 1960s? Are the dimensional and lateral distinctions leading toward polarity in the evaluation of a better quality of life of the Indian people?

COMPREHENSION

The dimensional and lateral distinctions among the elites in evaluating the quality of life of the people is of significant import to the need-based quality of life research, as illustrated and indicated in the global and nation-state contexts. It also has a profound bearing on the future of society, culture, and the people. To cite an extreme example, Marie Antoinette's alleged remark that the people should eat cakes if they have no bread points to a dimensional and lateral distinction in the evaluation of the quality of the people with catastrophic consequences. However, the proposed course of need-based quality of life research, beyond mere handling the 'social indicators' prepared by the experts, may be faulted on the following grounds:

1. The use of particularly chosen documentary materials to delineate variable valuations of the quality of life may be valid and relevant, but not sufficient. The appraisers may yield different structures of value if other documents are consulted.
2. The official documents of corporate bodies may not represent adequately, and even accurately, their valuations. Therefore, what the leaders and cadres of the political parties say in public meetings, etc., and the lines of action they implement in practice, comprise a comprehensive and a better source of valuations made by these bodies than what they put in documents.

3. The fact that the documents of a particular appraiser do not mention an item of information should not be interpreted as denoting the appraiser's neutrality to the information content of an indicator formulated on the basis of data items obtained from all the appraisers considered. It is quite possible that if the unmentioned data items were placed before the appraiser, he or she would have valued the corresponding indicator positively (+) or negatively (−) in place of the researcher attributing a neutral (0) valuation on behalf of the appraiser.

4. The content analyst would impose subjectivity on to the enumeration of need items from the documents and, therefore, on the formulation of need indicators and their valuation. On the contrary, the need indicators (viz., the 'social indicators') formulated by the experts on the basis of general consensus among them would be far more objective.

However, contrary to faulting the proposed course of need-based quality of life research, these arguments highlight its scope for the following reasons:

1. As for any course of research, additional material will ensure the findings already made or revise them. But this only means that the course of research should be rigorously devised and pursued systematically as regards the source materials. By thus conducting a course of research in the manner proposed above, the seeming lacunae in the appraisal of social reality by a scholar may be resolved or the apparent differences among a set of scholars may not be found valid or relevant; such as, with reference to the controversy on young and old Marx, and among the development theorists like Bendix (1964: 5–6), Moore (1967: 3), Shils (1962: 10), Weiner (1966: v), etc., as discussed elsewhere (Mukherjee 1978: 94–99).

2. Doubtless, the wishes expressed in the documents published by corporate bodies like a business agency, a transnational concern, etc., require validation in practice. However, the documents from such bodies as political parties are of a different kind, despite the euphemism they may contain. The genuineness of their appraisal of social reality for a better quality of life of the people they are concerned with need not be doubted. Of course, the elaboration and interpretation of a party programme or election manifesto in public meetings, etc., may deflect the

original valuation, and some lines of action may deviate from the professed standpoint. But these possibilities reflect processual variations in valuation over a time sequence, say, t_{ij}, while value changes in the programmes and manifestos referring to the time points t_i and t_j will capture these processual variations as illustrated for the major Indian political parties over the period 1970–77. The point, therefore, is not to reject the proposed course of need-based research but pursue it over the time sequence.

3. It is likely that if an item of information is placed before an appraiser, the person or the corporate body like a political party will attribute a positive or negative valuation to it. But that does not obliterate the fact that, on his/her own initiative, the appraiser did not attribute a datum to the need item and thus to the need indicator. This means that the item of information was not considered important enough by the appraiser for the appraisal of social reality in the context of a better quality of life of the people. This fact denotes that no mention of an indicator is itself a valuation, namely, the neutral valuation (0) which holds the systematic and systemic structure of the analysis.

4. Content analysis is a carefully designed course of research, meant for eliminating or, at any rate, reducing to the minimum the personal bias inevitable to a reviewer of a document. No doubt, the yield from one analyst may be of superior quality to that from another analyst, as is possible in any course of analytic research. On the other hand, subjectivity of experts is in-built in their formulation of indicators, as discussed in Chapter 1. Therefore, the substantive merit of the illustrations may possibly be improved, but that does not affect the illustrations adversely; nor does it undermine the efficiency of the proposed course of research.

The point, then, is to apply the analytic procedure evermore efficiently with direct reference to the standpoint of the elites on what the people need in order to attain a better quality of life, rather than to depend exclusively on the mediacy of the experts on the social indicators research.

• 3 •
• Mass Perspective: What Do People Want?

DATA COLLECTION

Data are not directly available for enumeration and formulation of indicators of what the people want for a better quality of life. Rigorously structured data base denoting the wants of the people is scarce. Therefore, almost always, the data space has to be structured from the information space of individuals by means of field investigation.

As mentioned in Chapter 1, the data space seems to be systematically and comprehensively structured by questions on 'domain satisfaction' of individuals with reference to 'numerous specific life concerns'. Therefore, like the need-based quality of life research, the want-based research is regarded as proceeding directly with valid want data. The procedure is applied by structuring the questionnaire-schedule with *precoded* responses of individuals, in order to record their range of agreement ('yea'-saying) or disagreement ('no'-saying) with the substance of the questions on an n-point scale. But the procedure cannot preclude the requirement of data formation from the information space of individuals, even though the information space seems to be systematically explored by the questions on 'domain satisfaction'.

The point deserves detailed examination because this commonly adopted procedure short-circuits the want-based quality of life research by starting from the data space provided by the researcher and not by the individuals concerned.

While perceiving a phenomenon, such as the quality of life, an individual explores the information space for the identification of some items of information as good, desirable, etc. ('yea'-saying), some others as bad, detestable, etc. ('no'-saying), and remains neutral (neither 'yea'- nor 'no'-saying) to all other items which enter into his/her field of sensation. The n-point scale takes this bidirectional valuation of a phenomenon into account. Along with the positive and negative responses to the data items graduated on the scale, the neutral responses of the interviewees are located at the *null* (zero) point of the scale between the precoded 'yea' and 'no' responses. Also, variable graduation of their responses along the range of positive and negative valuations amplifies the range of multilateral valuation of the data items. But the *predetermined* data items do not give the interviewees scope for an unconstrained exploration of their information space. They are directed to evaluate a selected set of information items which are posed before them as data items by the researcher.

The perception of quality of life is thus obscured because perception is not registered by the path formed by the relative emphasis laid by an individual on all the items of information that enter into his/her field of sensation. This path, reflecting the mechanics of the mind, will not be revealed from staccato responses to a streamlined battery of prestructured and precoded questions. The point can be illustrated from survey data on the quality of life in India.

During the survey the questions on a respondent's goal of a better quality of life were posed after steering him or her through life experience to appraise social reality for a better quality of life. It was found at the time of analyzing the collected information that specific life concerns of the respondents varied in importance with reference to what they wanted in order to attain the goal. In Calcutta, many respondents equated the goal with what they had first declared in response to the introductory and overall question: 'what do you want most in your life?' But, in the villages of West Bengal, many respondents equated the goal with their response to a specific concern posed later, namely, what they wanted in order to improve their 'personal career'. Moreover, with all the respondents characterized by gender, age, religion/ethnicity, or social status, other life concerns were seen to assume distinctively different positions nearer or farther away from what was declared as the goal. Details of the sample of respondents from West Bengal are given in Table 3.1.

It may be argued that so long as the want-based quality of life research proceeds along specific life concerns ('domain satisfaction') and leads ultimately to eliciting the all-inclusive perception of a better quality of life, findings of the kind recorded in Table 3.1 will be obtainable at the time of data analysis. But the point is that the findings cannot emerge in an unconstrained manner unless the course of research is so designed that it does not pre-empt the respondents' structure of value.

The structure of value is built from the correlated matrix of a respondent's perception of the life process. The nodal points in his/her life experience articulate the matrix. Therefore, a researcher's systematic and comprehensive enumeration of life concerns ('domain satisfaction') is *valid* in respect of an individual's valuation of the quality of life. But the *relevance* of some particular life concerns for the evaluation of one's quality of life and their *necessity* for the identification of a better quality of life cannot be predetermined by a researcher, as is done by enumerating a set of data items and enforcing the reduction of data by precoding the responses to the data items. In this case, the valuation of the researcher is *confounded* by that of the researchee in the sense Fisher (1949: 108–09) employed the term 'confounding' in a design of experiment, albeit, in a different context.

> . . .in the case of interactions involving 3 factors or more, the position is often somewhat different. Such interactions may with reason be deemed of little experimental value, either because the experimenter is confident that they were quantitatively unimportant, or, because, if they were known to exist, there would be no immediate prospect of the fact being utilized. In such cases we may usefully adopt the artifice known as 'confounding'.

For the quality of life research the issue of 'confounding' cannot be 'deemed of little experimental value' and, therefore accepted as an artifice. The fallacy of any such attempt is obvious in the context of elitist acceptance of *sufficiency* of the need-based quality of life research or a singular formulation of need indicators by an expert. Therefore, the first step in the case of want-based quality of life research is to decide on the form of field enquiry which can best explore the information space of individuals to yield valid data.

Failure to distinguish the data space from the information space for the enumeration of want data might result in the generation of false or fallacious data from the immediate responses of informants on what they want most in their life, their life goals, or any other leading issue to indicate their quest for a better quality of life. The point is illustrated by six cases of surveyed information from respondents in Calcutta to ascertain their evaluation of a better life quality:

1. In response to the overall question on what he wanted most in life, a well-established doctor replied 'professional eminence'. But by further probing this question and from answers to

Table 3.1

Decreasing Order of Importance of the Themes of Specific Life Concerns with reference to the Theme of Goal in Life, according to Percentage Incidence of the Themes by Sex, Age, Religion or Ethnicity, and Social Status of Respondents in West Bengal in 1980

Respondent	Decreasing order of importance of themes							
	1	2	3	4	5	6	7	8
(1)	(2)	(3)	(4)	(5)	(6)	(7)	(8)	(9)
				1 City				
Male	Want	Career	(GL 1	Family)	Lack	Work	WB	Peace
Female	Want	Career	Work	GL 1	Peace	(WB	Lack	Family
Young	Want	Career	GL 1	(Lack	Work	(Family	Peace	WB
Adult	Want	(Career	GL 1)	Family	(Lack	Work	WB	Peace
Old	(Want	Career)	WB	(Lack	GL 1	Work	Family	Peace
Hindu	Want	Career	GL 1	Lack	WB	(Work	Family	Peace)
Muslim	Want	(Career	GL 1	Work	Family	(WB	(Lack	Peace
Upper	Want	Career	(GL 1	(Work)	WB	Family	(Lack	Peace)
Middle	Want	Career	Work	(GL 1	Peace)	Lack	WB	Family
Lower	Want	Career	(GL 1	Family)	Lack	WB	Peace	Work
Total	Want	Career	(GL 1	Work	Lack	Family)	WB	Peace

2 Rural

Young	Career	Work	Family	Want	(Lack	GL 1	(WB | Peace)
Adult	Career	Want	WB	(GL 1	Work	Family)	(Lack	Peace)
Old	Career	(Want	GL 1	Family	Peace	Work	Lack	WB
Hindu	Career	Family	Want	(GL 1 | Work)	WB	Peace	Lack
Santhal	Career	(Want	Lack	GL 1	Work	Peace)	Family	WB
Upper	Career	(Want	GL 1	Family)	(Work	(WB)	Lack	Peace
Middle	Career	Want	(Work | Family)	GL 1	(WB	Peace	Lack
Lower	Career	Family	Work	(Want | GL 1)	Peace	WB	Lack
Total	Career	Want	Family	(GL 1 | Work)	WB	Peace	Lack

Note: 1. Bracketed themes record small differences in percentage.
2. GL 1 = good luck to meet want; WB = personal well-being; Lack = feeling of something lacking in life: it does not refer, positively, to a want item.

subsequent questions (including the life goal question), it was found that his prime concerns were his son's education and employment and his daughter's marriage, both befitting his social status.

2. A reasonably well-paid foreman in a reputable industrial enterprise repeatedly declared that all he wanted to achieve (and all that he wished to be removed from the path of attaining his life goal) was to be a university graduate. But by analysing replies to systematic questioning it was found that his goal was not the quest for knowledge or enhancement in social status as an 'educated' person. As his wife is a graduate, although employed at a much lower salary as a college teacher, his aim is to establish parity in familial prestige while maintaining economic superiority by earning more than his wife.

3. An engineer in a firm repeatedly declared that his goal was to find a husband for his sister, befitting his social status. But systematic questioning revealed that status maintenance was not his only concern. He was equally (perhaps more) concerned with improving his own career and his sister's marriage was not only a worry but also a hindrance to this achievement.

4. A reasonably well-paid skilled worker's spontaneous reply to all quality of life questions was 'money'. But his real concern, found from probing his responses, was to obtain suitable employment for his sons before his superannuation which was due shortly.

5. A young man serving as a waiter in a restaurant declared that to be a 'good man' was his life goal. But it was found from systematic questions and by probing his responses that he desires a well-paid job in Calcutta which will fetch enough money to buy land in his native village where he will be established as a respectable 'peasant'.

6. A middle-aged woman executive declared her life goal to live peacefully, happily, and amicably with all around her. But her real concerns, revealed from systematic questioning, were to separate from her husband's joint family of orientation, set up her own nuclear family of procreation, and attain the highest position in her career.

The clusters of information in the six examples can be categorized as false and true data in the manner shown in Table 3.2.

The collection of true data for the want-based quality of life

Table 3.2
Derivation of False and True Data from Apparent and Apposite Content of Information on the Perception of a Better Quality of Life, as obtained Spontaneously and from Exploration in the Information Space (vide, six examples from Calcutta in 1980)

Example	False	True
(1)	(2)	(3)
1.	Self-assertion in professional ability	Retention of social status by children
2.	Personal quest for knowledge/ Education to raise social status	Assertion of male superiority in conjugal life
3.	Retention of social status while meeting family obligation of sister's marriage	Career-building for higher economic status, against which stands the family obligation of sister's marriage
4.	Money for current comfort: personal and familial	Money to establish sons in life with suitable jobs and retain economic security
5.	Self-assertion as a 'decent' person in society	Self-assertion by attaining a better economic status
6.	Happy, amicable, and peaceful life	Higher social status by asserting authority in family and job place

research requires four considerations: (*i*) organization of the field of enquiry in such a manner that the information space for individual respondents is systematically explored, (*ii*) the responses are duly probed (and not prompted) in order to clarify the individuals' perception of the items of information, (*iii*) the investigators' ability is tested to verify the realiability of individual responses, and (*iv*) the researcher's bias is not introduced in the course of research.

The biographic method of survey appears to be free from the above limitations. According to this method, an individual is allowed to freely narrate the course of his/her life and, from this narration, his/her appraisal of the contemporaneous quality of life, awareness of and aspirations for a better life quality, and his/her expectations and achievements in that context are elicited by the researcher. The method is both expensive and time consuming and, therefore, usually covers a small sample. But it may provide substantial data for the quality of life research, as found from the Hungarian experience. However, the method is not free from the limitations mentioned above.

In the course of the first pre-pilot study (PR-1) we held non-
directive or only slightly directive interviews (lasting 6–8 hours
each, and the scenario contained only a list of some basic issues that
had been touched upon) with [120] employees of large-scale enterprises (Hankiss 1978: 61).

Admittedly, the biographic method cannot avoid 'slightly directive
interviews' because the researcher or an investigator may have to
intervene during a narration in order that it does not become inconsequential with irrelevancies. But, while helping in structuring the
course of narration, the intervention may also inadvertently prompt its
substance: a possibility acknowledged for the interview method of
survey.

Another advocated method is of participation and observation. But,
apart from the fact that this method also can deal only with small
samples within reasonable cost-time budgets, it prejudices an unbiased
exploration of the field of variation in concerned individuals. As
participation involves an 'insider's' role in a community of people, the
participant-observer requires a specific 'social entry' into the community.
Therefore, the participation-observation method is efficient only when
the community is homogeneous. Otherwise, the researcher is obliged
to enter into a community of heterogeneous interests by aligning
himself or herself with one of these interests. This rider is inescapable
in adopting the participation-observation method to collect
information on the quality of life.

Contemporarily, there is hardly any community of people which is
not composed of contradictory sectors. The homogeneity of
communities like the Trobriand Islanders (Malinowski 1922) and the
Malay Fishermen (Firth 1946), doubtful at any time of history, is
surely a myth today. This means that while one is obliged to choose a
homogeneous sector of the field of variation in order to participate
and observe, the heterogeneity of the field—which is of distinctive
relevance to the quality of life research—prejudices the enquiry.
Therefore, at best, the participation-observation method will yield
segmental evaluation of the life process; at the worst, biased data on
the quality of life. This is noticeable with respect to the evaluation of
the same place, time, and people bound configuration of a society by
two anthropologists, one of whom explicitly followed the participation-observation method (Beteille 1966; Gough 1981).

The limitation of the participation-observation method can be removed by evolving an interpenetrating network of participant-observers and the sectors of the field of variation in so far as sectoral heterogeneity can be identified on *a priori* grounds. The technique to be employed in this case is that of the *Interpenetrating Network of Subsamples* (IPNS) which was devised and demonstrated by Mahalanobis (1944) for the detection of investigators' bias in large-scale sample surveys. But the adoption of this technique will endorse that, like the biographic-narrative method, the participant-observer method is subject to above mentioned limitations.

The most suitable form of field enquiry is thus of interviewing the people, but not on the basis of *precoded responses to a set of data items posed in a closed* questionnaire-schedule. In order that the researcher's and the investigator's bias can be eliminated (at any rate, reduced to the minimum) and, at the same time, true want data elicited from the interviewees, the questionnaire-schedule should be standardized by posing a set of open-ended questions for the purpose of delving into the mind of the respondent and stimulating it for the respondent's own exploration of the information space to yield want data.

Therefore, the quality of life surveys conducted in India in 1980 and 1982 first posed six overall questions in order to gear the minds of the interviewees to the phenomenon of quality of life and direct them toward a better quality of life. These questions were laid on the axis of desire (positive valuation) and detestation (negative valuation), and their information content was distinguished as what one wants to *have* or to be *removed*. Also, in the context of both desire and detestation, riders were introduced to test the reliability of want data by posing hypothetical situations.

The next batch of eight questions referred to the nodal points in an individual's life, namely, personal career, life at work, family life, and the neighbourhood. The individual mind was thus tuned for the exploration of the information space specific to his/her life concerns. On each of these concerns, the questions referred to what one wants to have (positive information and valuation) and what one wants to be removed (negative information and valuation).

After thus traversing the information space from an overall perception to specificities, the individual mind was steered to a broader, non-specific aspect of one's life concerns. Six questions were considered appropriate to this aspect, which were successively wider in content and ended in generalities; namely, one's recreation and leisure, personal well-being, and leading a peaceful, happy, and progressive life.

Consistently, as before, the questions referred to the positive and negative nuances of life conditions.

With the information space explored in this manner from an overall perspective to specificities and then to generalities, the mind should be set on responding to all-inclusive questions on what one wanted to have, and to get rid of, in order that one may attain a better quality of life. Therefore, ten goal-of-life questions were now posed to ascertain what, in essence, is one's concept of a better quality of life, how it is to be attained, and why it is not yet attained.

Those questions posed for the quality of life surveys in India are given in Table 3.3.

Table 3.3
Open-ended Questions for Want-based Quality of Life Surveys

Overall

1. What do you want most in your life?
2. What do you feel the 'lack' of most in your life?
3. As you know, in olden times, the gods and saints used to appear in a dream and command a person to ask for a boon. Now, if you were to receive such a boon, what would you ask for?
4. What do you detest most in your life?
5. What would you like most to be removed in order that you are satisfied in your life?
6. If you were asked to receive a boon to remove from your life what you detest most and thus make you happy, what would you ask for?

Specific

7. What do you want most to improve your personal career?
8. What would you like most to be removed in order that you may improve your personal career?
9. What do you want most to improve your life at work?
10. What would you like most to be removed in order that you may improve your life at work?
11. What do you want most to improve your family life?
12. What would you like most to be removed in order that you may improve your family life?
13. What do you want most to improve the neighbourhood conditions?
14. What would you like most to be removed in order that your neighbourhood conditions are improved?

Generalized

15. What do you want most for recreation and leisure?
16. What would you like most to be removed in order that you may enjoy recreation and leisure?
17. What do you want most to improve your personal well-being?
18. What would you like most to be removed in order to enhance your personal well-being?

19. What do you want most for a peaceful, happy and progressive life?
20. What would you like most to be removed in order that you may attain a more peaceful, happy, and progressive life?

Focused

21. What is the goal in your life?
22. What do you do to attain the goal?
23. What prevents you from attaining the goal?
24. What do you do to remove that which prevents you from attaining the goal?
25. What kind of support do you desire to attain your goal?
26. What kind of support do you require to remove the obstacles in the way of attaining the goal?
27. Why have you not received the support you desire to attain the goal?
28. Why have you not received the support you require to remove the obstacles in the way of attaining your goal?
29. Do you think you will ever reach your goal?
30. (1) If 'yes', how?
    (2) If 'no', why?
    (3) If you 'do not know', why are you uncertain?

Once the mind of an individual is thus tuned to the phenomenon of quality of life and directed toward the perception of a better quality of life, leading questions may be posed in the light of variable appraisals of the need-based quality of life research so as to ascertain, in a direct manner, the extent to which the wants of the people synchronize with the stated needs.

Questions may also be framed to further explore the individuals' appraisal of a better quality of life concerning oneself, the community one belongs to, the nation-state to which one is affiliated, and, ultimately, humankind at large. However, in the course of progression from Ego to society, there are inherent limits to one's perception of the quality of life and appraisal of a better quality of life. These limits do not falsify the want data; on the contrary, they reveal the extent and the depth to which an individual is able to explore the information space and attribute *datum* to the items of information to produce the want data.

The limits to individual exploration of social reality for a better quality of life are also inherent to the basic questionnaire-schedule outlined in Table 3.3, and have a substantive bearing on the formation of want data, as will be examined later. But these limits should not be confounded with the possibility of failure on the part of investigators to help the informants in exploring the information space. Therefore, each of the questions in Table 3.3 requires probing. But, in order that probing is not different for respective investigators and different informants, as also to avoid indiscriminate probing which may turn into prompting responses, the method of probing each and all questions should be standardized.

During the 1980–82 surveys of quality of life in India, the course of probing was standardized in the following manner. After receiving a spontaneous answer to a question, the first probing question was 'what is it?' for a clear *description* of the content of the response. The second was 'how is it?', to reveal the *instrumentality* behind the spontaneous response, and the third was 'why is it?', to elicit the *causality* of spontaneous response.

For example, in response to the first overall question 'what do you want most in your life?', sometimes the spontaneous (S) response was 'money'. In that case, the first probing question was: 'what exactly do you mean when you say you want money the most in your life?'. The response (P1) was followed by the second probing question: 'how will you obtain money?', and the response (P2) was followed by the last probing question: 'why do you want money?'. The usefulness of probing such a spontaneous response has been noted with reference to Example 4 in Table 3.2.

In this manner, the informants can be helped, without investigators' bias, to explore their information space with respect to each question. Thus, subject to the limits of one's perception of a better quality of life, precise and comprehensive want data can be collected by adopting the stated version of the interview method of field investigation.

Doubtless, the method is more time and cost consuming than the conventional attitudinal surveys, but much less than the biographic-narrative or the participation-observation methods of field investigation. During the 1980 and 1982 surveys of 590 individuals in India it was found that, on an average, one man-day (spread over, if required, more than a calendar date to suit the convenience of the informant) was required per respondent.

DATA VERIFICATION

For the want-based quality of life research, verification of the information collected from field investigation as true want data is essential because fallacious responses may appear as true expressions of what an individual wants in order to improve the quality of life. The point has been illustrated in Table 3.2, and it has also been discussed that avoiding the issue by listing the data items in a questionnaire-schedule (as for attitudinal studies on an n-point scale) would restrict the flow of want data and is liable to researcher's bias. Therefore, the data collected by adopting a rigorous course of field investigation, as described and illustrated, should be tested to verify, first, the usefulness of the researcher's design of the open-ended questionnaire-schedule to reveal the mental process of the respondents. Second, the validity of the investigators' probing should be tested, as unbiased and effective in helping the respondents to appraise social reality systematically and meticulously for the evaluation of a better quality of life. Third, the reliability of the informants' responses as furnishing valid want data should be verified.

The efficiency of structuring the questionnaire-schedule will be tested by a steadily decreasing incidence of the necessity of probing the questions. The schedule outlined in Table 3.3 is so designed that it steers the mind of a respondent from an overall perception of what he/she wants to specificities, then to generalities, and, finally, to focus his/her mind on the goal of a better quality of life. Therefore, as the interview proceeds along these categories of questions, the respondents should require less and less probing to express their wants precisely and comprehensively. This means that the efficiency of the schedule design will be tested by fewer and fewer items of new information elicited from consistent and standardized probing by the investigators in the manner described.

The consistency of decreasing incidence of new information items elicited by the investigators' probing would also testify to an overall reliability of the investigators. Therefore, in the case of employing a few investigators directly trained by the researcher, the procedure will also adequately testify against the investigators' bias. Otherwise, when employing a large number of investigators, a more efficient technique should be used.

For the 1980 quality of life survey in West Bengal, one male and one female investigator were employed for the city of Calcutta, and one male investigator for the villages. With reference to these three investigators directly trained by the researcher, Table 3.4 testifies to the efficiency of the questionnaire-schedule and the effective role of the three investigators. It will be noticed from the Table that while the villagers required more probing than the city dwellers, for either category of respondents the questions with the positive information content of what one wants to have required more probing than the questions with the negative information content of what one wants

Table 3.4
Percentage of Responses Yielding New Items of Information by Probing
(total responses in brackets) for Different Categories of Questions noted in Table 3.3:
1980 West Bengal Survey

Category of question	Percentage	
	Calcutta	Villages
(1)	(2)	(3)
1. Overall	(407) 77	(450) 90
2. Specific: Positive	(258) 68	(296) 92
Negative	(231) 41	(296) 75
3. Generalized: Positive	(204) 52	(225) 78
Negative	(190) 25	(221) 58
4. Focused: Goal of life	(506) 7	(673) 10
Total	(1796) 43	(2161) 59

removed. Evidently, wants dominated the social scene, redundancy was shelved to the background. However, both ways and for successive categories of questions, the decreasing trend in percentage incidence is consistently maintained.

The 1982 survey of quality of life in the city of Delhi and the villages in its hinterland was based on the same questionnaire-schedule as applied in the West Bengal survey in 1980, but it involved a large number of investigators trained by two research associates who were previously trained by the researcher. Therefore, in this case, a stringent technique was applied to testify against the investigators' bias along with testing the efficiency of the schedule which was already verified in 1980 with respect to the West Bengal sample.

In place of noting the percentage incidence of responses which yielded new items of information by probing, the effect of probing the spontaneous (S) responses was put on a four-point scale. As there were three successive probings P1, P2, and P3 to each question, the effect of probing would be 0 in case of zero yield of new information item and 3, at the maximum, in case all the three probing questions yielded new information items. That is, with respect to each question, the effect of probing will score one of four values 0, 1, 2, or 3. The mean and standard deviation of these scores, with reference to the categories of questions noted in Table 3.3 and their positive and negative aspects (noted in Table 3.4 for the specific and generalized categories only), would be a more stringent test than mere percentage incidence.

Table 3.5
Mean and Standard Deviation of New Items of Information (0, 1, 2, 3) Yielded by Probing Spontaneous Responses to Each Question under Categories noted in Table 3.3: 1982 Delhi Survey

Category and aspect of questions		Mean		Standard deviation		Number of responses	
Positive	Negative	City	Rural	City	Rural	City	Rural
(1)	(2)	(3)	(4)	(5)	(6)	(7)	(8)
1 Men							
Overall		2.53	2.54	0.63	0.66	300	414
Specific		2.34	2.35	0.61	0.72	400	552
Generalized		2.21	2.04	0.69	0.77	300	414
Focused		1.91	1.81	0.75	0.79	594	781
	Overall	2.32	2.45	0.71	0.71	300	414
	Specific	2.23	2.26	0.64	0.76	400	552
	Generalized	2.17	1.99	0.50	0.84	300	414
	Focused	1.70	1.48	0.76	0.72	306	461
2 Women							
Overall		2.31	2.05	0.78	0.74	273	348
Specific		2.21	1.80	0.77	0.70	364	464
Generalized		1.98	1.73	0.76	0.71	273	348
Focused		1.56	1.38	0.75	0.67	542	661
	Overall	2.05	1.90	0.82	0.76	273	348
	Specific	1.93	1.72	0.84	0.68	364	464
	Generalized	1.67	1.55	0.74	0.72	273	348
	Focused	1.17	1.27	0.65	0.56	277	383

Table 3.5, which gives the city-rural and male-female distinctions of the respondents, and of the categories of questions with positive or negative information content, shows that the standard deviations are more or less of the same order for all mean values. The mean values do not register an appreciable difference by city-rural location of the respondents (unlike the difference found for the West Bengal sample), but the gender difference is notable to an extent. On the positive and negative information contents of the questions, the alignment of the Delhi sample is the same as for West Bengal, showing the respondents' greater concern with what they want to have than what is to be rejected. However, most importantly, the test bears out the efficiency

of the schedule design and overall reliability of the investigators for the 1982 Delhi survey.

Although found reliable on the whole, it will be useful to ascertain whether one or a few of the large number of investigators failed to interview the informants properly and, therefore, whether the reliability of data has been seriously affected. The technique of Interpenetrating Network of Subsamples (IPNS) devised by Mahalanobis (1944) may be employed for this intensive scrutiny. Applied to the 1982 Delhi survey by 12 investigators, the technique demonstrated its usefulness.

Three ethnic communities, namely, Gujar (**Gu**), Meo (**Me**), and Scheduled Castes (**SC**), were selected for interview in the city of Delhi (**C**) and its rural hinterland (**V**). The members of each community were further distinguished as male (**M**) and female (**F**). The reason behind this manner of identifying the social groups for the want-based quality of life research is explained before presenting Table 3.23. For the present purpose, it should be noted that 12 sets of respondents were identified as: **GuCM, GuCF, GuVM, GuVF, MeCM, MeCF, MeVM, MeVF, SCCM, SCCF, SCVM,** and **SCVF**.

Three male and three female investigators were selected to interview the male and the female respondents, respectively, in the city: and, correspondingly, three male and three female investigators for the male and female rural respondents. The investigators were formed into four batches of three investigators each. By their city (**C**) or village (**V**) location and as male (**M**) or female (**F**), the investigators may be labelled in the above order of batch formation as: **CM1, CM2, CM3; CF1, CF2, CF3; VM1, VM2, VM3;** and **VF1, VF2, VF3**.

The same number of sampled individuals were allocated to each one of 12 specified sets of respondents in the city and villages, and that number was allotted in half to two investigators. At the same time, the three investigators in a batch were rotated among the apposite three sets of respondents. The design is outlined in Table 3.6.

This manner of applying the IPNS technique is rather crude. Moreover, it encountered procedural difficulties in the course of the survey. Because of non-contact of respondents for a survey constrained by a fixed cost-time budget, the actual number of responses in each IPNS cell varied between 290 and 522 for the city sample and between 435 and 812 for the rural sample. Nevertheless, its usefulness in discerning some investigators' limitations in fully eliciting the informants' responses to the questions was demonstrated by the coefficient of variation of

Table 3.6
Allocation of Equal Number of Respondents in IPNS Design of Investigators and Respondent-sets: 1982 Delhi Survey

City					Village				
Investigator		Respondent-set			Investigator		Respondent-set		
Batch	Code	1	2	3	Batch	Code	1	2	3
(1)	(2)	(3)	(4)	(5)	(6)	(7)	(8)	(9)	(10)
1. Male	CM1	GuCM	MeCM		3. Male	VM1	GuVM	MeVM	
	2		MeCM	SCCM		2		MeVM	SCVM
	3	GuCM		SCCM		3	GuVM		SCVM
2. Female	CF 1	GuCF	MeCF		4. Female	VF 1	GuVF	MeVF	
	2		MeCF	SCCF		2		MeVF	SCVF
	3	GuCF		SCCF		3	GuVF		SCVF

the scores of effective probing explained earlier and shown in Table 3.5.

Variability in the probing scores depends on three factors: (*i*) nature of the question, (*ii*) informants' ability to provide new information items for data formation, and (*iii*) investigators' efficiency in probing. The IPNS technique is applied in such a manner that the informants' ability in the present context is of random variation, while variation by the nature of questions will be the same for investigators and informants because all the questions are taken into account. Therefore, the coefficients of variation, prepared from the mean and standard deviation values given in Table 3.7 and placed in Table 3.8, will indicate inter-investigator variability.

The slightly larger dispersion of probing scores for women rather than men in Table 3.7 can be explained by gender differences in exploring the information and data spaces for the appraisal of a better quality of life: a point which will be examined in the context of data formation. Otherwise, Table 3.8 shows that investigator-wise variability within the four batches, as pointed out in Table 3.6, is nearly always of the same order for the respective categories of male and female respondents. However, the noticeable although slight variations within the order portend interesting findings.

From the mean values given in Table 3.7, the difference in probing scores can be calculated for (*a*) two investigators with respect to a

Table 3.7
Mean and Standard Deviation (in brackets) of Probing Scores of Investigators and Respondent-sets: 1982 Delhi Survey

City				Village			
Investigator code	Respondent-set			Investigator code	Respondent-set		
	1	2	3		1	2	3
(1)	(2)	(3)	(4)	(5)	(6)	(7)	(8)
CM1	2.51 (0.67)	2.13 (0.70)		VM1	2.15 (0.72)	2.46 (0.71)	
2		2.01 (0.78)	1.91 (0.74)	2		1.88 (0.81)	2.13 (0.85)
3	2.17 (0.75)		2.18 (0.60)	3	1.78 (0.79)		2.08 (0.86)
CF1	1.99 (0.85)	1.43 (0.71)		VF1	1.41 (0.60)	1.55 (0.62)	
2		1.80 (0.76)	2.02 (0.81)	2		1.32 (0.53)	1.23 (0.47)
3	1.72 (0.86)		1.89 (0.90)	3	2.25 (0.68)		1.89 (0.82)

respondent-set or (*b*) two respondent-sets with respect to an investigator. These differences can then be expressed as percentages of the maximum possible difference of 3 between the mean probing scores of

Table 3.8
Coefficients of Variation of Probing Scores of Investigators and Respondent-sets: 1982 Delhi Survey

City				Village			
Investigator code	Respondent-set			Investigator code	Respondent-set		
	1	2	3		1	2	3
(1)	(2)	(3)	(4)	(5)	(6)	(7)	(8)
CM1	27	33		VM1	33	29	
2		39	39	2		43	40
3	35		28	3	44		41
CF1	43	50		VF1	43	40	
2		42	40	2		40	38
3	50		48	3	30		43

two investigators or two respondent-sets because the 4-point scale of probing scores is graduated 0, 1, 2, and 3. Table 3.9 gives these percentage values for pairs of investigators and respondent-sets, respectively, in batch formation.

The first half of Table 3.9 records three uncommon values of 28, 22, and 19. Investigator **VF3** is common to the values 28 and 22 which she registers with **VF1** and **VF2**, while **VF1** and **VF2** register a value of 8. The second half of the table shows that the two respondent-sets **GuVF**

Table 3.9

Difference in Two Mean Values of Probing Scores as Percentage of Maximum Possible Value of 3, between Two Investigators for one Respondent-set or Two Respondent-sets for one Investigator: 1982 Delhi Survey

Investigator	Respondent-set	Percentage
(1)	(2)	(3)
1 Variation between Investigators		
CM1 – CM3	GuCM	11
CM2	MeCM	4
CM2 – CM3	SCCM	9
CF1 – CF3	GuCF	9
CF2	MeCF	12
CF2 – CF3	SCCF	4
VM1 – VM3	GuVM	12
VM2	MeVM	19
VM2 – VM3	SCVM	2
VF1 – VF3	GuVF	28
VF2	MeVF	8
VF2 – VF3	SCVF	22
2 Variation between Respondent-sets		
CM1	GuCM – MeCM	13
2	MeCM – SCCM	3
3	GuCM – SCCM	0.3
CF1	GuCF – MeCF	19
2	MeCF – SCCF	7
3	GuCF – SCCF	6
VM1	GuVM – MeVM	10
2	MeVM – SCVM	8
3	GuVM – SCVM	10
VF1	GuVF – MeVF	5
2	MeVF – SCVF	3
3	GuVF – SCVF	12

and **SCVF**, which **VF3** interviewed, register a value of inter-interviewer variability of 12, while **GuVF** and **MeVF** interviewed by **VF1** and **MeVF** and **SCVF** interviewed by **VF2** record the values of inter-interviewer variability of 5 and 3. A case against **VF3**'s performance as an investigator is thus indicated.

VM1 registers the value of 19 with **VM2** in the first half of Table 3.9 and 12 with **VM3**, while **VM2-VM3** register an inter-investigator variability of only 2. The second half of Table 3.9 shows that inter-interviewer variability is nearly of the same order as 10, 8, and 10 between **GuVM-MeVM, MeVM-SCVM**, and **GuVM-SCVM**, respectively. Therefore, a case against **VM1** can be mooted but less strongly than against **VF3**.

Table 3.9 records, furthermore, that **CM3** registers a somewhat larger value of 11 with **CM1** and 9 with **CM2**, while **CM1-CM2** register 4. But **GuCM** and **SCCM**, with which **CM3** was concerned, register a value of only 0.3, while **MeCM-SCCM** registers a value of 3 and **GuCM-MeCM** of 13. Therefore, a case against **CM3**'s efficiency as an investigator could also be considered.

Contrariwise, although **CF1** registers a value of 12 with **CF2** and 9 with **CF3**, while **CF2-CF3** register 4, variability between **GuCF** and **MeCF** interviewed by **CF1** is as large as 19 while the same between **MeCF-SCCF** (interviewed by **CF2**) and **GuCF-SCCF** (interviewed by **CF3**) are 7 and 6. Therefore, **CF1** may be absolved of suspicion because of large inter-interviewer variability.

Findings of this sort help in collecting reliable information from the field by a second scrutiny of the schedules submitted by the suspects and, if required, by re-interviewing particular respondents. As regards the 1982 Delhi survey, the information collected from **VF3, VM1**, and **CM3** could thus be made acceptable.

The example points out that because of careful selection of investigators and their further training for a specialized investigation, variability among them may be reduced to the minimum and, on that ground, the reliability of surveyed data can be assured. But inter-investigator variability cannot be eliminated as it is while a number of technicians measure something with a precision instrument.

Subject to the same limiting condition, the reliability of surveyed data may be examined from the side of the informants. However, in this case, the procedure encounters a difficulty built into the quality of life research which would be unanimously accepted with respect to the want-based research.

Unlike the usual kind of social research, the quality of life research is concerned with the **perceptual** and not the **perceived** variables. The point of information is on things which one perceives as need or want; and not on the perceived things which one had, has, or is going to have, which are the usual objects of enquiry for social research such as the living conditions of the people (in particular, the standard of living). This distinction is ignored for the need-based quality of life research because an expert's (or an elite group's, like the power-wielding elites') perception of things is considered invariant to the things perceived. The perceptual variables are thus equated with the things perceived and, on this basis, the need data are assumed to be objective. Contrariwise, the want data are considered as subjective perceptual variables because the elitist bias does not operate in this context and the perception of things the masses want is not equated with the things perceived.

The fallacy of this non-perceptual—perceptual and the consequent objective—subjective dichotomy of need and want data will be examined later with reference to the contexts of data formation. Presently, the concern is with the difference between the usual kinds of social research and the quality of life research, with particular reference to the want-based research. In this respect, an inadequate, inconsistent, or irregular response to a question would be unhesitatingly rejected as unreliable data collection for the usual kinds of social research, but the 'fault' may indicate a distinctive dimension of data collected for the quality of life research. As the latter kind of social research deals in perceptual variables, the 'fault' revealed by systematic probing of the spontaneous answer to each open-ended question may point to distinctive limits to the perception of a better quality of life and, thus, charter the path toward defining specific contexts to the formation of data.

But these limits, ascertained from a scrutiny of the completed questionnaire-schedules as regards probing the spontaneous answers, may also be due to the extraordinary intelligence of an informant or may be engineered by a frivolous informant. Here, therefore, is an instance of confounding the true with the false want data. The verification of want data from the side of the informants should take this form of confounding into account and proceed accordingly.

The procedure begins with a classification of the effects of probing the spontaneous answers to the questions listed in Table 3.3. Each one of successive probings may or may not add to the information provided by the spontaneous answer. Therefore, as same or different, the spontaneous and probed responses **S, P1, P2**, and **P3** to a question may be related in $(2^4 - 1 =)$ 15 ways. Of these, eight relations are consistent and seven inconsistent, as shown in Table 3.10.

The eighth consistent relation $S = P1 = P2 = P3$ has been separated from the other seven in Table 3.10 because it registers no effect at all of probing the question. The remaining seven relations are clearly inconsistent because they record that at the second or the third state of

Table 3.10

Consistent, Inadequate, and Inconsistent Relations among S, P1, P2, and P3 Responses to a Question in Table 3.3

Relation	Stage of difference in item of information			Reversal in item of information
	1	2	3	
(1)	(2)	(3)	(4)	(5)
1 Consistent				
1. $S \neq P1 = P2 = P3$	P1	—	—	None
2. $S = P1 \neq P2 = P3$	P2	—	—	"
3. $S = P1 = P2 \neq P3$	P3	—	—	"
4. $S \neq P1 \neq P2 = P3 \neq S$	P1	P2	—	"
5. $S = P1 \neq P2 \neq P3 \neq S$	P1	P3	—	"
6. $S = P1 \neq P2 \neq P3 \neq S$	P2	P3	—	"
7. $S \neq P1 \neq P2 \neq P3 \neq S \neq P2 \neq P3 \neq P1$	P1	P2	P3	"
2 Consistent but Inadequate				
8. $S = P1 = P2 = P3$	—	—	—	None
3 Inconsistent				
9. $S \neq P1 \neq P2 \neq P3 \neq S = P2 \neq P3 \neq P1$	P1	P3	—	P2 to S
10. $S \neq P1 \neq P2 \neq P3 \neq S \neq P2 \neq P3 = P1$	P1	P2	—	P3 to P1
11. $S \neq P1 \neq P2 \neq P3 = S \neq P2$	P1	P2	—	P3 to S
12. $S = P1 \neq P2 \neq P3 = S$	P2	—	—	P3 to S
13. $S \neq P1 = P2 \neq P3 = S$	P1	—	—	P3 to S
14. $S \neq P1 \neq P2 = P3 = S$	P1	—	—	P2 to S
15. $S \neq P1 \neq P2 \neq P3 = P1 \neq S = P2$	P1	—	—	P2 to S and P3 to P1

probing the spontaneous answer to a question, the new item of information elicited is the same as one which was posited before, but was qualified by another item of information elicited at an earlier stage of probing. This is a case of reversal to an information item and not of successive accumulation of items of information by systematic probing.

The consistent relations 1–7 in Table 3.10 suggest that, except for the seventh, probing is less and less useful after a certain stage of proceeding with the interview, as found in Table 3.4 and 3.5, to attest to the efficiency of designing the questionnaire-schedule and the effective role of the investigators in conducting the interview. This association between the efficiency of the questionnaire-schedule and the effective role of the investigators, on the one hand, and the respondent-wise relation among **S, P1, P2**, and **P3**, on the other, would be a confirmation of the reliability of the collected information and the identification of respondents unambiguously aspiring for a better quality of life.

Conversely, a reversal in the decreasing trend of the effect of probing by successive categorization of the questions listed in Table 3.3 would point to irregularity in the collection of information as want data. But a particular form of this irregularity will register reliable want data in the context of confused or constrained perception of a better quality of life.

Confused perception would suggest that the informant is less aware than others of what is the goal of a better quality of life, how to attain it, and why. Constrained perception may or may not reflect the lack of awareness of the informant of a better quality of life, but it would register less aspiration to attain the envisaged goal than in the case of aware and aspirant informants. Therefore, with the less aspirant respondents also, the goal-related questions (Questions 21–30 in Table 3.3) should yield more inadequate or inconsistent answers from probing (vide, Relations 8–15 in Table 3.10) than the probed answers to the overall, specific, and generalized questions (Questions 1–20 in Table 3.3).

This hypothesis of detecting more 'faulty' responses to the goal-related questions than to the other questions because of a confused or constrained perception of a better quality of life by the less aware and less aspirant respondents was verified in the field situation, first in West Bengal in 1980 and next in Delhi in 1982. It was found that the reversed trend of the effect of probing was governed by the fact that the goal of a better quality of life is less meaningful to a person lacking in awareness of or aspiration for a better quality of life. What is more meaningful is what the person would want to have or be removed in respect of contemporaneous life concerns (domain satisfaction).

Incidentally, this is a clear example of domain satisfaction being a valid concern for the want-based quality of life research, but not a sufficient condition: a point which was raised in Chapter 1 and briefly discussed in this chapter in the context of collecting true or false want data.

Another form of irregularity in the decreasing trend of the effect of probing will be registered by the extraordinarily intelligent and serious informants. They will not register the decreasing trend of probing at all, and thus record seemingly inadequate data, because their probed responses to all or more of the questions in the schedule will bear no effect of probing as indicated by Relation 8 of Table 3.10.

Thus, by two specific forms of irregularity in the collected information, the extraordinarily intelligent informants aspiring for a better quality of life will be distinguished from the less aware or less aspirant informants. Both the groups will testify to the reliability of want data despite the apparent anomalies of irregular and inadequate data yielded by the former, and, irregular, inadequate, and inconsistent data yielded by the latter.

Irregularity in the trend of effective probing is overruled for the frivolous informants because they have the impetus to conform to the general pattern, in order to demonstrate their ability and willingness to participate in the interview. The point was verified during the two quality of life surveys in India, when the respondents who did not register any irregular trend but yielded inconsistent information (Relation 9–15 of Table 3.10) were re-interviewed. However, reliable want data would be obtainable from the frivolous informants if the investigator is on guard and these informants are convinced of the usefulness of the enquiry.

In any case and in the manner indicated, the frivolous informants can be distinguished from both the aspiring informants (extraordinarily intelligent or not) and the less aware and less aspiring informants for a better quality of life. Thus, from such conceivable aspects, unreliable want data can be detected from the collected information and rectified by re-interviewing the informant or rejecting the schedule.

In the light of these logically conceived and empirically verifiable postulates, a set of hypotheses can be formulated for the verification of want data. The hypotheses are given in Table 3.11.

Table 3.11

Data Verification on Informant's Reliability from Effect of Probing Spontaneous Answers to Questions in a Schedule as Listed in Table 3.3

(Trend: Regular	= Downward trend of effect of probing to questions under successive categories noted in Table 3.3.
Irregular I	= Incidence of Relations 8–15 of Table 3.10 larger for goal-related than other categories of questions listed in Table 3.3.
Irregular II	= Incidence of Relation 8 of Table 3.10 for all or most questions in Table 3.3.
Nature: Consistent	= Incidence of Relations 1–7 of Table 3.10.
Inadequate	= Incidence of Relation 8 of Table 3.10.
Inconsistent	= Incidence of Relations 9–15 of Table 3.10.)

Trend	Nature	Deduction	Explanation
(1)	(2)	(3)	(4)
Regular	Consistent	Reliable data	Respondent aspirant for a better quality of life
	Inconsistent	Unreliable data	Frivolous respondent
Irregular I	Inadequate and inconsistent	Reliable data	Respondent less aware of or less aspirant for a better quality of life
Irregular II	Consistent but inadequate	Reliable data	Extraordinarily intelligent respondent aspiring for a better quality of life

Certain other societal characteristics will adduce to the relevance and reliability of the hypotheses formulated in Table 3.11 for the verification of the informants' reliability in the collection of information from field survey as want data.

A massive incidence of frivolous informants in the sample is ruled out in the case of a properly designed and efficiently conducted field survey. Also, the presence of a large number of extraordinarily intelligent persons who do not require probing at all is rare in any society. Therefore, unreliable want data, because of the informants' lack of seriousness, or seemingly unreliable data because of the extraordinary intelligence of the informants, may occur in the sample, but if they do they will occur with low incidence and as random variables.

On the contrary, individuals who are less aware of or aware but less aspirant for a better quality of life emerge through social processes, as will be examined in the context of data formation. They are, therefore, located at distinctive points of the social structure. A few of them may be genetic products but, in the present context, such persons are prima facie rejected from a field survey. This means that the decreasing trend of no effect of probing, as shown in Tables 3.4 and 3.5, may be partly or fully replaced in one or a few social segments by the trend noted in Table 3.11 as Irregular I, but the irregularity will hardly occur at random in the society and in its sample coverage.

The formulated hypotheses and their confirmatory indications were tested for the 1980 West Bengal and 1982 Delhi surveys. The West Bengal survey comprised a sample of only 145 informants, and their answered questionnaire-schedules were found on scrutiny to contain very few 'faulty' responses (Relations 8–15 of Table 3.10). Therefore, a percentage calculation of informants faulted by registering the Irregular Trend I of Table 3.11 was not very meaningful. Also, schedules registering Relation 8 of Table 3.10 for responses to all or most questions in a schedule were not many; that is, the Irregular Trend II of Table 3.11 was virtually absent from the sample.

However, the scrutiny yielded 3.5 per cent of responses to the total of 4,060 questions bearing Relation 8 of Table 3.10, while Relations 9–15 were less represented. Finally, the faulted schedules referred mostly to Calcutta Muslim women in particular (a sample of seven) and Calcutta women in general (a total Hindu and Muslim sample of 32). The West Bengal sample did not contain rural women.

The Delhi survey presented a similar scenario, but more clearly because of a wider sample coverage in extent and depth. Relation 8 of Table 3.10 was recorded for 4.5 per cent of the total of 12,460 questions; the incidence of Relations 9–15 was lower. Also, a schedule seldom contained these 'faulty' relations for all or most of the questions. On the other hand, out of 97 schedules faulted by the occurrence of Relations 8–15 of Table 3.10, 89 referred to women in the rural hinterland of Delhi, eight only to rural men, and none to the city dwellers.

For the larger sample of Delhi informants (445) and a slightly larger incidence of Relation 8 of Table 3.10 in their responses, it was practicable to calculate the incidence of Irregular Trend I of Table 3.11; the incidence of Irregular Trend II was insignificant as noted. The village women were mainly found to register the trend by recording Relation 8 of Table 3.10 for 64 per cent of the goal-related questions, as against 36 per cent of the overall, specific, and generalized questions. Thus, Irregular Trend I reversed the regular trend noted in Tables 3.4 and 3.5.

In Indian society, as for many other configurations of world society, the social conditioning of women is expressed in their confusion and constraint in apprehending reality for a better quality of life while being engrossingly concerned with somehow maintaining the status quo. This characteristic is also more noticeable in the rural rather than urban areas, and in communities displaying stronger male domination. The verification of want data has highlighted this social segment for the want-based quality of life research in India, although the segment is found to be very small in size in respect of the totals of Calcutta women and the women of Delhi's rural hinterland.

However, as data verification in the context of informants' reliability is primarily concerned with detecting the frivolous ones, some more tests may be applied to confirm the consistency of the perceptual data. One of these tests may be with respect to the thematic content of the positive and negative aspects of the same topic.

It is seen from Table 3.3 that questions are paired for responses on what one wants to have (positive) and give up (negative); namely, Questions 1 and 2, 4 and 5, 3 and 6 under the overall category, Questions 7 and 8, 9 and 10, 11 and 12, and 13 and 14 under the specific category, and Questions 15 and 16, 17 and 18, and 19 and 20 under the generalized category. A respondent may dwell on the same or allied theme when responding to a pair of questions or posit different themes for the positive and the negative aspects of the same topic. But a random occurrence of thema parity and disparity with respect to paired questions can be hypothesized to be offset by the design of the questionnaire-schedule, because the schedule has been tested to steer the mind of a respondent systematically and the mental horizon of the respondents has been tested to have been consistently probed by the investigator.

Therefore, an alternate hypothesis may be formulated that as the perception of an individual is more and more geared to stating what he or she wants *most* to have or give up, the incidence of thema disparity for the positive-negative aspects of the same topic will systematically decrease as the interview proceeds from the class of overall questions to the class of specific and then to the class of generalized questions. The hypothesis is supported by the findings from the 1980 West Bengal and 1982 Delhi surveys, as seen from Table 3.12.

Another test, unknown to the investigators and the informants, may be particularly useful. For this reason, two 'good luck' questions (Questions 3 and 6) were inserted in the list of questions in Table 3.3.

Table 3.12
Incidence of Thema Disparity for Positive-Negative Aspects of the Same Topic in Paired Questions under Categories in Table 3.3

Class of questions in Table 3.3	Percentage of paired responses recording thema disparity to total paired responses			
	West Bengal		Delhi	
	City	Rural	City	Rural
(1)	(2)	(3)	(4)	(5)
Overall	41	37	58	51
Specific	18	31	43	31
Generalized	16	21	45	31

The investigators and informants might think that the two questions on receiving boons from preternatural sources have a direct bearing on the perception of a better quality of life in the light of the once popular schema of tradition to modernity; and, therefore, the responses to the two questions would register traditional belief while the refusal to respond to them would register modernity.

On the contrary, the response content of the two questions would have another significance, namely, eliciting the latent desire and detestation of the informants through a medium which is socially endemic but not highly controversial. The informants may therefore make use of it to express their hardly attainable wishes although not seriously believing in the medium, as it is in the case of daydreaming.

However, as mentioned earlier, the primary consideration in inserting the two questions among the overall questions listed in Table 3.3 was to test the reliability of want data, without the investigators and the informants being aware of it. Therefore, the two questions of positive (Question 3) and negative (Question 6) information content may be posed in a different manner as suited to the particular culture context. The point is to devise an ingenious tool to ascertain the seriousness of an informant participating in the interview.

Thus, with respect to Questions 3 and 6 in Table 3.3, an informant may or may not believe in good luck but might respond to them to express latent desire and detestation. On the other hand, the informant may totally refuse to respond. It is also possible that the informant may refuse to respond to the first good luck question (Question 3) but by being moulded into the interview, might respond to the second (Question 6). But, if one refuses to respond to Question 6 after responding to Question 3, it will be an indication of one's lack of seriousness to participate in the interview. This form of deliberate retraction would not be attributable to either an extraordinarily intelligent informant or a less aware and less aspirant informant perceiving a better quality of life in a confused or constrained but effort-making manner.

Therefore, two variates **p** and **p′** may be constructed as respective percentages of total respondents in the sample who have responded to Boon 1 (Question 3) and Boon 2 (Question 6), bearing in mind that **p** greater than **p′** would denote the inclusion of frivolous respondents in the sample. However, no such case was detected for the West Bengal and the Delhi samples, while the city males in both regions objected somewhat to responding to Boon 1 but not to Boon 2. The details are presented in Table 3.13.

The good luck questions may be made further use of, in respect of the themes of the boons and the themes of responses to the previous questions, namely, responses to Questions 1 and 2 with reference to the response to Question 3, and responses to Question 1–5 with reference to the response to Question 6 in Table 3.3. As the

Table 3.13

Detection of Frivolous Informants from Larger Percentage Incidence of Responding to Boon 1 (p) than to Boon 2 (p′) in the Sample

Social structural categories	West Bengal				Delhi			
	City		Rural		City		Rural	
	p	p′	p	p′	p	p′	p	p′
(1)	(2)	(3)	(4)	(5)	(6)	(7)	(8)	(9)
Bengali Hindu	81	89	100	100				
Bengali Muslim	81	86	–	–				
Santal ('tribal')	–	–	100	100				
Gujar (Hindu)					83	89	92	96
Meo (Muslim)					73	96	94	94
Scheduled Castes					86	87	98	98
Male	70	81	100	100	69	85	96	99
Female	94	97	–	–	96	96	92	92

respondents' perceptions are geared to the interview, thema identity (or alliance) will be registered more than thema difference, and that will be noticeable more for the second than the first good luck question because the respondents will be more conditioned to the interview. Table 3.14 substantiates the hypothesis by findings from the 1980 West Bengal and 1982 Delhi surveys.

Table 3.14

Percentage Incidence of Thema Identity (Alliance) in Response to Question 3 with Responses to Questions 1 and 2 (q) and Response to Question 6 with Responses to Questions 1–5 (q′) in Table 3.3

Social structural categories	West Bengal				Delhi			
	City		Rural		City		Rural	
	q	q′	q	q′	q	q′	q	q′
(1)	(2)	(3)	(4)	(5)	(6)	(7)	(8)	(9)
Bengali Hindu	72	74	64	66				
Bengali Muslim	52	76	–	–				
Santal ('tribal')	–	–	73	73				
Gujar (Hindu)					97	94	91	94
Meo (Muslim)					94	98	73	92
Scheduled Castes					98	98	92	87
Male	84	81	65	67	99	94	84	95
Female	45	68	–	–	95	99	88	87

In various ways, as illustrated, the reliability of want data collected from the field can be verified, and better techniques may be devised for the purpose. However, the point is that verification of data reliability from the side of the informants opens up a new dimension in the want-based quality of life research. Therefore, unlike for the common varieties of survey research, the course of research moves from the level of data enumeration and verification to that of data formation.

DATA FORMATION

Data formation for the want-based quality of life research is concerned with the contexts of awareness, aspiration, and orientation of the masses to attain a better quality of life. The contexts are clarified by looking into the generally accepted objective—subjective dichotomy of the need and want data in the light of conceiving a uniform but 'subjective' data space for the masses, analogous to the uniform and 'objective' data space for the change-promoting elites. The fallacies involved in these two seemingly valid assumptions of objective—subjective dichotomy and a uniform data space for the masses (as for the change-promoting elites) can be clarified by examining several points systematically. The clarification should provide precise and comprehensive definitions of the contexts of the formation of want data, without which the scope of quality of life research is impaired by yielding limited want data and, also, confused data.

As pointed out earlier, the quality of life indicators formulated by the elites to meet the needs of the people are called objective *social indicators*, and those formulated from the perception of the masses concerning what they want in order to attain a better quality of life are labelled subjective *quality of life (QOL) indicators*. It has also been discussed that, conventionally, the 'objective' need data reflect the valuations of a better quality of life made by the power-wielding elites in society, while the 'subjective' want data register the valuations of a better quality of life made by the masses aspiring for, but, as change-recipients, expecting changes to be introduced by the power *in situ* for improvements in their life conditions. The subjectivity attributed to the valuations made by the masses, and their restricted identification as *aspiring* for and *expecting* a better quality of life, adversely affects the formation of want data.

The attention on the aspiring and expectant masses for the want-based quality of life research was brought into focus while building *Quality of Life Models*. Hankiss (1978: 84) prepared two diagrams to indicate the necessity of considering the aspirations and expectations of the masses in a diachronic model as different from the synchronic model. As seen from Figure 3.1, which reproduces the two diagrams, aspiration is considered to have been generated from 'past experiences' in the context of the 'current situation' and, thus structured at a time-point, aspiration rouses 'expectations' for 'satisfaction' with the quality of life.

The diachronic model introduces dynamism in the want-based quality of life research by noting the antecedents to the generation of aspiration and the sequence of aspiration to expectation. But dynamism is incompletely rendered to define the contexts to the formation of want data because (*a*) aspiration is summarily structured as the

Figure 3.1: Two Models for Quality of Life Research

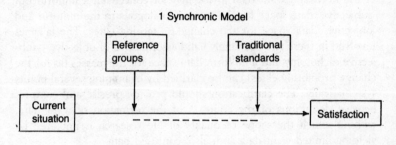

1 Synchronic Model

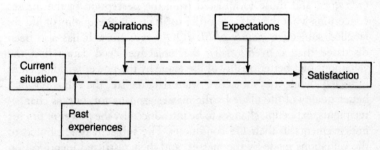

2 Diachronic Model

Source: Hankiss (1978:84)

product of interactions between the current situation and the past experiences, and (*b*) expectation is structured as the sole manifestation of aspiration. Thus, only two manifestations of the immanent social processes are accounted for while the processes are concerned with the entire gamut of awareness of a better quality of life, aspiration to attain it, and the orientation to fulfil expectations by receiving the gift of a better quality of life from external sources or achieving it through self-effort.

Life treats awareness, aspiration, and orientation to expect or achieve as processual variables of binary sequence. In the inexorable course of history, no one can survive, be secured in life, attain prosperity, and continue with progress unless one is evermore aware of a better quality of life, aspire for it with evergreater intensity, and eventually act for it instead of expecting it as a gift. But, in the cauldron of social processes, the sequence and the process may be reversed. One's achievement orientation may be replaced by that of expectation, as aspiration loses intensity. The orientation to expectations may disappear as aspiration fades away; and, eventually, one's awareness of a better quality of life may be obscured.

This binary sequence, epitomized by the masses as actors in the perennial course of social change, has a fundamental role in introducing a better quality of life in society. The role is forcefully revealed with reference to alliance or opposition of the valuations of the power-wielding elites with that of the majority of the masses for a better quality of life, both valuations rated against the cardinal valuations for humankind. The possible consequences in this respect can be broadly outlined, as shown in Table 3.15.

The hypothesis in Table 3.15 may seem tenuous, but history abounds in examples of consolidation or disintegration of an elite power bloc in the light of the differential will of the masses and of consequent frustration or further action of the masses to attain a better quality of life. The establishment of submissive or active democracies in ancient

Table 3.15
Hypothetical Formulation of Role and Effect of Expectation and Achievement Orientation of the Majority of Masses in the Light of Congruence or Contradiction of their and Power-wielding Elites' Valuations of a Better Quality of Life, Rated against the Cardinal Valuations for Humankind

Valuations rated against cardinal valuations for humankind		Orientation of the masses to attain a better quality of life	
		Expectation from external sources	Personal efforts for achievement
Elite's	Masses'		
(1)	(2)	(3)	(4)
Desirable	Desirable	Improved life quality leading to satiety, with less aspiration and awareness	Improved life quality arousing more aspiration and awareness
	Detestable	Acquiescence to power bloc, with fading aspiration and awareness	Social dissension, leading toward disintegration of society, possibly
Detestable	Desirable	(as above)	Social dissension with a view to reorganization of society
	Detestable	False social harmony	False but durable social harmony

India and Greece, the rise and fall of the Roman and the British Empires, the imposition of a dictatorial regime or the installation of a populist government, the factional strifes or the anti-oppressor wars, etc., attest to the validity of the hypothetical social consequences of the illustrated conjunctures of the power-wielding elites' and the majority of the masses' valuations of a better quality of life—both rated against the cardinal valuations for humankind.

Therefore, while the hypotheses may be better formulated, what cannot be denied is the fact that the formation of want data is distinguished along the spectrum of the social conditioning of the masses in respect of their awareness of, aspiration for, and orientation to attain a better quality of life. This fact is obscured by considering only the aspirant and expectant masses for the want-based quality of life research, especially because the processual variables of awareness, aspiration, and orientation operate under three conditions:

1. Awareness and aspiration are sequentially related over time but distinguishable at a time-point.
2. Orientation to expectation or achievement are distinctive manifestations at one time-point.
3. Awareness—aspiration and expectation—achievement are sequentially related to the course of alterations engineered by social processes to define the perception-action-perception syndrome of the phenomenon of quality of life.

This means that the systematic and sequential relations among awareness, aspiration, and orientation are not captured by the structural categories of current situation, past experiences, aspiration, and expectations, although the categories are placed sequentially in Figure 3.1. The sequences, with binary possibilities, may be different as shown in Figure 3.2.

Figure 3.2 points out that it is not only the masses' awareness for a better quality of life that changes in the course of perception (Sequences 1–3), action (Sequences 4–5), and perception (Sequence 6), but also aspiration or the lack of it as related facts. Figure 3.2 also points out that the orientation to expectation or achievement are interrelated and integrated to aspiration and, thence, to awareness.

Thus, Figure 3.2 suggests that the contexts to the formation of want data are delineated by a processual bell-shaped curve similar to the eternal cycling of the life process from 'dust to dust'. The curve is

Figure 3.2: Formulation and Reformulation of Awareness of a Better Quality of Life by Passing through the Sequence of Awareness, Aspiration, Achievement Orientation or Expectation, and Success or Failure of Consequent Action or Inaction

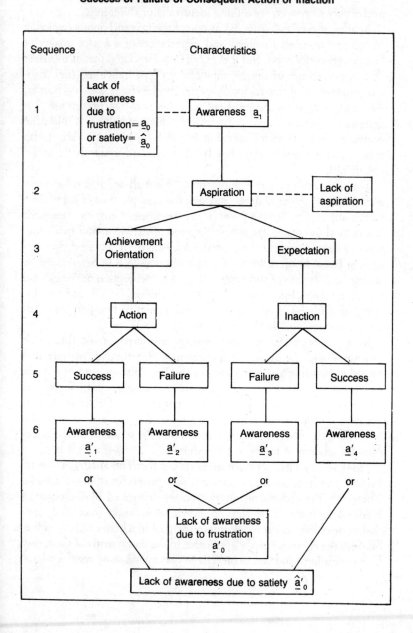

shown in Figure 3.3, which provides the base for resolving the anomaly of 'objective' indicators formulated by the elites and 'subjective' indicators formulated with respect to the masses, because the objective—subjective dichotomy is truly a continuum expressing the differential probability of perceiving a thing identically or differently.

Apathy, shown in Figure 3.3 as one of the two end points depicting frustration from achievement and expectation of a better quality of life, is well understood. But it may not be appreciated that at this state of non-perception of things, subjectivity of an individual (i.e., Ego-wise perception of things) totally overrules objectivity which is beyond Ego and, in that sense, non-Ego. It is this non-Ego perception that denotes the identical perception by individuals of a thing. A mundane example will be of an individual in a million (or tens of millions) who sees red as green and may thus be characterized as apathetic to the colour red.

The structuralists may feel uncomfortable with defining subjectivity and objectivity in this manner, and with the example cited of subjectivity versus objectivity. But the point is that the scope of empirical research is impaired by conceiving subjectivity and objectivity under two structural categories and dwelling on the subjective—objective dichotomy on that basis. Contrariwise, the scope of research is unconstrained by laying the concepts of subjectivity (Ego-wise perception of things) and objectivity (non-Ego-wise perception of things) on the axis of differential probability ending at two *null* points of non-perception of things, such as apathy and satiety in Figure 3.3.

Satiety is not a characteristic usually considered for social research in general and the quality of life research in particular, because it is regarded as a spiritual beatitude like the Buddhist concept of nirvana which negates objectivity and subjectivity. But satiety is built into the terminal conceptualization of an 'affluent society'. Therefore, from a negative standpoint of forestalling satiety of a 'modern' society, the concept 'post-modern' has been mooted in the sequence of the once-popular schema of tradition to modernity.

However, as a living organism, none can dwell on apathy or satiety. Neither the circulation of matter nor the conspectus of mind is static. Therefore, the process of binary changes delineated by the curve in Figure 3.3 implies, first, that no individual is totally frustrated (apathetic) or oblivious (from satiety) to the goal of a better quality of life. Second, the curve is equally applicable to the elites; many of them may be expectation (and not achievement) oriented, some may not have

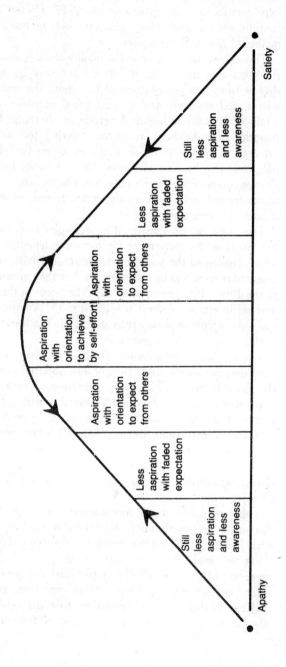

Figure 3.3: Binary Sequence of Awareness, Aspiration, and Orientation with Respect to a Better Quality of Life

expectations and register less aspiration for a better quality of life as traditionalists in true colour, and a few may be less aware of a better quality of life as obscurantists.

This means that in so far as the quality of life research is concerned, the need data and the want data are *perceived* by the elites and the masses from two perspectives, that is, both the need-based and the want-based research deal in perceptual variables. These variables attain objectivity by identical perception of things by a substantial majority of individuals aware of, aspiring for, and achievement-oriented to induce or infuse change in society for a better quality of life. It is on this consideration that the needs formulated by the change-promoting elites are objective. On the same consideration, the wants formulated by the aware, aspirant, and achievement-oriented masses are objective.

The point can be illustrated by examples from various aspects of life. Such as, the movement for India's Independence in the 1940s, which registered the wants of the aware, aspirant, and achievement-oriented masses, was no less objective than the imposition of British raj in the 18th—19th centuries to meet the needs of the aware, aspirant, and achievement-oriented British elites (Mukherjee 1974). Another example of contemporary relevance is the Black movement in South Africa against White domination.

The conclusion thus follows that the contexts to the formation of want data determine their (more or less) objectivity as the data refer to the characteristics of awareness, aspiration, and orientation from the apex of the curve in Figure 3.3 toward reaching either of the *null* points of apathy or satiety. As the curve descends on either side, subjectivity enters more and more into the formation of want data, just as achievement orientation is replaced by expectations, expectations disappear with dwindling aspiration, and awareness is obscured with fading aspiration. The course may also be in reverse from subjectivity to objectivity.

This perspective to the formation of want data is germane to the discomfort noticeable among the critical researchers from the onset of what has been labelled the conventional quality of life research (e.g., Campbell et al. 1976). In course of time, the scholars have become more explicit. Stone (1980) emphasized the problematic concern while underscoring the Durkheimian viewpoint, and Andrews and McKennel (1980: 152) acknowledged that 'the separate influences of affect and cognition also need to be explored at the level of evaluations of specific life concerns ("domain").' A UNESCO meeting of experts on the quality of life indicators suggested that the seemingly anomalous relation between objective and subjective indicators is due to specificity or non-specificity of awareness, aspiration, and orientation to concrete or abstract issues as dependent upon social structural distinctions:

> It has been observed that correlations between objective and subjective indicators are generally weak. It is not clear whether this is a weakness of measurement or whether the objective and subjective phenomena are really very different from each other. When the subjective reactions are concerned with fairly specific physical phenomena, there is a higher correlation between objective and subjective indicators.
>
> It has been observed that those persons who, objectively, have greater resources, such as education or income, often are more critical of the quality of their life than are persons who, objectively, have fewer resources. Those persons with greater resources probably also have a greater awareness; hence, a greater ability to be critical. This leads to the proposition that those with fewer resources have a 'false consciousness' [registering more subjectivity than objectivity?] which limits their ability to report accurately [with more objectivity?] on their satisfaction (UNESCO 1978: 92).

Moum came to the conclusion from researches into the reasons for a weak fit 'between objective and subjective indicators' that the issue of objective—subjective dichotomy of the need and want data reflects the 'problems of measurement' with reference to 'causal factors of substantive interest' (Moum 1981: 185, 194):

> It is necessary to draw a hard and fast line between *problems of measurement*, on the one hand, and a search for *causal factors of substantive interest* on the other. Biases in subjective indicators of well-being that arise because of response style (trait desirability, need for approval, response acquiescence, etc.) should not be confused with social psychological processes (such as aspirations, expectations, reference groups, etc.) that may contribute to the *true* variance in measures of subjective well-being, and which should, therefore, be *incorporated in one's causal model* on a par with objective living conditions . . . . results indicate that such factors as

response style ('yea-saying'), *generalized life ambition* ('resignation') and *personal value commitments* separately and in combination impinge upon the association between objective background variables and (global) subjective indicators of well-being.

The causal factors of social structural and other distinctions are the concern of want-based research at the level of comprehension of indicators formulated from want data and classified in distinctive ways. This means that the level of analysis is concerned with the problems of measurement as well. However, as discussed, the measurement problems emerge with reference to different contexts of formation of want data. Therefore, it is necessary to conceive the data space of the masses as *analogous* (parallel) to the data space of the elites at the level of data formation, and, furthermore, distinguish the data space of the masses into *homologous subspaces* of common origin at the level of reduction of data.

DATA REDUCTION

It is not necessary for the need-based quality of life research to distinguish the data space of the elites into subspaces, in order to locate the aware, aspirant, and achievement-oriented elites at the apex of the curve shown in Figure 3.3 and, successively, the less aware and the least aspirant elites at either end of the curve. The elites for this course of research are all aware of a better quality of life, aspire to realize it, and induce changes in society for its realization. But the corresponding segment of the masses is not automatically identified. Therefore, the reduction of want data should begin with the identification of the masses with reference to their awareness, aspiration, and expectation or achievement orientation to attaining a better quality of life, so as to capture intra-mass variability in distinctive manifestations of the immanent social processes yielding the processual categories shown in Figure 3.3.

Thus conceived, the want-based quality of life research will yield want data on par with the need data because these are all perceptual variables. At the same time, the relative objectivity of want data will be rated as falling under the segments shown in Figure 3.3 or in a more precise manner. The possibilities of truly or falsely introducing a better quality of life can then be inferred in the light of such hypotheses as are illustratively formulated in Table 3.15.

But the want-based quality of life research encounters a formidable difficulty in precisely defining the contexts to data formation. In any society a low awareness of a better quality of life would be of insignificant incidence in these days of rapid communication within and across societies and quick realization of social changes over time and space. The incidence of low aspirations without even the expectations of a better quality of life would be more than of low awareness; but consequent to the evermore evident unequal exchange in material and mental resources and products in any configuration of world society, it cannot be of a large magnitude.

Therefore, the less aware and the more aware but less aspirant masses may be distinguishable for specialized studies based on a small but selective sample of respondents. Useful 'clinical' studies of this kind will reveal a social concern but will not be able to gauge its impact on the society as a whole. On the other hand, a small-scale study with reference to the society *en bloc* is likely to fail in distinguishing these two segments of the masses occurring in tiny proportions in the sample, except by hesitant inferences drawn from the scrutiny of the respondents' probed answers to all questions listed in Table 3.3.

For instance, the less aspirant respondent without expectations of improving their quality of life will be more inconsistent with the second probing question of 'how' to improve than the third probing question of 'why' to improve, while any such distinction is irrelevant to the less aware respondents who are not concerned with either the instrumentality or the causality of attaining a better quality of life. If this hypothesis is valid, the ensemble of less aware and less aspirant respondents—identified at the time of data verification by recording Irregular Trend I of Table 3.11 and Relations 8–15 of Table 3.10—will be distinguished by the more frequent occurrence of Relations 9, 14, and 15 of Table 3.10 for the less aspirant rather than for the less aware respondents.

The inference may be precise in case the want-based quality of life survey involves a large sample of respondents, representing the social structural distinctions extensively and in depth, because, as discussed, low awareness and low aspiration are socially conditioned by deprivation. Also, in the case of a large-scale survey of the quality of life, apposite questions may be introduced in the questionnaire-schedule to distinguish the less aware from the more aware but less aspiring respondents. But large-scale surveys would be rare because of the relatively higher cost and greater time required, unless the utility of conducting an unconstrained want-based quality of life research is duly appreciated.

However, the least aspirant respondents may be distinguished from the less aspirant ones in the light of all the respondents' precoded replies 'yes', 'no', or 'don't know' to Question 29 in Table 3.3: 'Do you think you will ever reach your goal?'. Those replying 'yes' are undoubtedly aspiring for a better quality of life while the vacillating reply 'don't know' may be indicative of a lingering aspiration which is lost (or very feebly present) in the reply 'no'. The assumption may be challenged on the ground that under the prevailing social polity, a prudent aspirant may reply 'don't know' in place of 'yes'. However, this possibility will affect the distinction between aspiring and less aspiring respondents and not between the less and the least aspiring ones.

Therefore, consistent with the shortened communication gap and mounting awareness of unequal exchange in the world context, the least aspirant respondents should occur in very small number and as a random variable. On the other hand, the less aspirant respondents may occur in an appreciable but not a large number while, in conformity with the findings at the level of data verification, their incidence should be particularly noticeable at distinctive social segments such as the Calcutta women and the village women of Delhi, with respect to the 1980 West Bengal and 1982 Delhi surveys.

These possibilities are indicated by the findings from the quality of life surveys in India, as shown in Table 3.16.

Besides recording a large incidence of less aspiring respondents among Calcutta women and Delhi village women, Table 3.16 shows that except for the 'tribal' Santals and the old persons in the West Bengal sample, who register somewhat large incidences of the least aspirant respondents, variations in the incidence of least and less aspiring respondents by ethnicity, social status, and age are noticeable but not remarkably so. On the other hand, while the least aspirant respondents are found more in the rural than urban areas of West Bengal and Delhi, and so it is for the less aspirant respondents in the Delhi sample, the rural-urban alignment is reversed for the less aspirant respondents of West Bengal.

This may reflect the social polity of West Bengal with the Communist Party of India-Marxist forming the state government in 1977 and reportedly taking more concerted measures to uplift the rural rather than the urban masses. The policy measures may have thus

Table 3.16
Respondents' Definite (No) and Vacillating (Don't know) Lack of Aspiration for a Better Quality of Life as Deduced from Question 29 'Do you think you will ever reach your goal?' in Table 3.3

Respondents' gender, ethnicity, social status, age-grade	Percentage of respondents lacking aspiration for a better quality of life to total respondents							
	Definite (No)				Vacillating (Don't know)			
	West Bengal		Delhi		West Bengal		Delhi	
	City	Rural	City	Rural	City	Rural	City	Rural
(1)	(2)	(3)	(4)	(5)	(6)	(7)	(8)	(9)
Male	3	9	0	11	24	19	12	21
Female	3	–	4	7	32	–	7	26
Bengali Hindu	4	8			28	20		
Bengali Muslim	0	–			29	–		
Santal ('tribal')	–	18			–	9		
Gujar (Hindu)			3	15			16	13
Meo (Muslim)			4	8			12	28
Scheduled Castes			0	4			1	29
Upper status	4	8	0	9	25	18	11	19
Middle status	0	4	1	10	29	18	6	25
Lower status	5	7	4	8	32	20	12	29
Young	0	4	1	6	26	19	14	25
Adult	5	4	3	9	32	16	3	18
Old	3	21	2	12	28	21	11	27
Total	3	9	2	9	28	19	9	23
City and Rural	6		6		23		17	

counterbalanced the rural-urban distinction in the incidence of less aspiring respondents as noticed for the Delhi sample.

From findings of this nature it seems reasonable to accept that in the case of small-scale surveys the occurrence of least aspirant (and less aware) respondents would not seriously affect the reduction of want data although a notable context to data formation would not be considered. Also, the separation of the aspiring from the less aspiring respondents may not be precise, but that contingency cannot be avoided. Therefore, in the case of small-scale surveys, the primary concern for the reduction of want data is with the aspiring respondents distinguished by their orientation to achieve a better quality of life through self-effort or expecting it as a gift from others.

In this respect it is necessary to bear in mind that like awareness and aspiration defining the contexts to data formation, expectation or achievement orientation are processual categories. They can be distinguished but not treated as mutually distinct structural categories because, on the one hand, the achievement orientation does not deride help from beyond self and, on the other, expectation from external sources does not absolve one from some action. In other words, while the *null* situation is of a person governed by both self-effort and expectations, one governed equally by the two kinds of orientation will be in a state of confusion as to how to attain a better quality of life.

Therefore, the point is to ascertain the relative stress laid by the aspirant respondents on either of the two kinds of orientation. The point refers to the instrumentality of attaining a better quality of life, which can be deduced from the responses to Question 30(1) listed in Table 3.3 in reference to Question 29; namely, if the answer to question 'Do you think you will ever reach your goal?' is yes, then 'how?'.

As for awareness and aspiration of the respondents, the deduction on their expectation or achievement orientation is worth verification by the genuineness of the response to Question 30(1). This can be done by referring to the answers of the aspiring respondents to the Focused Questions 22–28 and to the 'how' aspect of responses to Questions 1–20 in Table 3.3. In this case, the content of response to the questions is to be examined, as different from the structure of response which was scrutinized for the verification of awareness and aspiration of the respondents. The analysis of the content of response may be based on some logical postulates.

With respect to virtually any aspect of the quality of life, one may perceive it in a purely egocentric manner, i.e., as referring to oneself and those with whom one has face to face relations. Another person may react in a purely sociocentric manner by perceiving the same aspect of life quality in terms of the society at large and not the Ego and Ego's circle of immediate encounter. A third person may consider both the egocentric and the sociocentric characteristics when perceiving the same aspect of the quality of life. These variations in the content of response can be examined with reference to endogenous or exogenous motivation to improve one's life quality and, on that basis, one may infer on the achievement or the expectation orientation of a respondent to attain a better quality of life.

A person governed by endogenous motivation will be inclined to achieve a better quality of life by his/her own efforts, along with channelizing the social forces in his/her favour through those with whom the person has, preferably, a direct and, otherwise, an indirect contact. A person governed by exogenous motivation will aspire for a better quality of life mainly by expecting help from others, with whom the person has direct or indirect association. Therefore, hypothetically, the content of response will be different in accordance with the endogenous or the exogenous motivation of respondents to improve their life quality.

One governed by endogenous motivation is likely to be egocentric in response to a question so long as the perception of the aspect of life quality posed by the question is largely within one's grasp. The same person is likely to be egocentric and sociocentric (= ego-sociocentric) when responding to a question which evokes perception involving those who are beyond his/her direct encounter as well. Relatively, however, that person is not likely to be entirely sociocentric because that would be against his/her endogenous motivation.

Contrariwise, one governed by exogenous motivation is likely to be consistently egocentric in response to the questions on life quality except when inexorably confronted with a perception involving those beyond Ego. In the latter situation, that person will be more inclined to depend on others than on self-effort. Relatively, therefore, the person will be entirely sociocentric and not ego-sociocentric in improving the quality of life.

In view of these hypothetical assumptions, a relatively large incidence of ego-sociocentric responses for the endogenous and a corresponding small incidence for the exogenous motivation would be the critical indicator. These large and small incidences should be particularly registered for the Focused Questions 22–28 listed in Table 3.3 and thus constitute the primary indicator. However, such incidences will also be generally registered for the preceding Questions 1–20 and may thus be regarded to constitute the secondary indicator.

The two indicators would be applicable to the grouping of respondents into motivation categories formed by their answers to 'how' in Question 30(1). The answers may be categorized into two alternatives, pointing to one or the other motivation. The answer may be to achieve a better quality of life by self-effort (with or without help from others) and thus denote the endogenous motivation. Alternatively, the answer may be to expect a better quality of life exclusively through help from others, which would denote the exogenous motivation. The two contrasting motivation groups formed by answers to Question 30(1) may be further distinguished as highly endogenous or highly exogenous depending upon the incidence of either motivation in any social group for, say, 70 per cent or more of its constituents. Otherwise, by registering an incidence rate between 50 and 69 per cent, a social group may be categorized as endogenous or exogenous.

Thus, the respondents distinguished by their social structural affiliations will display one of the motivations arranged in the sequence of highly endogenous, endogenous, exogenous, and highly exogenous; and, in the same sequence, the social groups should register less and less ego-sociocentric responses. In this way, the two indicators may attest to the consistency of the motivations deduced from responses to Question 30(1) in Table 3.3. The possibility is demonstrated in Tables 3.18–3.20.

For a further verification of consistent motivation grouping of the aspiring respondents, a set of tertiary indicators may be constructed with reference to different classes of questions labelled in Table 3.3 as overall (Questions 1–6), specific (Questions 7–14), and generalized (Questions 15–20).

The responses of persons with endogenous or exogenous motivation are likely to be mainly egocentric with respect to Questions 1–6 because of the nature of the formulation of these questions. However, those with the exogenous motivation to mainly expect improvements in the quality of life are likely to be more egocentric than those with the endogenous motivation, because while acting for improvements in the quality of life one cannot be oblivious to the necessity of securing help from others. Therefore, less and less ego-sociocentric responses to the overall questions, along the sequence from highly endogenous to highly exogenous motivation, will be a critical indicator to testify to the consistency of the motivation categories deduced from the answers of the aspiring respondents to Question 30(1).

The critical indicator with respect to Questions 15–20 should be the same as for Questions 1–6 because the generalized questions belong to the same genre as the general questions with which the interview began. But the critical indicator with respect to Specific Questions 7–14 will be different.

The specific questions deliberately steer the attention of respondents to forces beyond one's control, besides one's own; such as, improvements in personal career, life at work, family life, neighbourhood conditions, etc. Therefore, to a certain extent, the responses to these questions must be sociocentric. Nonetheless, those with the endogenous motivation are likely to react less sociocentrically than those with the exogenous motivation. Hence, more and more sociocentric responses to the specific questions along the sequence from highly endogenous to highly exogenous motivation will be the critical indicator to testify to the consistency of the motivation categories deduced from the answers of aspiring respondents to Question 30(1).

The Specific and Generalized Questions 7–20 may be examined further with respect to their positive (to have) and negative (to give up) information content, bearing in mind the decreasing importance of the indicators formulated as primary, secondary, and tertiary with respect to Questions 22–28, 1–20, and the three classes of questions. The tertiary indicators may be supported by an auxiliary indicator formulated with respect to the positive and the negative information content of the specific and the generalized questions.

In the case of endogenous motivation, the incidence of sociocentric response to the specific and generalized questions is likely to be smaller for the positive than the negative aspect of the topics. One with this motivation is likely to want to have those specific and generalized things and facilities which are realizable through self-effort, with or without help from others. But one will also appreciate that the removal of impediments to these concerns is more within the purview of faceless power than one's own (e.g., the public bodies and the government). Therefore, a sociocentric response is more likely to occur to the negative aspect of the specific and the generalized topics than to the positive aspect; i.e., the ratio of sociocentric response to the positive/negative questions should be a fraction.

This distinction in the incidence of sociocentric response to the positive and the negative aspects of the specific and the generalized topics is not meaningful to the exogenous motivation. Therefore, it should occur with equal frequency for either information content; i.e., the ratio of sociocentric response to the positive/negative questions should be 1. However, in a small sample of limited coverage of probable incidence of sociocentric response, it may be larger for the positive than the negative aspect of the topics or, conversely, record the relation posited for the endogenous motivation; i.e., the aforementioned ratio may be greater than 1 or a fraction.

For this anomalous possibility, the ratio of sociocentric response to the two sets of positive—negative questions as (1) Questions 7, 9, 11, 13, 15, 17, 19, and (2) Questions 8, 10, 12, 14, 16, 18, 20 of Table 3.3

should be regarded to provide an auxiliary indicator. However, subject to the limitation of a small sample coverage, the ratio of percentage incidences of sociocentric response to the specific and the generalized questions of the positive and the negative information content will be less and less a fraction, and ultimately become an integer, in the sequence from highly endogenous to highly exogenous motivation categories formed by the aspiring respondents' answers to Question 30(1).

Thus, against the *null* hypothesis that a person is equally motivated endogenously and exogenously for attaining a better quality of life, a series of alternate hypotheses of decreasing importance can be proposed for the formulation of indicators to test the consistency of the motivation categories deduced from the answers of aspiring respondents to Question 30(1) in Table 3.3. Table 3.17 shows in summary form what these indicators indicate.

Table 3.17

Indicators to Testify Categorization of Aspiring Respondents' Motivation (Orientation) to Attain a Better Quality of Life from Answers to Question 30(1) in Table 3.3, Denoting the Sequence: Highly Endogenous—Endogenous—Exogenous—Highly Exogenous

Indicator		Percentage incidence of nature of response in categories rated as highly endogenous to highly exogenous motivation
Rating	Formulated from Questions	
(1)	(2)	(3)
Primary	22–28	Less and less ego-sociocentric
Secondary	1–20	Less and less ego-sociocentric
Tertiary 1	1–6	Less and less ego-sociocentric
2	7–14	More and more sociocentric
3	15–20	Less and less ego-sociocentric
Auxiliary	(7, 9, 11, 13, 15, 17, 19)	Ratio of percentage incidence of sociocentric for positive to
(positive-negative information content)	versus (8, 10, 12, 14, 16, 18, 20)	negative questions from largest fraction to finally an integer

Alternate hypotheses may be formulated, and more efficiently, in the light of accumulating knowledge on individual perceptions as the quality of life research is conducted rigorously and systematically. However, the hypotheses formulated in Table 3.17 were found useful to test the consistency of the motivation categories formed by those respondents who had said 'yes' to Question 29 in Table 3.3, of 'Do you think you will ever reach your goal?', and had thus identified themselves as aspiring for a better quality of life. Their motivations are deduced from answers to Question 30(1) of 'how?' they will attain a better quality of life.

Table 3.18, which gives the deductions made from responses to Question 30(1) of the aspiring respondents in the West Bengal sample, shows that irrespective of gender, ethnicity, social status, and age differences (except a slight variation with regard to the Calcutta Muslims), the aspiring respondents of West Bengal register a highly endogenous motivation to attain a better quality of life.

Table 3.19 shows that the respondents from the city of Delhi aspiring for a better quality of life also register an endogenous motivation but less strongly than the West Bengal respondents, with a high incidence recorded for the men, the Scheduled Castes, the respondents in the lower status group, and the old persons. Contrariwise, the aspiring respondents from the rural hinterland of Delhi register an exogenous motivation with its high incidence for the women, the respondents in the lower status group, and the old persons.

Table 3.18 and 3.19 show that variations in endogenous or exogenous motivation by gender, ethnicity, social status, and age difference are more noticeable among the Delhi respondents than among the West Bengal respondents. However, the respondents of West Bengal, the city of Delhi, and those from Delhi's hinterland, can be placed in a sequence according to their motivations to attain a better quality of life, namely, from highly endogenous to endogenous to exogenous. Against this deductive finding, the indicators formulated in Table 3.17 are examined in Table 3.20 to test the consistency of the motivation groups.

In the manner illustrated, the contexts to data formation for the want-based quality of life research may be clarified at the level of data reduction, although in the case of small-scale surveys the efforts may largely be restricted to the orientation (= motivation) of the aspiring respondents to attain a better quality of life. As noted, the indicated course of analysis may only assure a negligible and random occurrence in the sample of the least aspiring (also less aware) respondents, and denote the linkage of less aspiring respondents with the aspiring ones. However, the context categories may thus be as clearly defined as is possible under the circumstances.

The 1980 West Bengal and 1982 Delhi surveys bear out the first

Table 3.18
Motivation Deduced from Content of Response to Question 30(1) in Table 3.3 of Respondents Confident of Attaining a Better Quality of Life: 1980 West Bengal Sample

Respondents' gender, ethnicity, social status, age-grade	Percentage of respondents confident of attaining a better quality of life by:		Deduction of respondents' motivation (High ≥ 70%)
	Self-effort, with or without help from others	Others' help exclusively	
(1)	(2)	(3)	(4)
1 City			
Male	88	12	Highly endogenous
Female	74	26	" "
Bengali Hindu	90	10	" "
Bengali Muslim	67	33	Endogenous
Upper status	94	6	Highly endogenous
Middle status	72	28	" "
Lower status	75	25	" "
Young	86	14	" "
Adult	80	20	" "
Old	75	25	" "
Total	82	18	Highly endogenous
2 Rural			
Male	84	16	Highly endogenous
Bengali Hindu	80	20	" "
Santal ('tribal')	100	—	" "
Upper status	82	18	" "
Middle status	87	13	" "
Lower status	82	18	" "
Young	85	15	" "
Adult	80	20	" "
Old	86	14	" "
Total	84	16	Highly endogenous

possibility by only 6 per cent occurrence of the least aspiring respondents in respective samples, as shown in Table 3.16. The table records 23 per cent and 17 per cent incidences of less aspiring respondents in the West Bengal and Delhi samples but, as surmised for

Table 3.19
Motivation Deduced from Content of Response to Question 30(1) in Table 3.3 of Respondents Confident of Attaining a Better Quality of Life: 1982 Delhi Sample

Respondents' gender, ethnicity, social status, age-grade	Percentage of respondents confident of attaining a better quality of life by:		Deduction of respondents' motivation (High ≥ 70%)
	Self-effort, with or without help from others	Others' help exclusively	
(1)	(2)	(3)	(4)
1 City			
Male	85	15	Highly endogenous
Female	53	47	Endogenous
Gujar (Hindu)	60	40	"
Meo (Muslim)	61	39	"
Scheduled Castes	82	18	Highly endogenous
Upper status	65	35	Endogenous
Middle status	69	31	"
Lower status	73	27	Highly endogenous
Young	69	31	Endogenous
Adult	64	36	"
Old	75	25	Highly endogenous
Total	69	31	Endogenous
2 Rural			
Male	45	55	Exogenous
Female	30	70	Highly exogenous
Gujar (Hindu)	39	61	Exogenous
Meo (Muslim)	39	61	"
Scheduled Castes	39	61	"
Upper status	43	57	"
Middle status	44	56	"
Lower status	23	77	Highly exogenous
Young	39	61	Exogenous
Adult	46	54	"
Old	30	70	Highly exogenous
Total	39	61	Exogenous

the Calcutta sample vis-à-vis the rural West Bengal sample, a substantial number of less aspiring respondents seem to be close to the

Table 3.20
Verification of Motivation Groups Deduced in Tables 3.18 and 3.19 by Inference Drawn from Indicators shown in Table 3.17

Indicator	Indication	Percentage incidence of nature of response to total response in group		
		West Bengal (Highly endogenous)	Delhi city (Endogenous)	Delhi rural (Exogenous)
(1)	(2)	(3)	(4)	(5)
Primary	Decreasing ego-sociocentric	22	3	1
Secondary	"	8	5	3
Tertiary 1	"	12	5	4
Tertiary 2	Increasing sociocentric	18	23	22
Tertiary 3	Decreasing ego-sociocentric	6	3	2
Auxiliary	Positive/negative sociocentric from fraction to 1	0.63	0.90	0.89

aspiring ones. This is suggested by the answers to the question 'why?' (Questions 30(2) and 30(3) of Table 3.3) posed before those respondents who had replied 'don't know' or 'no' to Question 29: 'Do you think you will ever reach your goal?'.

The answers could be classed under two categories: impossible and unpredictable. The 'unpredictable' response registers lingering aspiration and thus brings the respondent nearer the aspiring ones in the curve shown in Figure 3.3, while the 'impossible' response moves the respondent further down the curve, either toward apathy or satiety. Table 3.21 shows that for both West Bengal and Delhi, the majority of less aspiring respondents in the city and rural areas, both men and women, consider it unpredictable (not impossible) that they will attain the goal of a better quality of life. There is thus the suggestion of a possible alliance between the less aspiring and aspiring respondents, and the indication of a clear categorization of the West Bengal, Delhi city, and Delhi rural respondents being less and less endogenous in motivation and achievement orientation.

This manner of reduction of want data has a substantive bearing upon the comprehension of the want-based quality of life research

Table 3.21
Less Aware and Less Aspirant Respondents' Lingering Aspiration for a Better Quality of Life (Indicator: Unpredictable)

Sample	Percentage of respondents lacking confidence to attain a better quality of life because it is:					
	Impossible			Unpredictable		
	City	Rural	Total	City	Rural	Total
(1)	(2)	(3)	(4)	(5)	(6)	(7)
West Bengal						
Men	40	43	42	60	57	58
Women	9	—	9	91	—	91
Total	24	43	34	76	57	66
Delhi						
Men	0	34	27	100	66	73
Women	40	21	25	60	79	75
Total	18	28	26	82	72	74

because it indicates *how* the people wish to have *what* they want. Several social groups' appraisal of a better quality of life may be the same, i.e., the groups may want the same thing(s). But some of these groups may clearly aspire to obtain the thing(s), the others may be less aspiring, and there may also be those groups in society which are hardly aspiring for a better quality of life and may only be vaguely aware of the possibility.

These groups, emerged and emerging with reference to the immanent social processes would define the usefulness of the want-based quality of life research with respect to a place, time, and people bound configuration of world society. Also, the social groups expecting a better quality of life as change-recipients or wishing to achieve it as change-actors would clearly gear the want-based quality of life research to the perception—action—perception syndrome of appraisal of social reality for a better quality of life.

However, these findings at the level of reduction of want data should be examined, on the one hand, by their specific merit and, on the other, in association with what the people actually want in the context of the groups identified at the time of data collection and the groups they are found to form in the light of individual valuations of a better quality of life. These two possibilities of formation of value groups with respect to the predetermined social groups and the analytically evolved social groups may be examined at the levels of analysis and comprehension of the want-based quality of life research.

ANALYSIS

An individual's appraisal of social reality for a better quality of life can be distinguished as his/her primary and secondary valuation, according to the same conceptual construct as found useful to the need-based quality of life research. The primary valuation is denoted by the presently announced final objective of an improved quality of life, such as, the goal declared by a respondent in answer to Question 21 listed in Table 3.3. However, the all-inclusive notion of the quality of life may not be captured by the mere statement of a goal, as discussed earlier. It may acquire its full meaning by taking note of the strategy for reaching the goal. The strategy is indicated while evaluating the life quality in general and in its positive and negative aspects, such as, in response to Questions 1–6 listed in Table 3.3.

The secondary valuation is concerned with the modalities of meeting the strategy and reaching the goal. It ascribes priorities to the beneficiaries of the goal and points to the logistics of attaining it. The priorities may be recorded while stating the goal of a better quality of life; however, these are clarified from the responses of an individual while scanning his/her mental horizon with direct reference to the contemporaneous life concerns, such as, by posing Questions 7–20 in Table 3.3. The logistics should be registered in response to Questions 22–23 in Table 3.3; however, these also would be clarified by the responses to the aforementioned Questions 7–20.

This means that if the want data—collected, verified, formed, and reduced in the manner indicated earlier—are analyzed in the manner indicated above, the primary and secondary valuations of the want-based quality of life research would correspond to the primary and secondary valuations ascertained in Chapter 2 with respect to the need-based quality of life research, viz., the 'goal and strategy' and the 'priorities and logistics' formulated by the expert-elite groups. Therefore, the free responses to the questions listed in Table 3.3 should undergo the same procedure of content analysis as explained in Chapter 2, in order to formulate, succinctly, the primary and the secondary valuations of what the people want to have (positive) and what they want removed (negative).

Nine primary positive valuations could thus be formulated with respect to 590 respondents from West Bengal and Delhi in 1980 and 1982:

1. spiritual achievement; 2. spirit of love, universal harmony, mutual understanding; 3. respect, prestige; 4. education—including husbands' or sons' education from some female respondents and sons' education from some old male respondents; 5. happiness, satisfaction, comfort, and peace—including the desire for sons (for satisfaction) from a few female respondents; 6. development of one's ethnic community through social work or political activities; 7. money; 8. job career—including that of husband or sons from some female and old male respondents; and 9. economic stability.

A few respondents completely failed to express a positive primary valuation; however, what is more important to note is that Item 5 above (viz., happiness, satisfaction, comfort, and peace) was a theme common to all primary positive valuations. Referring to the two contexts, a consideration of the positive and negative aspects showed that all primary valuations were concerned with the ways of attaining happiness, satisfaction, comfort, or peace. This means that, on its own, the primary positive valuation registers an omnibus base, while the primary valuation as such is precisely expressed by taking note of its positive and negative aspects. Thus treated, a new value item was revealed from the joint consideration of the positive and negative aspects of primary valuation.

The spirit of love, universal harmony, mutual understanding, etc., were found coincidental with one's spiritual satisfaction through religion or non-materialist knowledge. Education was not merely for acquiring knowledge but to raise one's social or economic status. The two valuations rested on the assumption that higher education would command respect and prestige from the milieu (kingroup, neighbourhood, ethnic community, etc.) and thus raise one's social status *or*, higher education would fetch better paying jobs and the consequent rise in economic status would command respect and prestige from the milieu.

Similarly, mere possession of sons would not make the particular women respondents happy because the craving was that the sons, yet to be born, would grow up and bring money to the family. The desire to develop one's community was in fact the desire of particular respondents for enhanced social status, which would be achieved by generating the community's social and political consciousness or somehow persuading the community to demand material benefits from the public bodies and, command respect and prestige from the compatriots through social work and political activities.

Also, the desire for money was not for accumulation but for survival by securing material requisites from any source. Correspondingly, job career embraced improvements in current jobs or business enterprises (including agriculture) by means of better education and availability of necessary capital and ancillary facilities, for economic stability and security in life.

Thus, for 590 respondents from West Bengal and Delhi, six primary valuations of a better quality of life could be formulated, including those who had failed to provide a primary positive valuation. These valuation categories, with the number and percentage incidence for each one of them out of 590 respondents, are presented in Table 3.22.

The third category, which emerges only from a joint consideration of the positive and the negative aspects of primary valuation, may be placed between the categories of spiritual gain and social status on the one side, and economic status, security, and survival on the other, because it is clearly concerned with the issues of social existence. However, Table 3.22 points out that the majority valuation is for economic security, and next but in much lower importance are the valuations of economic survival, economic or social status, and well-being. A spiritual valuation of a better quality of life is negligible.

These primary valuations are seen to be truly expressed by taking note of their positive and negative aspects jointly, because only then may the notion of a better quality of life be posed in an all-inclusive manner. The secondary valuations, on the other hand, were found distinguished in their positive aspect by focusing on the priorities, and in their negative aspect for evaluating the logistics in terms of the impediments to attaining a better quality of life.

For the West Bengal and Delhi respondents, the secondary positive valuations brought into focus the self, the family, or the society (beyond self and family) as the direct beneficiaries of a better quality of life. The three structured categories are not, of course, mutually exclusive: one can hardly visualize a better quality of life for only the self, the family, or the society. Nonetheless, the distinctive emphasis reveals the mechanics of one's perception on the priorities of who should directly benefit from meeting the wants. The focus on self was

Table 3.22
Primary (Positive-Negative) Valuation of a Better Quality of Life, made by Respondents in West Bengal and Delhi in 1980 and 1982

Valuation Category	Respondents	
	Number	%
(1)	(2)	(3)
Spiritual gain through religion, spirit of love, universal harmony, mutual understanding, scriptural knowledge, etc.	20	3
Social status enhanced in the non-material sense by commanding respect and prestige from the milieu by generating social consciousness through education, reformist or political activities, etc.	61	10
Well-being ensured by maintaining the current life quality, living in one's own house, forming a nuclear from the present extended family, pleasant conjugal life, amicable behaviour of children, finding dowry for daughters' marriage, freedom from in-laws' oppression, personal freedom from patriarchal or male domination, pursuing a career virtually reserved for men, maintaining good health, etc.	44	8
Economic status enhanced by commanding respect and prestige from the milieu by acquiring wealth from anywhere or from a job career or business enterprise (including agriculture) which may require higher education.	61	10
Security in life established by improvements in job career or business enterprise (including agriculture) by means of better education, availability of necessary capital and ancillary facilities, etc.	308	52
Survival by receiving money from any source to meet immediate needs and eventually establishing a durable living by obtaining a job, running a business enterprise (including agriculture), etc.	96	17
Total	590	100

for 31 per cent of 590 respondents, on the family for 63 per cent, and on society for only 6 per cent.

The priorities revealed by the secondary positive valuations are seen to be closely associated with the inherent characteristics of the primary (positive—negative) valuations of the West Bengal and Delhi respondents. On the one hand, those aspiring for spiritual gain or enhanced social status are essentially self-centred (65 per cent and 54 per cent, respectively, of their total incidences). A non-Ego focus on society is zero for spiritual gain, but it occurs with 28 per cent respondent-incidence for the social status category—which is also the highest for any primary valuation category.

On the other hand, those asking for security or survival are essentially family-centred (77 per cent and 69 per cent, respectively, of their total incidences). Aspirations for well-being or enhanced economic status are also mainly family-centred (55 per cent and 51 per cent, respectively, of their respondent incidences). Society-centred respondent-incidences for these four primary valuation categories range from zero for well-being to 11 per cent for economic status, with 2 and 3 per cent, respectively, for security and survival.

The secondary negative valuation categories were found to cut across the primary (positive-negative) and the secondary positive valuation categories evolved for the West Bengal and Delhi respondents. Referring to the impediments to attaining a better quality of life, these categories occurred for a respondent with reference to separate kinds of impediments or in any combination of them. However, with or without mutual association, five secondary negative valuation categories could be formulated: (*i*) lack of employment; (*ii*) lack of education; (*iii*) lack of government aid; (*iv*) lack of equality of gender or age; and (*v*) lack of freedom of the poor from oppression by the rich, abetted by corruption in high places.

Lack of employment (viz., jobs for unemployed and improvements in jobs and business enterprises including agriculture) is the crucial secondary negative valuation accounting for 88 per cent of what the West Bengal and Delhi respondents want: even the 'spiritual' valuation is not exempted from it. However, it is combined with the other four valuations mentioned above for 31 per cent of all respondents, and in equal proportions of 19 per cent with lack of education alone or any combination of lack of government aid, equality by sex and age, and freedom from oppression of the poor by the rich. For only 19 per cent of all respondents, the lack of employment is valued exclusively.

Lack of education (including the lack of facilities for technical and higher education) is the next important secondary negative valuation of the West Bengal and Delhi respondents, accounting for 56 per cent of them; but it never occurred alone. It was found associated with the lack of employment for 50 per cent respondents, as noted above, and with the lack of other three kinds for the remaining 6 per cent respondents.

The other three secondary negative valuations of the West Bengal and Delhi respondents, viz., lack of government aid, equality by sex and age, and freedom from oppression of the poor by the rich, occurred for only 6 per cent of these respondents, separately or in any combination of the three.

Thus, as shown illustratively with reference to the want-based quality of life research in India, categories of primary and secondary (positive and negative) valuations can be evolved from the total space of want data under examination. These value categories can then be employed as indicators of what the predetermined social groups want for a better quality of life. As explained in Chapter 2, this course of analysis would be sufficient to conduct the want-based quality of life research to monitor the implementation of a policy or a programme sponsored by a particular appraisal of a better quality of life as made by an elite group such as the power-wielding elites.

For example, it can be ascertained from Table 3.23 and 3.24 that leaving aside the want of economic security, the emphasis on the 'family' and the lack of employment, along with the lack of educational facilities—which are the predominant primary (positive-negative) and secondary positive and negative valuations of the West Bengal and Delhi respondents—there are distinctive differences among the social groups examined under certain assumptions:

1. West Bengal and Delhi should register any geo-political dif-ference in the perception of a better quality of life because the state of West Bengal, ruled from 1977 by the Communist Party of India-Marxist in the main, is situated at the eastern periphery of the Republic of India while the core is at Delhi and is ruled by the Indian National Congress (Indira) barring a lapse between 1977–80.

2. City-rural habitation in West Bengal and Delhi should denote distinctive differences in the way of life despite the process of rural-urban continuum cutting across the rural-urban structural dichotomy which surely prevailed under the Raj (Mukherjee 1965: 15–58).

3. Ethnic community differences in the style of life, mode of life, etc., are still noticeable in West Bengal among the Hindus, the Muslims, and the de-tribalized people like the Santals; just as the Hindu Gujars and the Muslim Meos are distinguished in the Delhi region, although both belong to the 'Backward Commu-nities', and the Scheduled Castes not only symbolize economic

Table 3.23

Percentage Incidence in Social Structure Categories of Respondents' Primary (Positive-Negative) Valuations of a Better Quality of Life

Social structure category	n	Percentage of total respondents ($n = 100$) for each social structure category					
		Spiritual	Social status	Well-being	Economic status	Security	Survival
(1)	(2)	(3)	(4)	(5)	(6)	(7)	(8)
Location							
West Bengal	145	1	7	14	11	60	7
Delhi	445	4	12	5	10	50	19
Habitation							
City	261	5	18	12	15	42	8
Rural	329	2	5	4	6	60	23
Ethnic community							
Bengali							
Hindu	112	1	7	14	13	59	6
Muslim	22	5	9	18	9	45	14
Santal (tribal)	11	—	—	—	—	100	—
Gujar (Hindu)	159	4	20	5	11	40	20
Meo (Muslim)	133	5	3	2	9	62	19
Scheduled Castes	153	3	10	9	10	49	19

	N						
Gender							
Male	351	4	14	4	12	51	15
Female	239	2	5	12	8	54	19
Age							
Young (25+)	202	2	11	6	10	55	16
Adult (40+)	200	4	10	6	12	54	14
Old (55+)	188	4	10	10	9	48	19
Status							
Upper	220	2	20	14	14	35	15
Middle	203	4	5	4	10	59	18
Lower	167	4	5	2	7	66	16
Total	590	3	10	8	10	52	17

Table 3.24
Percentage Incidence in Social Structure Categories of Respondents' Secondary Valuations of a Better Quality of Life

Social structure category	n	Percentage of total respondents (n = 100) for each social structure category				
		Secondary positive			Secondary negative	
		Self	Family	Society	Employment	Others
(1)	(2)	(3)	(4)	(5)	(6)	(7)
Location						
West Bengal	145	30	70	—	91	9
Delhi	445	31	61	8	87	13
Habitation						
City	261	40	52	8	82	18
Rural	329	24	72	4	92	8
Ethnic community						
Bengali						
Hindu	112	29	71	—	91	9
Muslim	22	45	55	—	86	14
Santal (tribal)	11	—	100	—	100	—
Gujar (Hindu)	159	25	64	11	85	15
Meo (Muslim)	133	30	64	6	92	8
Scheduled Castes	153	39	56	5	84	16
Gender						
Male	351	38	54	8	89	11
Female	239	20	78	2	85	15
Age						
Young (25+)	202	30	64	6	91	9
Adult (40+)	200	28	66	6	90	10
Old (55+)	188	34	61	5	82	18
Status						
Upper	220	34	54	12	82	18
Middle	203	32	66	2	89	11
Lower	167	25	74	1	93	7
Total	590	31	63	6	88	12

and cultural deprivation in society since the British structured this group with a purpose in the 1930s (Mukherjee 1957: 80–102), but has also acquired a formidable political significance since the 1960s.

4. Gender difference prevails despite significant changes in Independent India through legislation and the rapidly advancing women's movement toward complementarity of sexes.

5. Age difference may register different perceptions of a better quality of life for (*i*) the young persons around 25 years of age, who have just entered the labour market, (*ii*) the adults around 45 years of age, who have grown into that market, and (*iii*) the old persons around 55 years of age, who are facing the prospect of retirement from the labour market.

6. Status difference, epitomizing the crystallization of the social, economic, and cultural forces, is likely to record different perceptions of a better quality of life; the difference in the Indian context being categorized in the following manner: (*i*) *upper*, comprising the high-ranking professionals and the managers and executives in organized industries in the cities, and the landed interests and the rural intelligentsia in the villages; (*ii*) *middle*, comprising the office personnel, shop assistants, and the like in the city, and the own-account workers in agriculture, crafts, and trade in the villages; and (*iii*) *lower*, comprising the skilled, semi-skilled, and unskilled workers in the cities and the villages (such as the sharecroppers and farm hands).

Bearing upon the identification of predetermined social groups for the above reasons, it is seen from Tables 3.23 and 3.24 that:

1. The primary valuation of well-being is a noticeable concern of the West Bengal respondents and social status of the Delhi respondents. Correspondingly, as regards the secondary valuations, the Delhi respondents are more concerned than the West Bengal respondents with 'society' and the lack of facilities other than for employment (and education which is largely associated).

2. The West Bengal valuation is applicable to the two communities of Hindus and Muslims but not to the very small sample of Santals who are all concerned with family-centred economic security and the lack of employment (and educational) facilities. However, the Hindus and the Muslims are distinguished by the primary valuation of economic status for the Hindus and economic survival for the Muslims. Also, the Muslims are more self-centred than the Hindus, and feel relatively more for the lack of facilities other than employment (and education).

3. The Delhi valuation is presented by the Hindu Gujars and the Scheduled Castes, mainly the Gujars, while the Muslim Meos tend to be nearer the Bengali Hindus and Muslims, particularly the Muslims, as regards their valuations of a better quality of life.

4. For all the respondents, the city folk are noticeably concerned with social and economic status and well-being as against the villagers who primarily want economic security and survival. Correspondingly, the secondary valuations of the city respondents are relatively more self- and society-centred than of the rural respondents, and they feel the lack of facilities other than for employment (and education) much more.

5. Interestingly, the men are noticeably concerned with social status and the women with well-being, along with the men being more self-centred (and even society-centred) than the women.

6. Age difference does not seem to differentiate the valuations of the respondents except that the young persons are the least concerned with the lack of facilities other than of employment (and education).

7. Status difference distinguishes the upper from the middle and the lower by the upper status group being concerned, in an appreciable measure, with social and economic status and well-being; by being more society-centred, and feeling the lack of facilities other than of employment (and education) much more. However, the three strata are clearly graded from upper to lower by being more and more concerned with family-centred economic security through employment and associated education.

A course of analysis of the predetermined social groups as above is also relevant to a comprehensively designed need-based quality of life research which would yield different valuations of a better quality of life as discussed in Chapter 2. In that context and irrespective of a more precise value-characterization of the social groups by their cross-classification than the small samples of Indian respondents would permit, it is seen that Meadows' need-valuation of 'moral resources' and JS's (Bharatiya Jana-Sangh) of 'integral humanism' (Chapter 2) hardly leave an imprint on the wants of the people. Only 3 per cent of the total sample of respondents have posited spiritual gain as the means to a better quality of life (Table 3.23). This is of particular significance to the Indian context which was regarded by Max Weber (1958b) and is still considered by like-minded scholars (e.g., Loomis and Loomis 1969) to present the 'other wordly' outlook on the quality of life.

On the other hand, it is seen that economic security of the family by means of employment and necessary education is the valuation of a better quality of life which rules the minds of the general mass of the people. The Indian political parties examined in Chapter 2 are all found to be concerned with this point. In this context, the stability of CPI-M rule in West Bengal may be largely due to its effective policy and programme, especially in the rural areas. It is also noticeable in the same context that the lack of government aid, equality by sex and age, and of freedom from oppression of the poor by the rich (abetted by corruption in high places) are felt more in Delhi than in West Bengal, possibly because expectations are generated more near the seat of power than at the periphery and are not met satisfactorily.

However, a synchronization of the valuations of the masses with those of the elites requires that the value groups of respondents emerge directly from the data space of the masses just as such value groups have been seen in Chapter 2 to have been formed for the elites. In this respect, the valuations of what the people want acquire an independent analytic role in place of its dependent qualifying role with respect to the predetermined social groups. This necessary course of analysis is indicated by the respondent-incidence of the evolved value categories in the predetermined social groups, as seen from Tables 3.25 and 3.26.

Table 3.25 shows that, however low in importance, the incidence of spiritual gain as the primary valuation is concentrated in the Delhi region, among the city respondents, the males; and it is more the valuation of adult and old persons, and of the middle and lower status groups, than of the young persons and of the upper status group. Similarly, Table 3.26 shows that society-centred secondary positive valuations are entirely a Delhi phenomenon and essentially the characteristic of the city, the Gujar, the male, and of the upper status group. However, except in respect of these two minimally represented value categories, Table 3.25 and 3.26 do not elicit significantly more information than what Tables 3.23 and 3.24 have already provided.

This may happen, in part, because of the unequal sample size of the social structure groups, which is an inevitable limitation to the time-cost constrained research projects as noted earlier with reference to the quality of life surveys in West Bengal and Delhi in 1980 and 1982. However, it suggests in any event that employing the evolved value

Table 3.25
Percentage Incidence of Primary (Positive-Negative) Value Categories of a Better Quality of Life in Each Social Structure Category

Social structure category	Percentage of total respondents under a value category to respondents in each social structure category					
	Spiritual	Social status	Well-being	Economic status	Security	Survival
(1)	(2)	(3)	(4)	(5)	(6)	(7)
Location						
West Bengal	10	16	45	26	28	10
Delhi	90	84	55	74	72	90
Habitation						
City	70	75	70	66	35	22
Rural	30	25	30	34	65	78
Ethnic community						
Bengali Hindu	5	13	36	23	21	7
Bengali Muslim	5	3	9	3	3	3
Santal (tribal)	—	—	—	—	4	—
Gujar (Hindu)	35	52	18	28	27	26
Meo (Muslim)	30	7	7	20	21	34
Scheduled Castes	25	25	30	26	24	30
Gender						
Male	70	79	36	69	58	53
Female	30	21	64	31	42	47
Age						
Young (25+)	20	38	27	33	36	33
Adult (40+)	40	33	27	39	35	30
Old (55+)	40	29	46	28	29	37
Status						
Upper	25	71	73	49	25	34
Middle	40	16	18	33	39	39
Lower	35	13	9	18	36	27
Total	100	100	100	100	100	100
(*n*)	(20)	(61)	(44)	(61)	(308)	(96)

categories as independent variables for analysis would not be efficient in the case of being restricted to the predetermined social groups. Obviously, as pointed out in Chapter 1, value as a processual (and not a structured) variable would cut across the predetermined social groups and thus distinguish and interrelate all individuals under consideration in a precise and comprehensive manner.

The input of processual variations in place of structural variations alone, which is the common procedure in social research, would automatically shift the level of analysis to that of comprehension of what the people want in an unequivocal manner. However, the shift is not applicable to the perceptual variables only, such as, the want data.

Table 3.26

Percentage Incidence of Secondary Positive and Negative Value Categories of a Better Quality of Life in Each Social Structure Category

Social structure category	Percentage of total respondents under a value category to respondents in each social structure category				
	Secondary positive			Secondary negative	
	Self	Family	Society	Employment	Others
(1)	(2)	(3)	(4)	(5)	(6)
Location					
West Bengal	24	27	—	26	18
Delhi	76	73	100	74	82
Habitation					
City	57	37	61	41	64
Rural	43	63	39	59	36
Ethnic community					
Bengali Hindu	18	21	—	20	14
Bengali Muslim	6	3	—	3	4
Santal (tribal)	—	3	—	2	—
Gujar (Hindu)	22	27	52	26	33
Meo (Muslim)	22	23	24	24	15
Scheduled Castes	32	23	24	25	34
Gender					
Male	73	50	88	61	51
Female	27	50	12	39	49
Age					
Young (25+)	33	35	36	35	25
Adult (40+)	31	35	36	35	29
Old (55+)	36	30	28	30	46
Status					
Upper	41	32	79	35	55
Middle	36	35	15	35	30
Lower	23	33	6	30	15
Total	100	100	100	100	100
(*n*)	(182)	(375)	(33)	(517)	(73)

It is equally applicable to the so-called objective behavioural variables, such as, the need data examined in Chapter 2, because based on the structure and the processes of a 'thing' or a phenomenon, the shift should lead to a precise comprehension of the subject and the object of enquiry: in the present context, who wants what for a better quality of life.

Therefore, the rest of this chapter will be concerned with the concept behind the shift from the level of analysis to that of comprehension, a suitable methodology for applying the concept to a real situation, and an illustration of the concept and the method with reference to the want data already analyzed and formulated into want-based quality of life indicators of primary (positive-negative) and secondary positive and secondary negative import.

COMPREHENSION

At the first stage of understanding a phenomenon, its essential properties, say, *p*, are enumerated and regarded as the *content* variables. Variability in these properties with reference to the phenomenon are located at some nodal points identified by one or more sets of *context* variables. The nodal points are composed of indivisible elements of the phenomenon, viz., individual human beings in the case of social phenomena. By the collation of elements (individuals), the nodal points assume a group character, say, **G, G′, ...** The groups are systematically articulated with reference to the context and the content variables in order to represent the structure of the phenomenon. On this basis a social structure is constructed to describe what a societal configuration is at a point in time, say, t_j.

The causal or concomitant relations drawn among the **G**-groups with reference to the *p* properties denote the operation of the social structure and, thus, answer the question: how the societal configuration functions within itself and across other homologous or analogous configurations. In this manner, the variability of a phenomenon is often explained at the static point t_j.

For a dynamic explanation, the social structure composed of the same context variables is constructed for successive points in time, say, $t_c, . . . , t_j$ and variations in the characteristics of the **G**-groups noted. For this purpose, the content variables and the context variables may be the same and, therefore, the group character remains static. Variations in this case refer to the varying number of elements (individuals) comprising the groups at different time-points.

For example, a set of groups may be constructed by identical characterization at all time-points of the mode of production in society, the state of the productive forces, the relations of production, and the relations of property. Then, the incidence of all the elements N in different groups is noted as n in G, n' in G', and so on; so that from variations in n/N, n'/N, . . . over t_{ci} an inference is drawn on whether the social structure has changed and the nature and extent of the change processes.

Greater dynamism is introduced in the course of analysis when the context and the content variables are distinguished. Pursuing the previous example, the context variables may remain the same four as noted, in order to define and systematically order a set of groups, viz., G, G', ... But, now, the content variables will refer to attributes denoting variability in the four parameters. So that, the central tendencies and dispersions of the content variables in respective groups may be calculated and the overall mean and standard error values may be derived; such as, $g \pm s$ for G and $g' \pm s'$ for G'. Then, at different time-points, any one of the possible relations $g \gtreqless g'$ is established and these relations of equality and inequality among the G-groups at successive time-points are assumed to denote change or no change, and the nature and extent of change, in the phenomenon.

This course of analysis is less equivocal and more precise and comprehensive than the one previously described. But this course of analysis, also, elicits only a quasi dynamic explanation of the processes the phenomenon is undergoing, which one looks into after describing the structure and the function of the phenomenon. Dynamism would be enforced in the course of explanation when interactions between pairs of groups with respect to the g-values, such as gg' for G and G', are also examined at each and all time-points. In that case, the course of analysis will take a simultaneous account of the relations between g and g', g and gg', and g' and gg', in place of the relation between g and g' exclusively.

The variable relations among g, g', and gg' as $g \gtreqless g' \gtreqless gg' \gtreqless g$ will point to what is happening at each and every time-point, while $g \gtreqless g'$ alone may point out what has happened over t_{ci}. From what is happening at t_i one can detect the probability of what the phenomenon is likely to be at t_j. Also, if one can ascertain what is happening at each time-point t_c to t_i, then the pointer to what has happened over t_{ci} would be safeguarded by checks and balances. In either case, the explanatory understanding of the phenomenon will become more precise and comprehensive.

However, the envisaged course of analysis involves a basic departure from the course usually undertaken. When only the proportional incidences of **N** in respective groups are considered, or exclusively the mutually distinct relations of **g**>**<g**′, the groups are the *items* as well as the *units* of analysis. Therefore, the statistical indicators are constructed with exclusive reference to **n, n**′, . . . individuals constituting the respective groups; such as, **n/N, n**′**/N**, . . .,

or $g = \sum_{1}^{n} (fx)/n$, $g' = \sum_{1}^{n} (fx)/n'$, ... But, the construction of the

indicator **gg**′ requires the consideration of **nn**′ individuals between a pair of groups (**G** and **G**′) in order to ascertain group interaction and, thus, the interrelations among all groups. And, in conformity with this perspective of mutually distinct but interrelated groups, the intra-group indicators require to be constructed with reference to all possible combinations of the elements (individuals) constituting the respective groups; such as, with respect to **G** and **G**′, n_{C_2} and n'_{C_2} pairs of individuals are now under reference and not merely **n** and **n**′.

Thus, for the concept mooted, the individuals (elements constituting respective groups) are the items of analysis and the groups are the units of analysis: a set of distinctions necessary for any course of classification or analysis (Mukherjee 1983: 55–111). The individuals are examined in pairs within and between groups so as to ascertain comparable values of **g**, **g**′, and **gg**′, bearing in mind that the total number of pairs for, say, **N** = **n**+**n**′ is given by $N_{C_2} = n_{C_2} + n'_{C_2} + nn'$.

The procedure is equally applicable to the 'objective' and the 'subjective' content variables. Since individuals are the points of reference to collect 'subjective' information, no one will doubt the feasibility of the proposed course of analysis in respect of 'subjective' variables. For example, with reference to the content variable *d* of individuals' 'subjective' disagreement in accepting the same out of the total of *p* attributes, pairs of contextually identified groups **G** and **G**′ may be distinguished by applying a test of significance to the mean and standard error of respective sets of *d* values as **g** ± **s**, **g**′ ± **s**′, and **gg**′ ± **s**″; the three statistics based on the constituents of **G** and **G**′ as n_{C_2}, n'_{C_2}, and **nn**′.

The 'objective' variables may appear to refer directly to respective groups, but all social groupings are composed of individuals and groups are not immutable. Therefore, intra-group and inter-group variations denoting the processes will be comprehensively revealed by regarding the constituents of the groups (the individuals) as the items of analysis. In that case, the proposed course of analysis is clearly applicable to the 'objective' attributes or a combination of 'subjective' and 'objective' attributes.

For example, with reference to the aforementioned context variables of production and property, the gainfully occupied persons in a societal configuration may be categorized into a set of industry-occupation groups **G, G'**, . . ., in accordance with the sector of the economy to which they are attached and the actual jobs they perform. Each one of these individuals may then be characterized by the 'objective' q attributes denoting variability in the parameters of production and property and/or other relevant content variables. Also, the 'objective' attributes may be combined with apposite 'subjective' attributes in order to ascertain the processes concerned with the concepts like 'class in itself' and 'class for itself' which have generated a good deal of polemics among the Marxist scholars.

Thus characterized, any two individuals within a group like **G** or **G'** and across any two groups like **G** and **G'** can be paired in accordance with the acceptance or rejection of each one of the 'objective' and 'subjective' attributes. Intra-group and inter-group variations can then be ascertained from proportional incidences of the discrete variables, and the central tendency and dispersion of the continuous variables, provided the content variables of all kinds are duly pooled to present the overall group characteristics.

It will be noticed that the procedure rests upon an inductive orientation to the course of analysis. The data space is conceived of all probable attributes depicting the object of enquiry, and the social space is conceived of all subjects of enquiry (individuals) to which the attributes refer. From these two spaces the available attributes for analysis and the available elements (subjects) of analysis are coordinated without imposing any constraint upon their selection and systematic arrangement. The course of analysis is, then, concerned with the items of analysis (viz., the group formation of the elements according to the attributes they depict) in order to ascertain whether or not the groups denote stably *structured* unities or indicate the probable formation of another set of unities in the immediate future because of the processual variations registered *across* the structured unities.

The method of analysis is based upon the following considerations:

1 Let there be two groups G and G' which are composed of n and n' members, respectively.

Let there be p number of attributes, each of which is accepted, subjectively or objectively, or rejected by each one of n and n' individuals.

One may amplify the extent of acceptance/rejection of the attributes. This would mean formulating a series of attributes from each one of the present set of p attributes, i.e., extending the total number of attributes.

It follows that any two individuals may agree or disagree in accepting each attribute. Therefore, for the p number of attributes and with reference to pairs of individuals, variations in *not* accepting the same attribute ($= d$) will be 0 at the minimum, p at the maximum, and the possible range of the d values will be $0, 1, 2, \ldots, (p-1), p$.

2 The mutually distinguished group characteristics of G and G' will be depicted by the statistical properties of the d values calculated for n_{C_2} and n'_{C_2} pairs of individuals within respective groups.

In case the central tendency and dispersion of the d values (i.e., $g \pm s$ and $g' \pm s'$) denote $g = g'$, then the two groups will be considered as structurally identified.

In case the central tendency and dispersion of the d values denote $g \neq g'$, then the two groups will be considered as structurally distinct.

3 Any *process* of change or no change from these deductions of structural identity or distinction will be registered by the d values calculated for pairs of individuals, one of the pair located in the G-group and the other in G'-group; that is, from nn' number of d values. In this case, the content of analysis (d values) and the items of analysis (n and n' individuals) are considered inductively from the bottom of the data and the social spaces; namely, each one of the p attributes evolved from the data space refers to each one of N individuals from the social space.

It will be seen that *a priori* grouping of N individuals into G and G' will provide n_{C_2} and n'_{C_2} d values, while the interactions between G and G' as given by nn' d values will complete all possible combinations of N individuals (to repeat: $N_{C_2} = n_{C_2} + n'_{C_2} + nn'$).

4 Let the central tendency and dispersion of nn' d values be noted as $gg' \pm s''$. When $gg' \pm s''$ is examined with reference to $g \pm s$ and $g' \pm s'$, the comparisons will indicate the process of change (or no change) in operation while the structural distinction (or identity) will be noted by the comparison of $g \pm s$ and $g' \pm s'$. Thus, the interaction

variances will indicate whether or not the structural distinction or identity is stabilized with reference to the respective sets of **n** and **n′** individuals.

5 On this basis, 13 possible relations can be drawn among **gg′**, **g**, and **g′**; eight of them are normatively valid and five more are statistically valid. The relations and the corresponding findings and deductions are given in Table 3.27.

The relations of structural and/or processual identity or distinction noted in Table 3.27 can be illustrated with reference to the West Bengal and Delhi respondents' valuations of a better quality of life, in order to substantiate their usefulness in place of usually ascertained exclusively structural distinction or identity. Each one of these 590 individuals has recorded 1 out of 6 primary (positive-negative) valuations elicited from the total data space, 1 out of 3 secondary positive valuations, and 1, 2, 3, 4, or 5 secondary negative valuations. Therefore, as the individuals in pairs may agree to none, any one, or more of these valuations, the range of disagreement d between the paired individuals may vary from 0 to 7.

Accordingly, $590_{C_2} = 173,755$ d values were calculated for the paired individuals while these individuals formed 11 context groups according to their affiliation to ethnic community, region, and habitation. These groups, with their symbols in brackets for purposes of identification in the tables that follow, are:

1. Bengali Hindu in Calcutta (BhC).
2. Bengali Hindu in West Bengal villages near a town (BhR).
3. Bengali Hindu in West Bengal villages far from a town (BhR+).
4. Bengali Muslim in Calcutta (BmC).
5. Santal in West Bengal interior villages (SaR+).
6. Gujar in Delhi city (GC).
7. Gujar in villages around Delhi (GR).
8. Meo in Delhi city (MC).
9. Meo in villages around Delhi (MR).
10. Scheduled Castes in Delhi city (SCC).
11. Scheduled Castes in villages around Delhi (SCR).

The individuals also formed 18 context groups by their gender (male M or female F) x status (upper U, middle M, or lower L) x age (young Y, adult A, or old O) as: MUY, MUA, MUO, MMY, MMA, MMO, MLY, MLA, MLO, FUY, FUA, FUO, FMY, FMA, FMO, FLY, FLA, and FLO.

For each of the two sets of 11 and 18 context groups the mean and

Table 3.27

Relations Formed among Group Means g and g′ and their Interaction gg′ (Operational assumption: g ≥ g′)

Relation	Finding	Deduction with symbol
(1)	(2)	(3)
1 Structural-processual distinction		
1. $g > g' > gg'$	Larger inter-group than across-group difference	Stable distinction of G and G′ (d)
2. $g > gg' > g'$		
2 Structural distinction but processual identity		
3. $gg' > g > g'$	Across-group difference supersedes inter-group difference	Strong process of amalgamation of G and G′ (i″+)
4. $gg' = g > g' = gg'*$	Inter-group difference significant but not across-group difference	Incipient process of amalgamation of G and G′ (i″)
5. $gg' = g > g' < gg'$	Along with inter-group difference, across-group difference registered with respect to G′ only	G′ tends toward identity with G, the group recording larger mean value (i′1)
6. $gg < g > g' = gg'$	Along with inter-group difference, across-group difference registered with respect to G only	G tends toward identity with G′, the group recording smaller mean value (i′2)
3 Structural identity but processual distinction		
7. $gg' > g = g'$	Larger across-group than inter-group difference, the latter insignificant	G and G′ under strong process of distinction from identity (d″)
8. $gg' > g = g' = gg'*$	Larger across-group than inter-group difference with respect to G or G′, but inter-group difference insignificant	G and G′ under incipient process of distinction from identity (d′)
9. $gg' = g = g' < gg'*$		
4 Structural-processual identity		
10. $g = g' = gg'$	Inter-group difference insignificant	Stable identity of G and G′ (i)
11. $g = g' > gg'$	Across-group difference not significant or less than inter-group difference with respect to G and/or G′	
12. $gg' < g = g' = gg'*$		
13. $gg' = g = g' > gg'*$		

* Statistical, not normative, possibility.

standard error of **d** values were calculated, as also for each pair of 11 and 18 social groups. Thus, the mean and standard error values were obtained for $11 + 11_{C_2} = 66$ cells of the region, habitation, ethnicity matrix of the perennial culture context, and $18 + 18_{C_2} = 171$ cells of the gender, status, age matrix of the *pervading* culture context. Next, *t*-test at the 5 per cent level of significance was applied to each set of $\mathbf{g} \pm \mathbf{s}$ and $\mathbf{g'} \pm \mathbf{s'}$, $\mathbf{g} \pm \mathbf{s}$ and $\mathbf{gg'} \pm \mathbf{s''}$, and $\mathbf{g'} \pm \mathbf{s'}$ and $\mathbf{gg'} \pm \mathbf{s''}$ values; that is, the test was carried out for 165 cases with reference to the perennial and for 459 cases with reference to the pervading culture context.

From the results of the test, the relation among $\mathbf{g}$, $\mathbf{g'}$, and $\mathbf{gg'}$ was drawn for each one of 55 cells of one matrix and 153 cells of the other. The relations depicted one or another variant of structural and/or processual distinction or identity of paired groups as given in Table 3.27 and each variant was represented by a symbol. Additionally, from the results of the test, inter-group distinction or identity was recorded with reference to $\mathbf{g}$ and $\mathbf{g'}$ alone, and the paired groups which registered significant distinction at the 5 per cent probability level were marked X while those which did not register that distinction were marked by the symbol of identity **0**.

Table 3.28 shows that in two clusters of *Sa* and *Sb* of three and four groups, respectively, the context variables of ethnicity, city-rural habitation, and regional location register structural identities in evaluating a better quality of life. In the same respect the remaining four context groups, placed in the heterogenous cluster *Sc*, register structural distinction among themselves and with the other seven groups except in one case. However, the two clusters of structural identity do not

Table 3.28
Structural Identity or Distinction of Context Groups formed by Ethnicity, Rural-Urban Distinction and Regional Location

Context group*	Structural identity (0) or distinction (x)										
	SCR	GR	BmC	MC	MR	BhR+	BhC	BhR	GC	SCC	SaR+
1 SCR	—	0	0	x	x	x	x	x	x	x	x
GR		—	0	x	x	x	x	x	x	x	x
BmC	*Sa*		—	x	x	x	x	x	0	x	x
2 MC				—	0	0	0	x	x	x	x
MR					—	0	x	x	x	x	x
BhR+						—	0	x	x	x	x
BhC				*Sb*			—	x	x	x	x
3 BhR								—	x	x	x
GC									—	x	x
SCC										—	x
SaR+								*Sc*			—

* Context groups are described on page 183.

indicate any notable pattern of integration by the perennial culture context of ethnicity, city-rural habitation, or regional location.

Table 3.29 records a different alignment from Table 3.28 for the same context groups and points to two cluster formations of **Pa** and **Pb** of nine groups (in place of seven) by their processual identity in evaluating a better quality of life.

As for structural distinction, the Scheduled Caste respondents from Delhi city (SCC) and the West Bengal rural Santals (SaR+) stand apart from all other context groups and between themselves. The only indication of processual identity of the city Scheduled Castes is with their rural counterpart (SCR) and the rural Gujars (GR). Similarly, the rural Santals tend toward identity with only the Bengali city Hindus (BhC). The remaining nine context groups form an intricate network of processual variations.

Ethnic identity of the Bengali Hindus (BhC, BhR, and BhR+) and of the Gujars in the Delhi Region (GC and GR) is registered, irrespective of their city-rural habitation. Moreover, a processual identity of these two ethnic groups is noticeable across their regional locations.

Table 3.29

Structural-processual Identity or Distinction of Context Groups formed by Ethnicity, Rural-Urban Distinction and Regional Location

Context group**	Structural-processual identity or distinction*										
	SCC	SCR	GR	GC	BhC	BhR	BhR+	MC	MR	BmC	SaR+
1 SCC	—	i"+	i"+	d	d	d	d	d	d	d	d
2 SCR		—	d'	i"+	i"+	i"+	i"+	i"+	d	d"	d
GR			—	i"+	i"+	i"+	i"+	i"+	d	d"	d
GC				—	i"+	i'1	i'1	d	i'1	d'	d
BhC					—	i'1	i	d"	i"+	d	i'1
BhR		*Pa*				—	i"+	i'1	i"+	d	d
BhR+							—	d'	d'	i'1	d
3 MC								—	d"	i'1	d
MR									—	i'1	d
BmC								*Pb*		—	d
4 SaR+											—

* Table 3.27 describes the symbols of identity or distinction.

** Context groups are described on page 183.

The rural Scheduled Caste (SCR) respondents in the Delhi region are seen moving toward their city counterpart (SCC) in evaluating a better quality of life, but the rural Scheduled Castes (SCR) are still allied to the rural Gujars (GR) in this respect.

On the other hand, the Bengali city Muslims (BmC) are moving away from the rural Scheduled Castes (SCR) and Gujars (GR) in their evaluation of a better quality of life, and moving toward the Meos (MC and MR) who, in their turn, are in the process of evaluating the life quality differently depending on whether they inhabit the city of Delhi (MC) or its rural environs (MR).

Table 3.29 shows, however, that the total network of processual variations cannot be captured in unidimensional cluster formation. Even so, the clustering shown in Table 3.29 is more efficient than the clear-cut clusters found in Table 3.28. It is seen from Table 3.30 that with reference to different valuations of a better quality of life, the central tendencies of percentage incidence in the context groups included in different clusters are more mutually distinct for cluster formation by processual than by structural identity. It will also be noticed that although the standard errors are not small in magnitude, they tend to be smaller for cluster formation by processual rather than by structural identity.

Table 3.31 and 3.32, prepared in the same manner as Tables 3.28 and 3.29, show the structural and processual identity clusters of context groups formed by the pervading culture of gender, social ηtatus, and age difference of respondents. As in the case of perennial culture groups, the processual identities place the pervading culture groups in a discernible pattern unlike the structural identities.

Compared to Table 3.31, Table 3.32 shows that the upper (U) status males (M) and females (F) of all ages (Y, A, or O) are distinguished from the middle (M) and low (L) status males and females of all ages. The latter ones are placed in the fourth cluster **P'd** except (*a*) the middle status old females aligned to the upper status young females and (*b*) the low status young females remaining distinct from all other context groups.

The upper status respondents are further distinguished by their gender and age in the first three clusters shown in Table 3.32. The first cluster (**P'a**) is composed of young and adult males only (MUY and MUA); the second, **P'b**, of adult and old females along with the old males (MUO, FUO, and FUA); and the third, **P'c**, of young females (FUY) along with the middle status old females (FMO) as noted before.

Thus, while the fourth cluster (**P'd**) locates the middle and low status persons except the two noted exceptions, the second and third clusters locate, in the main, the upper status females and the first

Table 3.30
Mean ± s.e. of Respondents' Percentages in Context Groups* in a Cluster for Valuation of a Better Quality of Life (V)

V**	Structural identity		Processual identity	
	Cluster *Sa*	Cluster *Sb*	Cluster *Pa*	Cluster *Pb*
	SCR GR BmC	MC MR BhC BhR+	SCR GR GC BhC BhR BhR+	MC MR BmC
(1)	(2)	(3)	(4)	(5)
I S j	0.67 ± 0.33	1.75 ± 1.44	0.83 ± 0.48	2.33 ± 1.86
o	0.33 ± 0.33	0.50 ± 0.50	1.00 ± 0.52	0.00
F j	1.67 ± 1.67	0.75 ± 0.48	0.00	2.67 ± 1.20
o	0.33 ± 0.33	0.00	0.17 ± 0.17	0.00
R S j	5.33 ± 3.18	3.50 ± 2.60	7.00 ± 2.86	1.67 ± 1.67
o	1.67 ± 1.67	1.25 ± 0.75	1.50 ± 0.72	1.67 ± 1.67
F j	0.67 ± 0.67	0.75 ± 0.48	1.00 ± 0.68	1.00 ± 0.58
o	0.00	1.00 ± 1.00	0.50 ± 0.50	1.33 ± 1.33
E S j	3.00 ± 3.00	2.75 ± 2.75	1.83 ± 1.83	3.00 ± 3.00
o	3.33 ± 2.85	2.50 ± 2.50	1.83 ± 1.64	3.00 ± 3.00
F j	2.00 ± 1.15	4.50 ± 2.18	4.83 ± 1.35	1.33 ± 0.67
o	0.00	0.50 ± 0.50	0.83 ± 0.54	0.00
R' S j	2.67 ± 1.20	4.50 ± 1.55	3.50 ± 1.34	4.00 ± 1.53
o	0.00	1.50 ± 0.65	0.50 ± 0.50	1.00 ± 0.58
F j	2.33 ± 1.45	3.50 ± 0.65	6.00 ± 2.96	4.67 ± 0.33
o	0.33 ± 0.33	0.00	0.17 ± 0.17	0.00
E' S j	11.33 ± 3.28	14.50 ± 4.56	8.17 ± 2.18	18.67 ± 3.18
F j	38.67 ± 4.10	43.50 ± 8.67	45.33 ± 7.77	35.00 ± 2.31
o	0.33 ± 0.33	2.00 ± 2.00	0.17 ± 0.17	2.67 ± 2.67
M S j	5.33 ± 3.18	3.25 ± 1.38	3.00 ± 1.79	3.67 ± 1.86
o	2.67 ± 1.45	1.50 ± 0.96	1.83 ± 0.87	2.00 ± 1.15
F j	14.67 ± 1.20	5.00 ± 3.79	8.00 ± 2.59	9.67 ± 4.91
o	2.67 ± 2.19	1.00 ± 0.58	2.00 ± 1.06	0.67 ± 0.67
Total	100.00	100.00	99.99	100.02

* Context groups are described on page 183.
** Primary: I = spiritual, R = social status, E = well-being,
      R' = economic status, E' = security, M = survival.
Secondary positive: S = self and society, F = family.
Secondary negative: j = employment with/without other impediments.
            o = impediments other than employment and education.

Table 3.31
Structural Identity or Distinction by Gender, Status and Age

Structural identity (0) or distinction (x)

Context group*	MUY	MUA	FUA	FUY	FMO	MMY	MLO	MMA	FMA	MLY	FLO	MMO	FMY	FLA	MLA	MUO	FUO	FLY
1 MUY	—	0	0	x	x	x	x	x	x	x	x	x	x	x	x	x	x	x
MUA		—	0	x	x	x	x	x	x	x	x	x	x	x	x	x	x	x
FUA			—	x	x	x	x	x	x	x	x	x	x	x	x	x	x	x
2 FUY				—	0	0	0	x	x	x	x	x	x	x	x	x	x	x
FMO					—	0	0	x	x	x	x	x	x	x	x	x	x	x
MMY						—	0	x	x	x	x	x	x	x	x	x	x	x
MLO							—	x	x	x	x	x	x	x	x	x	x	x
3 MMA								—	0	0	0	x	x	x	x	x	x	x
FMA									—	0	0	0	x	x	x	x	x	x
MLY										—	0	0	0	x	x	x	x	x
FLO											—	0	0	0	x	x	x	x
MMO												—	0	0	x	x	x	x
FMY													—	0	x	x	x	x
FLA														—	x	x	x	x
4 MLA															—	x	x	x
MUO																—	x	x
FUO																	—	x
FLY																		—

Boxed regions labelled: S'a (group 1), S'b (group 2), S'c (group 3), S'd (group 4).

* Context groups are described on page 183.

Table 3.32

Structural-processual Identity or Distinction by Gender, Status and Age

Context group**	Structural-processual identity or distinction*																	
	MUY	MUA	MUO	FUO	FUA	FUY	FMO	MMA	FMA	MLY	FLO	MMO	FMY	FLA	MLA	MLO	MMY	FLY
1 MUY	—	i	d	i'1	d"	i'1	i'1	d	i'1	d	d	d	d	d	d	d	i'1	d
MUA	P'a	—	d	r"+	d"	i'1	i'1	d	i'1	d	i'1	d	d	d	d	d	i'2	d
2 MUO			—	i'1	i'1	d	d	d	d	d	d	d	i'1	d	d	d	d	d
FUO			P'b	—	i'1	i'1	i'1	i'1	i'1	i'1	d	i'1	i'1	i'1	i'1	i'1	d	r"+
FUA					—	r"	r"	d	d	i'1	i'1	i'1	i'1	i'1	i'2	r"	r"+	i'+
3 FUY						—	i	i'1	r"	i'1	r"	i'1	d	d	d	d"	d"	d
FMO					P'c		—	i'1	r"	i'1	r"	d'	d	d	d	d'	d"	d
4 MMA								—	i	i	i	i'2	i'1	i'1	d	i'1	d	d
FMA									—	i	i	d'	r"	r"	i'2	r"	r"+	i'+
MLY										—	i	i	i	i	i'2	r"	d	d
FLO											—	i	i	i	i	i	d	d
MMO												—	i	i	i	r"	d	d
FMY													—	i	i	i	i'1	d
FLA							P'd							—	i	i	i'1	d
MLA															—	i	i'1	d
MLO																—	d	d
MMY																	—	d
5 FLY																		—

* Table 3.27 describes the symbols of identity or distinction.

** Context groups are described on page 183.

cluster the upper status males. The two exceptions are also worth noting, namely, the association of upper status old males and females in the second cluster and of middle status old females with the upper status young females in the third.

Table 3.33
Mean ± s.e. of Respondents' Percentages within Context Groups* in Structural Identity Clusters for Valuation of a Better Quality of Life (V)

V**	Cluster $S'a$	Cluster $S'b$	Cluster $S'c$
	MUY MUA FUA	FUY FMO MMY MLO	MMA MMO MLY FMY FMA FLA FLO
(1)	(2)	(3)	(4)
I S j	1.67 ± 0.88	1.25 ± 0.75	1.29 ± 0.61
o	0.67 ± 0.67	0.75 ± 0.75	1.29 ± 0.64
F j	0	0.75 ± 0.75	1.29 ± 0.64
o	0	1.75 ± 1.03	0
R S j	11.67 ± 6.01	5.00 ± 3.39	1.43 ± 0.69
o	3.33 ± 1.76	1.75 ± 1.75	0.71 ± 0.47
F j	2.33 ± 2.33	1.00 ± 1.00	1.14 ± 0.74
o	0	1.50 ± 1.38	0
E S j	4.00 ± 2.65	1.00 ± 1.00	0.86 ± 0.59
o	3.00 ± 2.08	0	0
F j	6.00 ± 1.00	5.75 ± 3.61	2.86 ± 1.24
o	1.00 ± 1.00	1.00 ± 1.00	0
R' S j	5.33 ± 1.86	4.00 ± 2.82	2.57 ± 1.45
o	0.67 ± 0.67	1.25 ± 0.75	0.57 ± 0.57
F j	9.00 ± 2.52	3.25 ± 0.48	4.00 ± 0.69
o	1.00 ± 1.00	0	0.43 ± 0.43
E' S j	10.33 ± 2.40	9.25 ± 2.06	17.71 ± 2.08
F j	25.00 ± 4.04	32.50 ± 2.47	48.00 ± 2.30
o	1.00 ± 1.00	0	1.43 ± 1.02
M S j	3.00 ± 2.08	6.25 ± 3.61	1.43 ± 0.75
o	0.67 ± 0.67	5.00 ± 2.55	0.86 ± 0.59
F j	9.33 ± 5.33	14.00 ± 1.73	10.00 ± 1.45
o	1.00 ± 1.00	3.00 ± 3.00	2.14 ± 0.99
Total	100.00	100.00	100.01

* Context groups are described on page 183.
** Primary: I = spiritual, R = social status, E = well-being,
      R' = economic status, E' = security, M = survival.
Secondary positive: S = self and society, F = family.
Secondary negative: j = employment with/without other impediments.
      o = impediments other than employment and education.

However, like Table 3.29, Table 3.32 shows that the total network of processual cluster formation cannot be captured in one dimension. Nevertheless, Tables 3.33 and 3.34, prepared in the same manner and for the same purpose as Table 3.30, substantiate the efficiency of cluster formation by processual rather than structural identity.

Now, the clusters formed in the perennial and the pervading culture contexts may be put together for a more precise comprehension of the respondents' different valuations of a better quality of life. It has been found for the two quality of life surveys in India that the predominant primary valuation of the people is for economic security, the corresponding secondary positive valuation is for the family to attain economic security, and the secondary negative valuation is the lack of employment facilities and opportunities to attain economic security. Besides these three predominant valuations, the other primary and secondary valuations may occur at random within the sample of respondents or indicate distinctive value-group formation by the respondents. Therefore, efficiency in comprehending what the people want for a better quality of life would be indicated by the procedure of value-group formation which can identify the corresponding social groupings of respondents most precisely.

With reference to this context, Tables 3.35–3.37 have been prepared by arranging the structural and the processual clusters according to an increasing respondent-incidence in them of security as the primary valuation, family as the secondary positive valuation, and the lack of facilities and opportunities for employment as the secondary negative valuation. It will be seen from the three tables that the processual clusters distinguish the valuations of the respondents much more precisely than the structural clusters.

At one end of the spectrum of value-group formation by processual variations are placed the rural West Bengal Santal (SaR+) men of all ages, who are family-centred, job-oriented, and aspire for economic security. Nearest to this social group are the lower status young women (FLY) of all other context groups while at the other end of the spectrum are placed the upper status Scheduled Castes of Delhi city (SCC), but with interesting variations among them by gender and age.

The upper status Scheduled Caste women (P′b and P′c) of Delhi consider the lack of equality by gender and age the main constraint against attaining a better quality of life, along with the upper status old men in P′b cluster and the middle status old women in P′c cluster. The better life quality is perceived by the adult and old women (P′b) as self-centred well-being, and as family-centred economic security by the young (**P'c**). The young and adult men (**P'a**) belonging to the upper status Scheduled Caste group in Delhi city are also self-centred, but they all want a higher social status and mainly education to achieve the goal.

Between these social groups at polar ends, the value groups identified by the processual clusters are cross-classified by the contexts pre-determined for group formation of the respondents, as described before Tables 3.23–3.26. These analytically evolved social groups confirm the unilateral findings from the above mentioned tables in a comprehensive manner while pointing out that neither the perennial context to group formation (viz., Delhi or West Bengal region, city-rural habitation, and ethnicity) nor the pervading context (viz., status, age, and gender) gain an upper hand in the formation of value groups.

The upper status groups (**P'a, P'b,** and **P'c**) of **Pa** and **Pb** clusters tend to be differentiated from the middle and lower status groups (**P'd**), but the **P'd** group of the Scheduled Castes in the city of Delhi (SCC) cuts across this trend. On the other hand, the gender difference registered by **P'a** versus **P'b** and **P'c** clusters is noticeable, as also the age difference registered particularly by **P'b** and **P'c** clusters; but neither denotes any sequence between the **Pa** cluster (formed by rural Delhi Scheduled Castes and Gujar and West Bengal city-rural Hindu) and the **Pb** cluster (formed by Delhi city-rural Meo and West Bengal city Muslim). Like the middle and lower status Scheduled Castes of Delhi city cutting across the upper status value groups formed by **Pa** and **Pb** clusters, the gender and age differences of the upper status respondents of **Pa** and **Pb** clusters tend to equate the male valuation of one cluster to the female valuation of another and the valuation of the old persons of one cluster to that of young and adult of another.

These discernible alignments of the value groups would be established or new alignments revealed by examining the g, g', and gg' values (vide Table 3.27) calculated for the combined clusters shown in Tables 3.35–3.37. But that requires a large sample of respondents which would be available only if a comprehensive course of the want-based quality of life research is encouraged despite it being rather expensive and time consuming. However, the processual comprehension of a small but apposite collection, verification, formation, reduction, and analysis of want-data points to the following characteristics tentatively revealed by the quality of life surveys in India:

Table 3.34

Mean ± s.e. of Respondents' Percentages within Context Groups* in Processual Identity Clusters for Valuation of a Better Quality of Life (V)

V**	Cluster P'a (MUY MUA)	Cluster P'b (MUO FUO FUA)	Cluster P'c (FUY FMO)	Cluster P'd (MMY MMA MMO MLY MLA MLO FMY FMA FLA FLO)
(1)	(2)	(3)	(4)	(5)
I S j	1.00 ± 1.00	1.00 ± 1.00	0	1.70 ± 0.47
o	1.00 ± 1.00	0	0	1.20 ± 0.51
F j	0	0	0	1.20 ± 0.51
o	0	1.33 ± 1.33	2.00 ± 2.00	0.30 ± 0.30
R S j	17.50 ± 2.50	6.33 ± 6.33	7.50 ± 7.50	2.20 ± 0.73
o	5.00 ± 1.00	3.00 ± 3.00	0	1.20 ± 0.73
F j	0	3.00 ± 2.08	2.00 ± 2.00	1.10 ± 0.57
o	0	2.00 ± 1.15	2.00 ± 2.00	0.20 ± 0.20
E S j	4.50 ± 4.50	2.33 ± 1.20	2.00 ± 2.00	0.60 ± 0.43
o	1.00 ± 1.00	10.67 ± 3.67	0	0
F j	5.50 ± 1.50	4.33 ± 1.45	11.50 ± 3.50	2.00 ± 0.95
o	0	3.33 ± 2.03	2.00 ± 2.00	0
R'S j	6.50 ± 2.50	4.67 ± 1.20	2.00 ± 2.00	3.30 ± 1.41
o	1.00 ± 1.00	0.67 ± 0.67	0	0.90 ± 0.48

F j	6.50 ± 0.50	8.33 ± 2.96	4.00 ± 0.00	3.60 ± 0.52
o	0	1.00 ± 1.00	0	0.30 ± 0.30
E' S j	12.00 ± 3.00	6.00 ± 1.00	6.00 ± 2.00	16.50 ± 1.58
F j	29.00 ± 1.00	23.67 ± 3.53	32.00 ± 6.00	45.70 ± 2.72
o	0	1.00 ± 1.00	0	1.00 ± 0.77
M S j	4.50 ± 2.50	3.00 ± 3.00	0	3.50 ± 1.59
o	1.00 ± 1.00	2.33 ± 2.33	6.00 ± 6.00	1.40 ± 0.62
F j	4.00 ± 0.00	9.67 ± 5.36	15.00 ± 0.00	9.90 ± 1.44
o	0	2.33 ± 1.20	6.00 ± 6.00	2.20 ± 0.80
Sample	100.00	99.99	100.00	100.00
	93	101	52	318

* Context groups are described on page 183.

** Primary: I = spiritual, R = social status, E = well-being,
             R' = economic status, E' = security, M = survival.

Secondary positive: S = self and society, F = family.

Secondary negative: j = employment with/without other impediments.
                       o = impediments other than employment and education.

Table 3.35

Respondents' Percentage Incidence ($n = 100$) in Primary (positive–negative) Value Categories for Clusters in Tables 3.28, 3.29, 3.31, and 3.32

Clusters		n	Spiritual	Social status	Well-being	Economic status	Security	Survival
(1)		(2)	(3)	(4)	(5)	(6)	(7)	(8)
1 Structural Clusters in Tables 3.28 and 3.31								
Sc	S'a	38	–	40	13	16	26	5
Sa	S'a	40	5	12	10	10	35	28
Sc	S'd	41	–	19	15	27	39	–
Sb	S'b	47	2	8	11	11	40	28
Sa	S'b	40	5	3	2	3	42	45
Sc	S'b	39	8	18	5	15	44	10
Sb	S'a	45	2	7	15	20	49	7
Sa	S'd	45	2	18	5	–	53	22
Sc	S'c	67	7	7	5	15	57	9
Sb	S'd	42	2	7	12	5	62	12
Sa	S'c	67	–	–	5	5	67	23
Sb	S'c	79	5	3	1	5	76	10

2 Processual Clusters in Tables 3.29 and 3.32

SCC	P'a	8	–	100	–	–	–	–
SCC	P'b	12	–	25	67	8	–	–
Pb	P'c	12	–	8	17	8	25	42
Pa	P'b	68	4	20	13	14	30	19
Pa	P'a	60	2	20	12	17	39	10
Pa	P'c	32	–	12	19	3	38	28
SCC	P'd	40	7	8	2	30	46	7
Pb	P'b	19	–	5	5	21	47	22
Pb	P'a	23	4	4	13	14	52	13
Pa	P'c	8	13	12	–	13	62	–
SCC	P'd	180	2	7	3	6	63	19
Pa	P'd	91	6	3	1	6	67	17
Pb	FLY	26	–	3	–	11	80	6
All	*All*	11	–	–	–	–	100	–
SaR+			–	–	–	–	–	–
Total		590	3	10	8	10	52	17
(Sample)			(20)	(61)	(44)	(61)	(308)	(96)

1. Although family-centred and job-oriented economic security is the predominant valuation of the respondents, all the three value characteristics are clearly segregated from none or rudimentary to 100 per cent incidence by the analytically evolved value

Table 3.36
Respondents' Percentage Incidence ($n = 100$) in Secondary Positive Value Categories for Clusters in Tables 3.28, 3.29, 3.31, 3.32

Clusters		n	Society	Self	Family
(1)		(2)	(3)	(4)	(5)
1 Structural Clusters (Tables 3.28, 3.31)					
Sc	S'a	38	21	32	47
Sa	S'a	40	10	37	53
Sb	S'a	45	9	33	58
Sb	S'b	47	2	38	60
Sc	S'b	39	5	33	62
Sc	S'd	41	7	29	64
Sb	S'd	42	3	33	64
Sa	S'd	45	11	24	65
Sc	S'c	67	3	31	66
Sb	S'c	79	3	30	67
Sa	S'b	40	–	30	70
Sa	S'c	67	2	22	76
2 Processual Clusters (Tables 3.29, 3.32)					
SCC	P'a	8	37	63	–
SCC	P'b	12	17	75	8
Pb	P'a	23	17	48	35
Pa	P'a	60	15	32	53
SCC	P'd	40	5	40	55
Pa	P'b	68	9	28	63
Pb	P'b	19	5	32	63
Pb	P'd	91	3	34	63
SCC	P'c	8	–	37	63
Pa	P'd	180	1	30	69
Pa	P'c	32	3	19	78
Pb	P'c	12	–	17	83
All	FLY	26	–	4	96
SaR+	*All*	11	–	–	100
Total (Sample)		590	6 (33)	31 (182)	63 (375)

groupings with reference to the processual (and not merely the structural) distinctions in society.

2. Complementing this course of differentiation, the primary valuation of survival is found linked to security while the other valuations (including spiritual gain) are considered by the upper status groups in particular, which are also relatively more concerned with the self than the family and with the other impediments to attaining a better quality of life than employment.

3. The status distinction, noticeable between the upper and the middle-lower status, is influenced by gender difference and age distinction of the old against the young and adult, as also by ethnic distinction, city-rural habitation, and location near the centre of power (Delhi city) or the periphery (West Bengal).

4. As a result, from the cauldron of value-group formation, two kinds of polar groupings are discernible: (*i*) the Delhi city-based upper status and rather newly emerged ethnic category of the Scheduled Castes, and particularly the young and adult males among them; and (*ii*) the deprived rural West Bengal Santals and the lower status young women of all other ethnic communities in the city or rural areas and in Delhi or West Bengal.

5. Although the other value groupings are not clearly distinguishable by the societal characteristics of the respondents, a spectrum of valuation tends to be defined and locates the two kinds of polar groupings at its terminal points; namely, from family-centred and job-oriented security and survival to self- (and even society) centred higher economic status or to well-being and, next, to enhanced social status; all of which are to be achieved not merely through employment but also in the light of education, equality by gender and age, freedom of poor from oppression by rich (abetted by corruption in high places) and, of course, government help.

Thus, the 1980 and 1982 quality of life surveys in India serve the purpose of demonstrating how the want-based quality of life research should be conducted in order to ascertain what the people want for a better quality of life and how they want it, which would be revealed at the level of reduction of duly collected and verified want data as expectation-oriented change-receivers or achievement-oriented change-actors. The point, now, is of a systemic treatment of the elites' valuations of what the people need and the masses' valuations of what they want, so that, the quality of life research may fulfil its role as outlined in Chapter 1.

Table 3.37

Respondents' Percentage Incidence (n = 100) in Secondary Negative Value Categories for Clusters in Tables 3.28, 3.29, 3.31, 3.32

Clusters	n	Inequality by gender and age	Exploitation of poor and corruption	Absence of government help	Lack of facilities and opportunities for	
					Education	Employment
(1)	(2)	(3)	(4)	(5)	(6)	(7)
1 Structural Clusters in Tables 3.28 and 3.31						
Sc S'd	41	39	15	15	59	76
Sc S'b	39	26	15	15	59	79
Sc S'a	38	34	18	13	63	79
Sa S'd	45	31	24	62	62	82
Sb S'd	42	33	7	19	48	86
Sb S'b	47	28	11	28	53	89
Sa S'a	40	28	28	68	83	88
Sa S'b	40	45	13	58	55	88
Sb S'c	79	19	5	11	49	91
Sc S'c	67	31	9	7	55	91
Sb S'a	45	29	7	27	44	96
Sa S'c	67	40	21	63	55	96

2 Processual Clusters in Tables 3.29 and 3.32

SCC	P'b	12	83	25	8	33	17
SCC	P'a	8	50	37	25	75	50
Pa	P'b	68	46	24	49	59	78
Pa	P'c	32	63	9	41	56	81
Pb	P'c	12	42	–	33	75	83
SCC	P'd	40	23	15	13	58	85
Pb	P'a	23	30	17	35	43	87
SCC	P'c	8	63	–	12	63	88
Pb	P'b	19	32	15	32	58	89
Pa	P'd	180	32	8	36	53	92
Pb	P'd	91	8	4	21	49	93
All	FLY	26	27		27	77	96
Pa	P'a	60	27	15	32	63	97
All	SAR+	11	9	18	18	64	100
Total		590	31	14	31	56	88
(Sample)			(185)	(81)	(184)	(332)	(517)

· 4 ·
· Elite-Mass Perspectives: Need and Want·

RELEVANCE

A **valid and** comprehensive understanding of the elites' perspective of what the people need in order to attain a better quality of life should follow from the principles of the need-based research outlined and illustrated in Chapter 2. The same will be the outcome of the want-based research in case the principles outlined and illustrated in Chapter 3 are duly attended to. However, as pointed out at the end of Chapter 1, the relevance, necessity, and efficiency of the quality of life research would not depend only upon a valid presentation of the elites' and the masses' perspectives. The relevance will be appreciated from a synchronization of the value-loads elicited from the sides of the elites and the masses; the necessity and efficiency will be substantiated by an examination of the relatively relevant valuations of the elites and the masses against the cardinal valuation for humankind.

The value-loads can be synchronized on the basis of the bidirectional scale of positive (desirable), negative (undesirable), and neutral (neither desirable nor undesirable) valuations of an item of information. The available information and data spaces on the quality of life can thus be fully and precisely explored to delineate different valuations of a better quality of life. The procedure, demonstrated in Chapter 2 with reference to the need-based quality of life research, is equally applicable to the want-based research because the masses' individual valuations of an item of information as positive, neutral, or negative can be ascertained from their responses to the questions listed in Table 3.3 of Chapter 3 with respect to what one wants to have or what one wants removed in a general, specific, generalized, and the ultimate life goal context of attaining a better quality of life.

However, although the information space of life experience would be the same for the elites and the masses in a place, time, and people bound configuration of the world society, the formation of their respective data spaces may follow the principles of a macro understanding of social reality by the elites and a micro understanding by the masses. As a result, the respective categories of the elites and the masses may be concerned with different gamuts of information-items selected as data for the evaluation of a better quality of life.

This may appear to adversely affect synchronization of the elites' and the masses' valuations of a better quality of life in the sense that the elites' valuations would be largely relegated by the masses to the neutral area of the bidirectional value scale and, conversely, the valuations of the masses by the elites. The information content of the elites' valuations noted in Chapter 2 and the masses' valuations noted in Chapter 3, both in the context of India, seems to attest to this unbridgeable dichotomy. But the dichotomy is not real.

Chapters 2 and 3 have pointed out that the overall spectrum of valuations of a better quality of life is not fundamentally different for the Indian political parties and the masses because the two social categories of the elites and the masses, which must interact to establish a better quality of life of the people, are primarily concerned with the sequential issues of economic security (and survival) of the individuals to raising their economic status and well-being, assuring a higher social status and providing scope for spiritual (ideological) attainments. The spectrum may vary in compositional detail and emphasis for different configurations of the world society, in the light of relative emphasis laid upon the four cardinal valuations for humankind, which have been stated and discussed in Chapter 1. But the spectrum for different configurations would not assume altogether different forms because it refers, ultimately, to the human society *en bloc*. This is substantiated by the global views on human society, which have been examined in Chapter 2.

As pointed out in Chapter 1, the spectrum of valuations of a better quality of life cannot be formidably antagonistic in respect of the elites and the masses in one configuration of world society, because the configuration would then burst asunder. But, as noted, the treatment of the spectrum by the elites and the masses would be from counter perspectives. The frame of reference to the elites is from society (collectivity) to individuals, and to the masses from individuals to society. Therefore, the details of information may appear different for the elites and the masses because these two social categories may posit in different ways the modalities of attaining a better quality of life and, also, allot different priorities to the items of information pertaining to one modality.

This means that prior to the synchronization of value-loads of the elites and the masses, the items of information elicited from respective sides should be made comparable, especially with respect to the modalities and priorities for attaining a better quality of life. But that will not be possible in case the masses' valuations of a better quality of life are encapsulated in a number of quality of life (QOL) indicators, which is the common practice.

The practice follows from the subsidiary role usually allotted to the want-based quality of life research vis-à-vis the need-based enumeration of social indicators by the change-promoting elites. As discussed in Chapter 1, the elites furnish an extensive series of social indicators (with, of course, variations among the expert-elite groups) while the QOL indicators are elicited from the masses in order to monitor whether or not the changes induced in society by the elites are reciprocated by the people.

It would, of course, be useful to juxtapose against the valuations made by the expert-elite groups the QOL indicators thus formulated. It would be particularly useful if the QOL indicators refer to the analytically evolved social groups the masses form in this context. This means that the want-based quality of life research should be rigorously conducted to elicit the primary and secondary valuations of the masses and the positive and negative aspects of these valuations, as pointed out in Chapter 3.

However, the synchronization of value-loads of the elites and the masses to this extent only will not be efficient because it will not cover, precisely and comprehensively, the value spaces of the elites and the masses. There will be gaps in monitoring the identities and distinctions in the structures of different valuations.

The gaps will be substantially fulfilled by formulating QOL indicators extensively from the details of individual responses to the questions listed in Table 3.3 of Chapter 3. For example, it is seen from Tables 2.9, 2.10 and 2.13 of Chapter 2 that the Indian political parties have suggested varied and contrary policy measures to generate employment on a centralized or decentralized base and varied emphasis on the rural versus the urban sector of Indian society. Tables 2.10 and 2.13 of Chapter 2 also show that these political parties are becoming more concerned than before with education, linked to or delinked from employment, inequality by gender and age, exploitation of the poor abetted by corruption, and specific government help to remove these and other impediments toward attaining a better quality of life of the people. Correspondingly, it was found from the detailed responses of the individuals surveyed and reported in Chapter 3 that the analytically evolved social groups mention distinctive modalities and priorities to attain a better quality of life.

It would be of little use to enumerate these details obtained from a small sample of respondents, which has been examined in Chapter 3 essentially for illustrative purposes. The point is that the items of information elicited from each individual with reference to his/her general, specific, generalized, and the ultimate perception of a better quality of life can be reorganized in terms of different goals, strategies, modalities and priorities in attaining a better life quality.

Therefore, the impression that the elites' and the masses' valuations of a better quality of life are dichotomous from the two sides or are disparate is false. On the contrary, corresponding to the elites' valuations, the masses' valuations need not be located largely in the neutral area of the bidirectional value scale, and vice versa with respect to the elites' valuations corresponding to those of the masses.

Moreover, in case the quality of life research is conducted in concert of the elites' (need) and the masses' (want) viewpoints, their value structures may be better standardized than is presently possible from assorted need and want data, with which Chapters 2 and 3 have been concerned. For such a course of research, the elites' value structures will be revealed with reference to the goal, strategy, modalities, and priorities they enumerate in respective group formations, as illustrated in Chapter 2. Also, while pursuing the same objective with respect to the masses, their minds would be fully geared to the matter of a better quality of life by posing the questions listed in Table 3.3 of Chapter 3. Therefore, as mentioned in Chapter 3, supplementary questions may be framed to ascertain the masses' valuations of the elites' valuations.

The concerted course of research may also be extended to collecting field data from the elites, rather than depending entirely on the content analysis of the documents they have produced. In that event, it will be possible to ascertain directly the elites' valuations of the masses' valuations of a better quality of life. Thus, in various ways and with or without the aforementioned interactions between the categories of the elites and the masses to evaluate their standpoints, their value structures may be made comparable.

However, there is another rider to organizing the value structures of the masses before synchronizing the value-loads from the sides of the elites and the masses. The elites' valuations are posited as of respective experts or of specified groups, either of which are not too many in number. Therefore, it should be possible to examine the elites' value structures in their original distinct forms. But the masses' valuations cannot be so treated in view of the very large number of different value structures they would form individually. Of necessity, therefore, their value structures should denote group characteristics.

This means that a precise demarcation of value-groups formed by the masses is a prerequisite to the synchronization of the value-loads of the elites and the masses. Obviously, by conforming to the logic of group formation, the groups should register homogeneity within themselves, respectively, and heterogeneity among them; that is, intra-group variations should be significantly less than inter-group variations. Therefore, as discussed and demonstrated in Chapter 3, the groups predetermined structurally would not be efficient; on the contrary, the groups should be structurally and processually distinct, as indicated under subheading 1 of Table 3.27. However, in case combined structural and processual characteristics fail to yield value-groups systematically and comprehensively, the processual clusters (like those shown in Table 3.29 and 3.32 of Chapter 3) would present the value groups as the next best alternative.

Now, formed and made comparable in this manner, each one of the value groups of the masses and each one of the expert-elite groups will present a structure of valuation of a better quality of life. On the bidimensional value scale, each structure will be laid out by 100 per cent fulfilment of the items of information valued 'desirable' and 0 per cent fulfilment of the items valued 'undesirable', with the neutrally valued items of information placed between the two sets of desirable and undesirable information items.

All these items, which in totality will represent the information space for the elites and the masses, will change places on the value scale in the light of the data spaces formed by respective expert-elite groups and the analytically evolved groupings of the masses. As illustrated in Chapter 2, one, some, or all positively valued items of information by one appraiser may be neutrally valued by another appraiser, and negatively valued by a third. Similar alterations will occur with respect to the first appraiser's neutrally and negatively valued items of information in reversed sequences of positive—neutral —negative valuations.

Therefore, with reference to the ensemble of items of information considered, the value structures given by 100 per cent and 0 per cent fulfilment of the items may assume three *extreme* forms with respect to any set of three appraisers, say, A, B, and C. As shown in Figure 4.1, Curve A delineating the valuation of Appraiser A may be reversed by Curve B delineating the valuation of Appraiser B, while Curve C formed by Appraiser C may record casual fluctuations on the value scale and thus register neutral valuation of the items of information valued contradictorily but positively or negatively by Appraisers A and B.

Figure 4.1: Extreme Possibilities in Evaluating a Better Quality of Life (Items of information arranged with reference to Curve A)

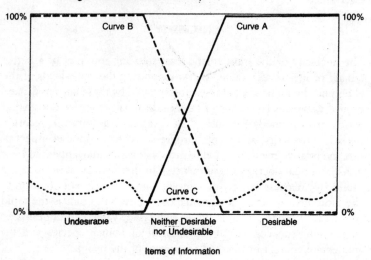

Within the limits set by Curve A and Curve B of Figure 4.1 and the *null* situation depicted by Curve C, the valuations made by Appraisers D, E, F, . . . will record variable formations of the value curve. The nature and extent of identity and distinction among all these curves are measurable in the manner demonstrated in Chapter 2, because the graduation points of each curve record +, **0,** or − valuation of the

items of information and are thus comparable for pairs of appraisers as
$++$, 00, $--$, $+0$, -0, or $+-$.

The value-loads of the elites and the masses will thus be synchronized, and the proximity or distance of the value structures would be measured in the manner shown in Tables 2.8, 2.12 and 2.15 of Chapter 2. Also, the relative distances among the value structures will be appreciated in the manner shown in Figures 2.3 and 2.4.

This means that the relevance of a comprehensive course of quality of life research (viz., need-based and want-based) will be indicated by the synchronization of all valuations of a better quality of life because the stated measurement will precisely record which valuations made by the elites and the masses are the same, allied, or more and more different from one another. As stated at the end of Chapter 1, the relative relevance of all appraisals of a better quality of life will thus be ascertained.

NECESSITY

The necessity of the most to the least relevant appraisal of a better quality of life, as ascertained by synchronizing the value-loads of the elites and the masses, would be substantiated by these appraisals, i.e., ordinal valuations conforming to the cardinal valuations for humankind which are succinctly formulated in Chapter 1 as survival, security, material prosperity, and mental progress. In one or another aspect of life, the relative relevance of elite-mass valuations may appear to have attained a high degree of congruence, but that may be superficial and ineffective because the highly relevant valuation may not conform to the aforementioned cardinal valuations. A case in point is the rapid population growth which is almost universally valued as 'undesirable' in the long-run context of the survival of human species and the immediate context of material prosperity of the people.

Presently, there is hardly any contrary valuation of the people's need and want for a 'small' family on the part of the elites and the masses, except from the standpoint of the shrinking social segments of the 'traditional' elites and the totally down-trodden masses surviving on their own and the labour of their progeny. At any rate, for Asia in general and India in particular, the assumptions are invalidated (Mukherjee 1976: 14–30) of an innate or culturally motivated parental impulse to produce as many children as possible (Chandrasekhar 1955: 67–68; Radhakamal Mukherjee 1938: SA5), the desire for more and more sons to meet the requirements of 'after life' or for social prestige in present life (Clare and Kiser 1951: 440).

But the concept of a 'small' family is differently evaluated by the change-promoting elites and the large mass of people, while the 'traditional' merchants and industrialists want many children to uphold their 'family business' for material prosperity and the down-trodden folks want many children to be employed from a young age for the survival of the family (Mukherjee 1976: 51–53).

The common valuation of demographers and planners is of a family at the replacement level of the parents or below that level, i.e., a nuclear unit of parents and one or two children. But the valuation of the large mass of the people is of parents with three to four children. They want two sons, one to ensure security in old age and the second as an insurance against the earlier demise of either of them. They also know from experience that to achieve the target they have to produce one or two daughters, i.e., a total of three to four children. At the same time, they are aware of the fact that they cannot afford to bring up more than three to four children satisfactorily under the present circumstances. Therefore, they frequently declare that three to four children form the 'ideal' family size (Mukherjee 1976: 31–54).

The result is that the rapid population growth is checked somewhat by family planning practices, because of the common valuation of the elites and the masses to have a 'small' family. But the state of zero or negative growth is not achieved to meet the cardinal valuations of survival of the species and the material prosperity of the people. In the absence of effective social security enforced by the government, the relevance of an optimally desirable small family is overruled by the necessity of ensuring economic security in the life span of common individuals.

The necessity of a relevant valuation may be indicated in other ways also, besides the extreme situation pointed out in Chapter 1 of a highly relevant valuation (e.g., in Nazi Germany) being contrary to the cardinal valuations for humankind. The relative relevance of a valuation may be low at a time-point because either a minority of the elites supports a major valuation of the masses or a major valuation of the concerned elites may find little response from the masses. However, the necessity of the valuation in the context of cardinal valuations for humankind may enforce a high degree of its acceptance by the elites and the masses at a distant time-point. The two kinds of alignments of the elites and the masses mentioned earlier, both recording low relative relevance of a valuation, can be illustrated with reference to any configuration of world society over time, such as, from the contemporary history of the Indian subcontinent.

The East Wing of Pakistan was formed in 1947 from the undivided British Province of Bengal because the want of the general mass of Bengali Muslims coincided with the needs of the Bengali Muslim elites in the perspective of a secure, materially prosperous, and progressive life. But the aspirations of the masses in East Pakistan were thwarted by the imposition of the elites from the West Wing of Pakistan. In consequence, what the people wanted was first symbolized by the demand for Bengali as the state language.

However, the mass movement, culminating in the march of 21 February 1952, was formidable but did not receive overwhelming support from the elites. Nevertheless, the people's want for a better quality of life eventually coincided with the needs formulated by the elites, and the highly relevant valuation—commensurate with the cardinal valuations for security, prosperity, and progress—led to the emergence of the state of Bangladesh in 1971. The changes thus made effective in Bengali society from the days of the raj to the state formation of Bangladesh have been described elsewhere (Mukherjee 1978: 181–206).

In the late 1920s and early 1930s, a band of elites in the British Province of Bengal began organizing the peasantry under the banner of 'land to the tillers'. The peasantry joined the organization in increasing numbers, but hardly responded to the valuation of 'land to the tillers'. Their valuation was against rack-renting and not against rent per se. Therefore, the mass movement of the disintegrated peasantry became very powerful by 1945 for a two-thirds share of the crops cultivated for the landowners but with the sharecroppers' own plough, cattle, seeds, and manure.

Thus, in the 1930s and 1940s in undivided Bengal, the relevance of the proclaimed valuation from the side of the elites was of a low order with respect to the masses, and in a converse elite-mass order of the low relative relevance of the previously cited valuation in the East Wing of Pakistan up to 1952. However, the necessary valuation of 'land to the tillers' for security, prosperity, and progress attained a high degree of relative relevance in West Bengal in course of time, as attested to by the Naxalbari Movement of the radicals in the 1960s and the reform movement entitled 'Operation Barga' in 1970–80 which was led jointly by the Communist Party of India-Marxist and the Government of West Bengal (Mukherjee 1981b).

As mentioned, similar examples can be cited from all configurations of world society to indicate that the quality of life research is not only concerned with the relative relevance of valuations for a better quality of life, as obtained by synchronizing the value-loads from the sides of the elites and the masses. It is equally concerned with the necessity of these valuations in the light of the cardinal valuations for humankind. Therefore, the conjunction of relative relevance and necessity, which are independent of each other, will determine the relative efficiency of the valuations of a better quality of life, as stated at the end of Chapter 1.

Schematically, the deductions on relative efficiency of a value structure, with reference to its relevance and necessity, are given in Table 4.1.

Table 4.1
Schematic Deductions on Relative Efficiency of a Value Structure on Better Quality of Life from Its Relevance and Necessity

Necessity: Conformation of value structure to cardinal valuations	Relevance: Elite-mass synchronization of the value structure	Deductions on relative efficiency of the value structure
(1)	(2)	(3)
None	None	Zero
	Noticeable	Negative potentially
	Appreciable	Negative presently
Noticeable	None	Zero but potentially positive
	Noticeable	Low presently and potentially
	Appreciable	High but potentially low
Appreciable	None	Zero but highly positive potentially
	Noticeable	Low presently but high potentially
	Appreciable	High presently and potentially

EFFICIENCY

An appraisal of the relative efficiency of value structures, in the context of their synchronization from the sides of the elites and the masses and their necessity with reference to the cardinal valuations for humankind, opens up a more or less untrodden path of quality of life research. The relative efficiency will be assessed from (*a*) the coincidence of valuation of none, some, or all segments of the elites and the masses to none, some, or all points delineating each value structure, and (*b*) the necessity of the value structure as indicated by its conformation to the cardinal valuations at none, some, or all points of its delineation. These points, schematically presented in Figure 4.1, are not only mutually distinct but also of distinctive meaning to the appraisal of a better quality of life. Therefore, the appreciation of relative efficiency of the elite-mass value structures is a matter of comprehension from a course of analysis involving several spheres of variation.

The quality of life research on the combined elite-mass perspective of need and want is thus raised to a derived order of comprehension on the basis of secondary analysis of the results obtained from the primary analysis of need and want data. Like the primary analysis, discussed and demonstrated in the preceding chapters, the secondary analysis would treat value as an analytic and measurable variable. However, this course of analysis will be concerned not only with the ordinal valuations of the elites and the masses but the cardinal valuations for humankind as well. Therefore, the point that emerges is the feasibility of treating all cardinal valuations analytically as a measurable proposition.

The cardinal valuations enumerated as survival of the human species, security in the life span of individuals, and their material prosperity may not raise problems, on their own, in yielding behavioural and perceptual variables amenable to measurement. This has been discussed and demonstrated in the preceding chapters, for instance, with reference to the global perception of the future of humankind. But an analytic evaluation and measurement of the valuation of mental progress, as denoted by unfolding the potentialities of individuals, generates formidable controversy. The controversy also affects the other three cardinal valuations and points to the necessity of a more precise and comprehensive formulation of behavioural and perceptual variables.

Progress, as defined, may be sequentially placed in a schema of survival to security, prosperity, and then to progress, as suggested by Galtung and Wirak (1977) and mentioned in Chapter 1. However, this ultimate valuation for the human species is systemically related to the other three cardinal valuations as indicated by common sayings, like, man does not live by bread alone, security in a confined society is not a sign of progress, and Epicureanism or satiety is not the goal of life.

Therefore, the analysis and measurement of cardinal values generates problems not only with respect to the valuation of progress but also the antecedents.

The problems related to the valuations of survival, security, and prosperity may be illustrated with reference to binary opposition built into the value attributes, the repercussion of one attribute upon another in the context of totality of cardinal valuations, and the efficiency of formulating an attribute in order to express this totality. For example, as undernourishment and overnourishment are both contra-indicated to the valuation of survival, the apposite attributes should not indicate 'well-fed' people but 'optimally fed' people. As priority for security in the life span of an individual may undermine his/her valuation of material prosperity, the attributes to indicate decline in population growth should not refer to mere family planning practices but to the modalities of family and its planning (Mukherjee 1976). As the poverty-line—a statistical rendering of the valuations of survival, security, and prosperity—may only partially denote the extent of deprivation in a society because it merely truncates the Lorenz curve of inequality (Sen 1983: 381), the attributes of deprivation should be formulated from the composition of contradictory social segments constituting the curve, as discussed elsewhere (Mukherjee 1983: 99–103) and schematically shown in Figure 4.2.

The examples show how from the positive and the negative aspects of evaluating the cardinal valuations of survival, security, and prosperity, the valuation of progress can be evaluated by a series of measurable attributes. Thus, with reference to the negative and positive aspects of survival as illustrated by the possibilities of under or overnourishment, attributes may be formulated to indicate the 'satisfaction' of want of food and need for food. In the context of population growth, attributes may be formulated to denote more 'happiness' from meeting the want of security *and* attending to the need for prosperity than from security alone. Rather than employing the poverty-line as a generalized indicator of 'deprivation', more efficient indicators may be constructed with reference to the polarized social segments, in order to denote how and *why* poverty operates to deprive specified social groups from attaining 'freedom' from want, meeting the need for prosperity, and thus developing the potentiality of individuals belonging to these groups, which is progress.

The ordinal measurement of value attributes (as 'more' or 'less') in the positive aspect implies, also, a corresponding formulation and

Figure 4.2: Lorenz Curve of Inequality Incorporating Contradictory Segments Polarized by Segments 1 and 6

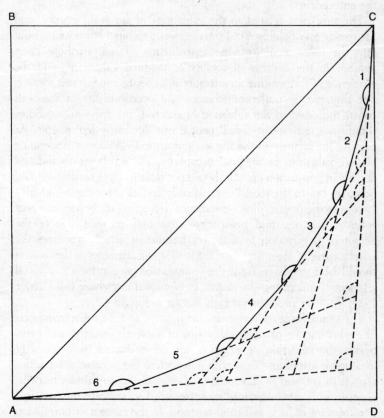

measurement of attributes in the negative aspect, and vice versa. For example, with respect to reducing population growth, less happiness in current life for old-age security may slide down to unrestricted production of children for the survival of a social group, as illustrated for the downtrodden masses in society, just as more happiness from prosperity of the traditional businessmen accelerates rapid population growth. The poverty-line not only indicates the negative valuation of 'deprivation' in a diffused manner but also fails to indicate, as pointed out, the positive valuation of 'freedom' of the deprived social segments from oppression by the exploiting segments.

The formulation of analytic attributes for the measurement of the valuation of progress can proceed by following the principles behind the variabilities illustrated, and beyond the immediate concern with the valuation of survival, security, and prosperity. This is also noticed in practice. For example, from the 1960s, Women's Lib has emerged as a movement in the context of evaluating progress. In that context, proceeding beyond rejection or acceptance of 'Women's Studies' on the basis of primary valuation of this attribute of progress, an attribute entitled 'Men's Studies Modified' (Spender 1981) has been mooted.

However, a number of scholars are of the view that the attempt would merely scrape the surface of unfathomable variability in the valuation of progress. Scott (1978: 8) takes this stand with respect to the valuation of 'human freedom' proposed by the UN experts in the context of measuring the standards and the levels of living (United Nations 1954). Many scholars are similarly sceptical of Galtung's suggestion that 'joy' should be translated into quality of life indicators. In sum, the opposition to treating the valuation of progress as an analytic and measurable proposition boils down to its definitive properties which are claimed to be neither precisely and comprehensively enumerable nor unequivocally measurable.

The viewpoint has somewhat lost its virulence because of the rigorous nature of the quality of life research undertaken by some psychologists and sociologists on the issues of 'satisfaction' and 'happiness' as mentioned in Chapters 1 and 3, some worthwhile peace and conflict research, the contemporary attempts of some economists to relate quantified ordinal valuations of choice and welfare to cardinal valuations (e.g., Sen 1983), etc. Nevertheless, the view that the cardinal valuations cannot be analytic and measurable, especially with reference to the valuation of progress, deserves careful examination.

A synoptic valuation of the cardinal valuations, which would afford a conspectus, a general appreciation of the values enumerated, is endorsed by this viewpoint. On the same account, the scholars extend their objection to treating the ordinal valuations analytically, as discussed in Chapter 1. The objection is based mainly on three grounds:

1. Value is ingrained in the perception and behaviour of individuals and their collectivities. Therefore, it cannot be isolated from apposite information except artificially.
2. Valuation is synoptic and diachronic in concept, i.e., it refers to the totality of a phenomenon and neither to its parts segmentally

nor synchronically to its manifestation at a particular place and
time and with respect to a specified people only. Therefore,
valuation is not the mere sum of evaluation of some selectively
observable components of a phenomenon.

3. Value is multilateral and multidimensional in expression; it is
not unilateral and unidimensional. Therefore, any attempt at
appraising value, except in its *original* multilateral and multidimensional state, would be unreal.

The conclusions drawn by the scholars, as noted, are fallacious; but
the enumerated features of value are valid. Therefore, they require
meticulous treatment as illustratively demonstrated in Chapter 2
under 'Analysis'. The point to note further is that value is doubtless
ingrained in the perception and behaviour of individuals and their
collectivities; but that denotes the synoptic, diachronic, multilateral,
and multidimensional appraisal of value at the level of comprehension.
This state of ultimate evaluation, which is submerged in the mental
process, should not be superficially equated to the spontaneous
appreciation of a phenomenon.

This means that the level of comprehension does not represent
spontaneity, nor should it be permitted to jeopardize the level of
analysis for sciencing society and the people. In this context, the level
of analysis is of paramount importance, which the mental process
takes note of invariably but not ostensibly (and may not also do so
meticulously) with respect to any phenomenon.

Therefore, in course of research, it is necessary to treat the level of
analysis distinctly and meticulously to ascertain the binary characteristics of a phenomenon; namely, (*i*) dividing the spontaneous synoptic
valuation by its value characteristics and reducing it to segmental,
synchronic, unilateral, and unidimensional value items, and (*ii*) collecting the value items from their irreducible state and reproducing
the totality of the value in such a manner that its comprehension is
now precise, comprehensive, and unequivocal.

The first half of the binary characteristics is almost universally
acceptable to scholars for a segmental, synchronic, unidimensional,
and often unilateral appraisal of reality; such as, from opinion and
attitude studies on a particular topic. But the second half of the binary
characteristics for reproducing the synoptic, diachronic, multidimensional, and multilateral valuation of a phenomenon at the level of
comprehension, after analysis, generates controversy. This happens

although the two complementary characteristics of valuation are implicitly accepted in everyday life, as discussed in Chapter 1 by citing examples of valuation of music, literature, and painting, the value preference for colours in the *vibgyor* spectrum, and the valuation of what is beautiful despite the common saying that beauty lies in the eyes of the beholder. Therefore, the point may deserve further examination with reference to binary characteristics of evaluating a specific subject like 'beautiful woman'.

Although the valuation of a beautiful woman varies from person to person, it registers commonality in various ways, such as, the beauty contests held in place-time-people specific societies and in the world context. However, up to this extent only, the use of value as an analytic and measure variable is acceptable to virtually all scholars. This form of universal acceptance is due to (1) the synchronization of value with information at the level of primary valuation of a phenomenon, and (2) the class of information taken into account which keeps the scope of valuation confined to a segmental, synchronic, unilateral, and unidimensional appraisal of the phenomenon.

For beauty measurement, the additive items of information on the somatometric characters (height, bust, hips, etc.) are unilateral and unidimensional on an interval scale of unit distances. The corresponding items on the somatoscopic characters (e.g., skin, hair, and eye colour, shape of face, nose, ear, etc.) are also additive on a unilateral and unidimensional ordinal-numeral scale. Finally, the measurement of all these items of information is standardized for the valuation of a woman as beautiful or not beautiful, more or less beautiful, or beautiful of a particular order like the first and the second beauty queen. Thus, the information and valuation are synchronized for a place, a time, and a people; and the scope of valuation is not only unilateral and unidimensional but also (a) segmental by referring only to the physical appearance of a woman, and (b) synchronic by being concerned with one particular standard of beauty.

Raising the level of valuation to a synoptic, diachronic, multilateral, and multidimensional appraisal of a beautiful woman would mean treating the subject of beauty beyond a standardized physical appearance with reference to some pre-selected attributes. In that case, variable characters and standards of physical appearance would remove the segmental, synchronic, unilateral, and unidimensional valuation of a beautiful woman. Correspondingly, a synoptic, diachronic, multilateral, and multidimensional valuation would be enforced by enumerating other value items which, by themselves, may be quite separate from the consideration of beauty; such as (a) the mental disposition of the person as haughty and independent or mild-tempered and submissive, (b) the particular kind and colour of dress, jewellery, etc., worn by the person, and (c) even her association with a particular species of animal (e.g., an Alsatian or a swan), flower (e.g., rose or lotus), and so on.

In this way, a beautiful woman may l e described as a tall, blue-eyed blonde, wearing a bottle-green silk dress, a platinum necklace of medium length, large coral earrings, high-heeled alligator shoes, accompanied by an Alsatian, and displaying a rather haughty and independent temperament. Conversely, a beautiful woman may be described as of medium height, olive colour skin, dark brown eyes, wearing a white saree with a lotus in black hair, playing with a swan, and displaying a mild, submissive temperament.

The illustrated primary, secondary, and tertiary properties for the evaluation of a beautiful woman are found in classical and modern romantic literature and painting from all over the world. Besides registering commonality in valuation for specific configurations of human society, the variability denotes that a particular combination of such properties forms a value structure which is equated to the data structure built by selecting certain items of information from the infinite but enumerable information space. This is how a beautiful woman is evaluated at the level of spontaneously synoptic observation and valuation.

It is necessary to underscore the point because to disregard the distinctions among the levels of observation (= spontaneous synoptic valuation), analysis, and comprehension (= deliberated synoptic valuation) of a phenomenon would be to impair the efficiency of social research in general and of the quality of life research in particular. It would merely allow value to be treated as a classificatory (and not an analytic) variable for providing a diffused or contradictory valuation of the phenomenon by means of mutually exclusive value structures. The value structures will draw a nominal distinction as 'this' or 'that' is beautiful, and so on with the valuation of other phenomena as desirable or detestable, good or bad, leading to satisfaction or dissatisfaction, conducive of happiness or unhappiness, etc.

As noted, the enforced limitation to social research follows from the fact that spontaneous synoptic valuation refers to *primary* evaluation of a structure of information. Social research has reached the stage,

from the days of Humanities and passing through the state of Human
Sciences, at which there is more or less unanimity on building a
structure of information on an ordinal (qualitative or numeral) or an
unit-interval base, as noted in Chapter 1. Therefore, there is also
general consensus among scholars on the evaluation of a phenomenon
analytically at the stage of primary valuation because the notion of
value is overlooked by its synchronization with the selection of items
of information.

But if the analytic valuation of a phenomenon is thus eschewed by
the spontaneous synoptic valuation, the yield will be of exclusive
unilateral, unidimensional, synchronic, and segmental value structures
which are equated to mutually exclusive data structures and are
commensurate with different structures of information. The procedure will gloss over the distinction between an information space and
the corresponding data space by ignoring variability in the data space
arising out of different translations of cardinal valuations with reference
to the valuation of the phenomenon. The approach will not lead to a
precise, comprehensive, and unequivocal valuation of the phenomenon
from a deliberated comprehension of its synoptic, diachronic, multilateral, and multidimensional aspects.

The point can be illustrated by considering two major instrumental
value premises for realizing the cardinal valuation of progress; (*i*) by
means of consensus among individuals and their collectivities, or (*ii*)
by the resolution of conflicts arising out of the social processes which
group individuals into contradictory collectivities.

The formulation of social class by Max Weber and class by Karl
Marx depends on analytic and measurable structures of information
built from the jobs performed by individuals with reference to the
sectors of economy with which the jobs are concerned. The selection
of jobs in two different ways, viz., by either their attributed status and
prestige or their expression of relations of production and property, is
acceptable to all scholars although the selection means primary evaluation of structure of information for data formation in the context of
presenting the phenomenon of social stratification. But, exclusively on
this basis, the appraisal of social stratification is disparate, as 'this' or
'that', because of the mere transformation of structure of information
into two unilateral and unidimensional data structures.

The two data structures are governed by the translation of the
cardinal valuation of progress in terms of consensus or resolution of
conflict, as clearly stated by Talcott Parsons (1954: 323–35). This

means that the two unilateral and unidimensional data structures present two segmental and synchronic value structures of progress. The point, then, is how to treat them in the context of a synoptic, diachronic, multilateral, and multidimensional valuation of progress.

The point draws attention to a comprehensive frame of reference to the phenomenon of social stratification, of which social class and class are two out of all probable and available formulations, such as, Pareto's (1963: 1915–18) elite-mass stratification. Against this frame of reference, a course of analysis should lead to the comprehension of the most efficient of all these available and possible data (= value) structures for a precise, comprehensive, and unequivocal valuation of progress from this aspect of reality.

Obviously, the validity, relevance, and necessity of these value structures will first be assured, as is found for social class and class, respectively. Afterwards, the course of analysis will rest upon the relational matrix formed by all these value structures, which would thus be multilateral, multidimensional, diachronic, and synoptic in character. In fact, the social scientists draw such a relational matrix with reference to two or more forms of social stratification; for example, Weber's and Pareto's formulations of social stratification are compounded for the identification of the 'traditional' and the 'modern' elites. The point is to draw the relational matrix from the irreducible state of dividing all available value items, as noted earlier.

On this base for the phenomenon under consideration, it should be possible to elicit an evermore precise and unequivocal valuation of the subject examined (e.g., progress in the present instance) in the light of the relative efficiency of all value structures brought to analysis for apprehending reality by their respective manifestations or any combination among them.

The relational matrix will encompass the homologous (common in origin) and analogous (parallel in origin) attributes of all value structures, commensurate with dividing them into an irreducible state of the aforementioned binary characteristics of a phenomenon at the level of analysis. This is possible because the value structures cannot emerge disparately with respect to a phenomenon or a class of phenomena as these are all interrelated. But at any stage of its reduction, each and every attribute collected from all available and possible value structures may be differently valued positively as, say, d, or negatively as, say r, or neutrally as O. Therefore, by noting the distinctions and interrelations of the value structures up to the irreducible state of the ensemble of attributes by the subscripts of d and r valuations, the relational matrix may be presented as in Figure 4.3, the construction of which has been explained elsewhere in detail (Mukherjee 1978: 120–31).

The distinctions and interrelations among all value structures will be precisely registered by their agreement and disagreement in evaluating the attributes in Figure 4.3 at any stage from their undivided to the ultimately divided state. Therefore, the mutual distinctions and inter-relations will be measurable by following the procedure outlined in Chapter 2, and in view of the principle of measurement explained in Chapter 1 for drawing progressive distinctions from the nominal to the ordinal (qualitative or numeral) and, then, to the interval scale of unit distances.

In that context it may be noted, with particular reference to the scholars opposed to the measurement of value, that in the light of widely accepted *Oxford Concise Dictionary* meanings reproduced below, measurement ascertains the 'extent or quantity of [things] by comparison with fixed unit or with object of known size.' Obviously, 'this' will not be distinguished from 'that' in the absolute (nominal) or relative (ordinal) term of 'more' or 'less' unless the comparison is with an 'object of known size': size defined by 'dimension, magnitude, weight or measures'. This means that finally, but not initially, measurement equates to full-fledged quantification when size equates to 'fixed unit' with reference to weights and measures, because quantity is defined as the 'property of things estimable by some sort of measure, the having of size, extension, weight, amount, or number.'

It follows that the viewpoint is not tenable, that because all pro-perties of a phenomenon have not been enumerated and the enumerated properties are not measurable, value can only be classificatory at the level of spontaneous synoptic evaluation. Obviously, the unknown properties will be increasingly revealed with the accumulation of knowledge on social reality from rigorous *research* and not from mere *search* for some 'data' in order to only substantiate a particular valu-ation. Since research (and not search) is the objective of sciencing the immanent reality, if it proceeds on to the secondary valuation of a phenomenon after the primary spontaneous valuation, the known and knowable properties will register mutually distinct and interrelated valuations of the phenomenon in a multilateral and multidimensional complex whole, as discussed and illustrated in the preceding chapters.

Figure 4.3
Diagrammatic Presentation of Relational Matrix of Value Structures of a Phenomenon

...												...
$^r112.1$	$^r112.2$	$^r112.3$	$^r111.3$	$^r111.2$	$^r111.1$	$^d111.0$ / $^r111.0$	$^d111.1$	$^d111.2$	$^d112.1$	$^d112.2$	$^r112.3$	...
$^r122.1$	$^r122.2$	$^r122.3$	$^r121.3$	$^r121.2$	$^r121.1$	$^d121.0$ / $^r121.0$	$^d121.1$	$^d121.2$	$^d122.1$	$^d122.2$	$^r122.3$	...
$^r132.1$	$^r132.2$	$^r132.3$	$^r131.3$	$^r131.2$	$^r131.1$	$^d131.0$ / $^r131.0$	$^d131.1$	$^d131.2$	$^d132.1$	$^d132.2$	$^r132.3$	...
...	...	...	...	...	...	...	...	...	...	...	...	...
$^r212.1$	$^r212.2$	$^r212.3$	$^r211.3$	$^r211.2$	$^r211.1$	$^d211.0$ / $^r211.0$	$^d211.1$	$^d211.2$	$^d212.1$	$^d212.2$	$^r212.3$	...
$^r222.1$	$^r222.2$	$^r222.3$	$^r221.3$	$^r221.2$	$^r221.1$	$^d221.0$ / $^r221.0$	$^d221.1$	$^d221.2$	$^d222.1$	$^d222.2$	$^r222.3$	...
$^r232.1$	$^r232.2$	$^r232.3$	$^r231.3$	$^r231.2$	$^r231.1$	$^d231.0$ / $^r231.0$	$^d231.1$	$^d231.2$	$^d232.1$	$^d232.2$	$^r232.3$	...
...	...	...	...	...	...	...	...	...	...	...	...	...
$^r312.1$	$^r312.2$	$^r312.3$	$^r311.3$	$^r311.2$	$^r311.1$	$^d311.0$ / $^r311.0$	$^d311.1$	$^d311.2$	$^d312.1$	$^d312.2$	$^r312.3$	...
$^r322.1$	$^r322.2$	$^r322.3$	$^r321.3$	$^r321.2$	$^r321.1$	$^d321.0$ / $^r321.0$	$^d321.1$	$^d321.2$	$^d322.1$	$^d322.2$	$^r322.3$	...
$^r332.1$	$^r332.2$	$^r332.3$	$^r331.3$	$^r331.2$	$^r331.1$	$^d331.0$ / $^r331.0$	$^d331.1$	$^d331.2$	$^d332.1$	$^d332.2$	$^r332.3$	...
...	...	...	...	...	...	...	...	...	...	...	...	...

The valuations will not remain discrete and unamenable to measurement of their distinctions and interrelations.

Thus, there is no conceptual or methodological constraint to treating value as an analytic and measure variable in the context of cardinal or ordinal valuations. On the other hand, it is necessary to treat value in this manner for the appreciation of the relative efficiency of different valuations of social reality and the consequent appraisal of a better quality of life. This necessity charters the untrodden path of quality of life research, but with a rider on treating the cardinal valuations in this context.

As explained, the necessity of an ordinal valuation made by the elites and/or the masses will be verified by its conformation to the cardinal valuations at none, some, or all points of delineation of the ordinal valuation in Figure 4.1. But the cardinal valuations are themselves translated into ordinal valuations in accordance with the meanings and modalities they convey in theory and practice. Therefore, the translated versions of the cardinal valuations are to be rated on their efficiency in presenting the succinctly formulated cardinal values, namely, survival, security, prosperity, and progress. Such as, in pursuance of an example already cited, is the value structure of social class or of class the more efficient for the realization of human progress in present times?

But appraising the relative efficiency of the ordinal translations of the cardinal values cannot follow the schema outlined in Table 4.1. Unlike for the elite-mass ordinal valuations of a better quality of life, the validity, relevance, and necessity of these ordinally translated valuations would depend upon their efficiency to mould reality toward the realization of the succinctly formulated cardinal values. This means that the course of secondary valuation of the previously discussed primary valuations of social reality involves two simultaneous operations: (*i*) synchronization of the ordinal value structures of the cardinal valuations with the elite-mass ordinal valuations shown schematically in Figure 4.1, and (*ii*) sustained monitoring of perception and behaviour of all in society with reference to the relational matrix formed by the ordinal value structures of the cardinal valuations so as to ascertain their relative efficiency, respectively or in any combination, in the quest for realizing the cardinal values.

The two tasks would be indicated by changing the heading of column 1 of Table 4.1 to: 'Monitoring efficiency of a value structure translating cardinal valuations'. However, the second task deserves special consideration, because it would establish the usefulness of quality of life research in the realm of social science, as it is intimately concerned with the social theories which are built upon the cardinal valuations for humankind and the social practice emerging from these theories, which have a profound effect on society and the people. A new prospect for the quality of life research is thus revealed.

PROSPECT

The prospect for the quality of life research in the context of social theories and the consequent social practice may not be readily appreciated. The theories are commonly regarded as explaining social reality in a place-time-people bound configuration of world society or human society as a whole. That the explanations stem from one or another form of translating the cardinal values into ordinal value structures is seldom brought to light.

However, the social theories are not disparate, although they would be mutually distinct, complementarily or contradictorily, because of their common origin from the cardinal values. But the reflective minds of the pathfinders and the pace-setters are found to treat the translated ordinal valuations of the cardinal values in a discrete manner. This attempt bears a crucial relation to the appraisal of contemporary social reality and unfolds the prospect for quality of life research beyond its topical utility.

Neither this prospect nor the topical utility of quality of life research was of paramount importance to social research in ancient and medieval times. The world in those days was largely an aggregate of discrete societies, relatively unique in themselves. Therefore, human concern with the cardinal values for the species was displayed within narrow perimeters of variation in the place, the time, and the people. As a result, the translation of the cardinal values into ordinal value structures was less diverse than it became when the global perspective became the predominant concern of humanity. To that end, the scenario underwent a drastic alteration with the advent of capitalism and the emergence of a global market in men, materials, and ideas.

The global reality, relevant to world capitalism in the 18th and 19th centuries, particularly as substantiated by its role in Asia and Africa (Mukherjee 1974, 1985), became a necessary condition to humanity in the 20th century. The necessity was first felt after World War I, with the emergence of duality between the capitalist and the socialist world systems. It has become essential after World War II, with (*a*) labour and capital assuming an international dimension under the rubric of various ways of describing the developed and the underdeveloped sectors of the world society, and (*b*) the schism in international politics resulting in the identities of the First, the Second, and the Third World in one or another manner. Therefore, on one side, the peoples of the world have come closer than ever before and, on the other, the differences in appraising social reality for the betterment of humanity have never been more clearly revealed than now.

The world economy and politics have set forth unprecedented transactions and movements of the people within and across the long established, newly emerged, and the emergent nation-states. Along with these global facilities and necessities, the items of information on respective configurations of the world society have remarkably accumulated in extent and depth. As a result, the appraisal of social reality has surmounted the divisive barriers of specialization (like economics, psychology, political science, and sociology) and the task of interpreting the cardinal values for humankind has come to bear the concept of social science in place of social sciences (Mukherjee 1983: 1–54). At the same time, multiple theories and consequent practice have emerged to explain the structure and function of human society, and alter its causality and processes.

As noted, at the basic level of valuation, the future of humankind is frequently evaluated in the light of consensus or conflict: (*i*) the modernizing ideals are bringing the social classes together for peaceful coexistence, growing affluence, and sustained progress, or (*ii*) the decisive shifts in class conflict and the struggle of workers and peasants in alliance with the middle class intelligentsia and the ghetto population are posing powerful concerns at the local, regional, and international levels and will eventually establish a world of peace, prosperity, and progress. The appraisal of social reality is correspondingly in different directions. It deals essentially in either the selectively acquired contemporaneous culture processes or the social processes emerging from the contemporary cauldron of society. The distinction is particularly manifest in viewing the phenomena of class and nation, the two indubitably important social products of the present day, in terms of complementarity or contradiction.

On the one hand, the Weberian concept of social classes, identified by the cultural attributes of status and prestige, is regarded to register social change by consensus. On the other, the Marxist concept of classes, identified by the interplay of social processes (in the course of which the cultural processes may intervene as, conversely, the social processes with respect to social classes), is regarded to register social change by the resolution of conflicts arising out of contradictory alignments in the mode of production, the state of productive forces, the relations of production, and the relations of property.

On the other prime axis of appraisal of social reality, either the consolidation of a nation-state is examined in terms of complementarity of its culture-specific subnational unities or the evolution of nation and the formation of state are considered in terms of resolving the contradictions arising out of the operation of social processes among the ethnic and national unities. As a result, nation-building has become the key concept for consensus, and the plasticity of nation formation and state formation for conflict resolution.

At the succeeding levels of valuation, the ideologies of consensus and conflict include notable variations for the evaluation of the social products and the processes regarded as of primary importance to the appraisal of social reality. Also, the products and the processes valued as of ancillary importance to the primary ones are not treated in the same manner, irrespective of the fact that these secondary variables may appear to be of prime importance in a local or regional setting; such as, the castes in India, the Islamic sects in the Muslim world, and the ritually or otherwise enforced cultural ranks in Africa, South America, and the Pacific. All these variations in appraising social reality are clearly evident in the viewpoint of the development theorists, on the one hand, who are regarded to be ardent followers of the ideology of consensus, and of the Marxists, on the other, who acknowledge adherence to the ideology of resolving the social conflicts.

The development theorists value a nation-state, their *unit of analysis*, as traditional or modern but differently evaluate the social products. The traditional society is characterized as an inert mass (Mende 1959), an entity for vegetative reproduction only (Rostow 1962: 4–5), or bearing internal potentialities to become modern (Rudolph and Rudolph 1967). The modern society may be clearly valued as the societies in West Europe and North America (Moore 1967: 3) or the valuation may be extended to include, in parenthesis, the socialist societies of Europe and the USSR in so far as they resemble the 'modern' society of the North Atlantic Region (Shils 1962: 10) or it may include any 'industrial society' (Bendix 1964: 3–6).

The process of change from the culture of traditionalism to modernity is also evaluated differently by the development theorists, although based on the primary valuation of nation-building; such as, according to the model of 'consociation' (Daalder 1973), distinctions and interrelations among subnational unities as among 'eight Spains' (Linz and Miguel 1966), and the future of Burma and 'Whither Africa' with reference to consensus within (Silverstein 1959, Coleman 1960) or across (Leach 1963; Servoise 1963) the nation-states.

Unlike the development theorists, the world-system theorists (acknowledged or not as Marxists) shift their level of analysis from the nation-state to the core-periphery axis of world society and appraise social reality by valuing capitalism as the overwhelming social process (Wallerstein 1974, 1979; Hopkins 1977, 1978). However, the identification of the semi-periphery, which denotes dynamism in the world-system theory and which may emerge from either the core or the periphery (Mukherjee 1980), remains a matter of subtle differences in valuation by the world-system theorists (e.g., Chase-Dunn and Rubinson 1979; Hopkins and Wallerstein 1980; Arrighi et al. 1983).

The acknowledged Marxists profess to take into account both the national state and the core-periphery identities because the seat of revolutionary change in the world-system is in a national state but the feasibility of revolution is concerned with forces beyond a national state as well. However, the social process of capitalism is not evaluated by means of the simple frame of reference to the three classes of the bourgeoisie, the petty bourgeoisie, and the proletariat. The three class categories are further evaluated, but variably within and across them, by the inclusion of categories of peasants in the schema, the category of lumpen bourgeoisie along with those of the lumpen proletariat and the labour aristocracy (Frank 1972), and so on.

Thus, while there are some attempts to conjugate different appraisals of social reality by interfacing them, such as, from the sides of the Weberians and the Marxists, the dominant note is struck by the evaluation of world society and its configurations in different and sometimes antagonistic ways. This is noticeable both at the basic and the succeeding levels of valuation.

With reference to the examples cited, while the theory of development is propagated by a large number of social scientists specializing in economics, political science, sociology, etc., the 'dependency model' is mooted by some other social scientists and some of them may castigate the theories of development as 'development of underdevelopment' (Frank 1970, 1975). Among the radicals also the valuation of reality may be so different that the world-system theory would be castigated as 'neo-Smithian Marxism' (Brenner 1977) while one brand of acknowledged Marxists would denounce another as 'bourgeois deviationists' and even as 'social fascists'.

However, the wide range of variability in translating the cardinal values into ordinal valuations points to various ways of exploring the value space on social reality in the context of a better future for humankind. Social science has attained the stage at which the data space for social research is more and more revealed as representing the primary value space of selecting items from the information space and the secondary value space for differently evaluating the items of information. Therefore, contemporary social research will be productive if the social theories presenting allied or opposed value structures are interrelated in a systemic manner in place of generating futile or less rewarding polemics by considering them disparately.

Along with this course of systemization, the relative relevance of the social theories will be indicated by the support they receive from the elites and the masses in society. Concurrently, the necessity of these theories will be evaluated by their efficiency in realizing the cardinal values, which is independent of their relative elite-mass relevance as discussed earlier. Thus, on these two accounts, sciencing society comes within the purview of the quality of life research, and the usefulness of the project is ultimately substantiated by meeting the basic objective of social science to appraise social reality for the betterment of humankind in an evermore precise, unequivocal, and comprehensive manner.

But to meet this basic objective of social science at its contemporary state of accumulation of knowledge, a change is required with respect to the approach and orientation to social research. To date, social research has been predominantly positivistic according to the value premises of the respective scholars, which may be formally character-ized as evolutionary, idealistic, etc. The value premises are enforced by the scholars' orientation to viewing society from the top, as it were, of the social space and thus deducing reality.

Therefore, a deductive and positivistic approach and a value-acceptor's orientation have ruled the realm of social research by positing one or another value structure. This has followed from an almost unanimous realization that value-free research is deceptive while, as discussed, a clear distinction has not been drawn between the information space and the data space which is formed by the meaning (datum) attributed to respective items of information (which is valuation).

The approach and the orientation have been acclaimed to be inherent to sciencing society and people, so that, on an obscure value base, the course of research has occasionally delved into metaphysical appreciation of reality on the plea of dealing with the nuances of 'human' emotions and spirit. However, the dominant deductive-positivistic approach and the value-acceptor's orientation, along with their logical aberrations, are not new in the realm of science and not unique to social science. The commonly classified physical and biological sciences have also passed from the value-free and through the value-accepted orientation to that of value accommodation in order to draw probabilistic inferences on an inductive base on 'what will it be?' of the aspect of reality under examination.

With reference to physical reality, Friedrich Engels pointed out in the 19th century that:

> It is however precisely the polar antagonisms put forward as irreconcilable and insoluble, the forcibly fixed lines of demarcation and distinctions between classes, which have given modern theoretical natural science its restricted and metaphysical character. The recognition that these antagonisms and distinctions are in fact to be found in nature, but only with relative validity, and that on the other hand their imagined rigidity and absoluteness have been introduced in nature only by our minds—this recognition is the kernel of the dialectical conception of nature (1939: 19).

Albert Einstein (1916: 101) pointed out the pernicious implications of value acceptance in physical science, and the need for value accommodation in view of an inductive appraisal of physical reality:

> Concepts which have been proved to be useful in ordering things easily acquire such an authority over us that we forget their human origin and accept them as invariable. Then they become 'necessities of thought', 'given a priori', etc. The path of scientific progress is then, by such errors, barred for a long time. It is therefore no useless game if we are insisting on analysing current notions and pointing out on what conditions their justification and usefulness depends, especially how they have grown from the data of experience. In this way their exaggerated authority is broken. They are re-

moved, if they cannot properly legitimate themselves; corrected, if their correspondence to the given things was too negligently established; replaced by others, if a new system can be developed that we prefer for good reasons.

Bertrand Russel (1931: 33) emphasized the need for inductive-inferential orientation to develop the scientific outlook, and implied against value acceptance for appraising reality, with the statement: 'The conflict between Galileo and the Inquisition is . . . a conflict between the spirit of induction and the spirit of deduction.'

Max Born (1956: vi–vii) journeyed from 'value-free' positivist deduction to value-accommodated inductive inference as a physicist:

> In 1921 I believed—and I shared this belief with most of my contemporary physicists—that science produced an objective knowledge of the world, which is governed by deterministic laws . . . . In 1951 I believed in none of these things. The border between object and subject had been blurred, deterministic laws had been replaced by statistical ones . . . . The final criterion of truth is the agreement of a theory with experience, and it is only when all attempts to describe the facts in the frame of accepted ideas fail that new notions are formed, at first cautiously and reluctantly, and then, if they are experimentally confirmed, with increasing confidence. In this way the classical philosophy of science was transformed into the modern one, which culminates in Niels Bohr's Principle of Complementarity.

However, the shift in the approach from deductive positivism to inductive inference, and the orientation from value acceptance to value accommodation, is not uncontroversial, especially where 'life' and 'individual' are concerned, such as, with respect to the appraisal of biological and social reality. At the end of the 19th century, the savants of the Royal Society of London declared it injudicious to mix mathematics with biology in the context of inductive and probability inference on 'evolution'. Reacting to this dominant viewpoint in those days, W.F.R. Weldon, K. Pearson, and C.B. Davenport brought out the journal *Biometrika*, stating its objective in the first issue (1901: 1) as:

> [to] serve as a means not only of collecting under one title biological

data of a kind not systematically collected or published in any other periodical, but also of spreading a knowledge of such statistical theory as may be requisite for their scientific treatment.

But several authorities, like Karl Popper (1968: 52), hold on to the viewpoint that it is not 'possible to decide, by using the methods of an empirical science, such controversial questions as whether science actually uses a principle of induction or not.' Nevertheless, with respect to a course of research, he agrees (1968: 44) that 'the *objectivity* of scientific statements lies in the fact that they can be *intersubjectively tested.*' This is precisely what has been discussed in the context of testing the relative efficiency of deductively and positivistically formulated value structures on an inductive, inferential, and value-accommodated base.

Thus, there is no reason why, for an efficient appraisal of social reality with a view to meeting the cardinal values for humankind, social science cannot cross the deductive, positivistic, value-accepted barrier and adopt the inductive, inferential, value-accommodated course of research, by treating all available and possible value structures as components of, theoretically, an infinite but enumerable value space which is also the corresponding data space. Indeed, the pathfinders, whose theories are presently contended, are seen to provide the scope for such a shift in the approach and the orientation to social research.

Max Weber, one of the most notable pathfinders for contemporary social research, had declared (1949: 68) his negative value premise for the appraisal of social reality as 'the so-called "materialistic conception of history" as a *Weltanschauung* or as a formula for the causal explanation of historical reality is to be rejected most emphatically.' Positively, he had pointed out (1949: 53) to the researcher that:

Science can make him realise that all action and naturally, according to the circumstances, inaction imply in their consequences the espousal of certain values—and herewith—what is today so willingly overlooked—the rejection of certain others. The act of choice itself is his own responsibility.

However, while he thus adopts a deductive, positivistic, and value-accepted stance for himself and the researcher, his instrumental value premise points to an inductive, inferential, and value-accommodated

232 · _Quality of Life_

course of research. With respect to the researchees he states (Gerth and Mills 1970: 152) that 'if we are competent in our pursuit . . . we can force the individual or at least we can help him, to give himself an _account of the ultimate meaning of his own conduct._'

Evidently, Max Weber's proposed course of research will deal with a multiplicity of individual valuations of social reality, emerging from an infinite but enumerable value space. As explained, these numerous but identifiable value structures will be inductively grouped and their relative efficiency will be testably inferred; so that, some of these inferences may refute Max Weber's or the researcher's value premise in place of supporting it.

Karl Marx, another most notable pathfinder for contemporary social research, viewed the resolution of class conflicts as the primary means of establishing a better humanity. He took note of behavioural and perceptual variables for the formulation of 'class in itself' and 'class for itself', but is commonly regarded to have abjured the need for valuation in social research because of his famous statement in the 'Preface' to _A Contribution to the Critique of Political Economy_ (1859):

> In the social production of their life, men enter into definite re-lations that are indispensable and independent of their will; . . . It is not the consciousness of men that determines their being, but, on the contrary, their social being that determines their consciousness.

The deterministic value premise of Marx on the role of the collectivity, in place of individuals, for the appraisal of social reality is endorsed by Emile Durkheim (1897), another notable pathfinder for contemporary social research, although from a totally different standpoint of evalu-ating what he described as 'social fact':

> I consider it extremely fruitful this idea that social life should be explained, not by the notions of those who participate in it, but by more profound causes which are unperceived by consciousness, and I think also that these causes are to be sought mainly in the manner according to which the associated individuals are grouped. Only in this way, it seems, can history become a science, and sociology itself exist.

However, while Durkheim evaluated 'social fact' as a thing in itself, for itself, and by itself, he advocated (1938: 135, 141) the inductive, inferential, and value-accommodated approach and orientation against the deductive, positivistic, and value-accepted approach and orientation, for sciencing society:

> It is necessary to compare not isolated variations but a series of systematically arranged variations of wide range, in which the individual items tie up with one another in as continuous a gradation as possible. For the variations of a phenomenon permit inductive generalizations only if they reveal clearly the manner in which they develop under given circumstances.
>
> Sociology does not need to choose between the great hypotheses which divide metaphysicians. It needs to embrace free will no more than determinism. All that it asks is that the principle of causality be applied to social phenomena. Again, this principle is enunciated for sociology not as a rational necessity but only as an empirical postulate, produced by legitimate induction.

Similarly, while Marx and the Marxists adhere to the valuation stated in the *Manifesto of the Communist Party* (Marx and Engels 1848) that 'the struggle of all hitherto existing society is the history of class struggles', Marx had clearly noted at the same time (1844) the role of value differentials for the appraisal of social reality:

> A class must be formed which has *radical chains*, a class in civil society which is not a class *of* civil society, a class which is the dissolution of all classes, a sphere of society which has a universal character because its sufferings are universal, and which does not claim a *particular redress* because the wrong which is done to it is not a *particular wrong* but *wrong in general*. There must be formed a sphere of society which claims no *traditional* status but only a *human status* . . . a sphere finally which cannot emancipate itself without emancipating itself from all the other spheres of society, without therefore emancipating all these other spheres; which is, in short, a *total loss* of humanity and which can only redeem itself by a *total redemption of humanity*. This dissolution of society, as a particular class, is the proletariat.

And, while elucidating the implications of Marx's 'Preface' to *A Contribution to the Critique of Political Economy*, V.I. Lenin (1951:

28), one of the foremost interpretors of Marxism, advocated an inductive, inferential, and value-accommodated approach and orientation to social research:

> By examining the whole complex of opposing tendencies, by reducing them to precisely definable conditions of life and productions of the various *classes* of society, by discarding subjectivism and arbitrariness in the choice of various 'leading' ideas or in their interpretation, and by disclosing that all ideas and all the various tendencies, without exception, have their *roots* in the condition of the material forces of production, Marxism pointed the way to an all-embracing and comprehensive study of the process of rise, development, and decline of socio-economic formations.

It will be superfluous to examine the views of other pathfinders and pace-setters, whether or not concerned with any specific form of specialization in social science, in the context of undertaking a rigorous course of social research. The point is, all researchers have their own value premises and, initially, they may appraise social reality from the top, as it were, of the social space. But social research, especially at the contemporary state of accumulation of information and consequent multiple formulation of value structures, demands appraising social reality from the bottom, as it were, of the social space, which is the value space comprising, theoretically, infinite but enumerable value structures on the betterment of humanity.

Valuation in social science is, thus, the crux of contemporary social research; but, as yet, it is virtually a virgin field for systematic and systemic exploration. It is in this context that the quality of life research can fulfil its topical and decisive obligations.

· Bibliography ·

Andrews, F.M., McKennel, A.C., 1980, Measures of Self-reported Well-being: Their Affective, Cognitive, and Other Components, *Social Indicators Research* 8(2): 127–55.

Andrews, F.M., Withey, S.B., 1976, *Social Indicators of Well-being.* New York, Plenum Press.

Arrighi, G., Hopkins, T.K., Wallerstein, I., 1983. Rethinking the Concepts of Class and Status-Group in a World-System Perspective, *Review* 6(3): 283–304.

Bendix, R., 1964, *Nation-building and Citizenship.* New York, John Wiley.

Bestuzhev-Lada, I.V., 1980, Why of Life and Related Concepts as Parts of a System of Social Indicators, *in* Szalai, A., Andrews, F.M. (eds.), *The Quality of Life: Comparative Studies,* pp. 159–70. Beverly Hills, Sage.

Beteille, A., 1966, *Caste, Class, and Power: Changing Patterns of Stratification in a Tanjore Village.* Berkeley, University of California Press; Bombay, Oxford University Press.

Bharadwaj, L.K., Wilkening, E.A., 1980, Life Domain Satisfactions and Personal Social Integration, *Social Indicators Research* 7(1–4):337–51.

Bharatiya Jana Sangh, 1965, *Principles and Policy.* Delhi, Bharatiya Jana-Sangh.

Blumer, M., 1983, The Methodology of Early Social Indicator Research: William Fielding Ogburn and 'Recent Social Trends', *Social Indicators Research* 13(2): 109–30.

Born, M., 1956, *Physics in my Generation: A Selection of Papers.* London, Pergamon Press.

Brenner, R., 1977, The Origins of Capitalist Development: A Critique of Neo-Smithian Marxism, *New Left Review* (July–August): 25–91.

Campbell, A., Converse, P.E., Rodgers, W.L., 1976, *The Quality of American Life.* New York, Russel Sage Foundation.

Chandrasekhar, S., 1955, Cultural Barriers to Family Planning in Underdeveloped Countries, *Report of the Proceedings of the Fifth International Conference on Planned Parenthood.* London, International Planned Parenthood Federation.

Chase-Dunn, C.K., Rubinson, R., 1979, Toward a Structural Perspective on the World-System, *Politics and Society* 7: 453–76.

Clare, J.F., Kiser, C.V., 1951, Social and Psychological Factors Affecting Fertility. XIV. Preference for Children of Given Sex in Relation to Fertility, *The Milbank Memorial Fund Quarterly* (New York) 29(4): 440–92.

Cole, D., Lucas, H., 1979, *Models, Planning and Basic Needs.* Oxford, Pergamon Press.

Cole, S., Gershuny, J., Miles, I., 1978, Scenarios of World Development, *Futures* (February): 3–20.

Coleman, J.S., 1960, The Politics of Sub-Saharan Africa, *in* Almond, G., Coleman, J.S. (eds.), *The Politics of the Developing Areas,* pp. 247–368. Princeton, Princeton University Press.

Communist Party of India (CPI), 1968, *Programme*, New Delhi, Communist Party of India.

————, 1977, *Election Manifesto*. New Delhi, Communist Party of India.

Communist Party of India-Marxist (CPI-M), 1972, *Programme and Statement of Policy*. Calcutta, Communist Party of India (Marxist).

————, 1977, *Manifesto on Elections to Lok Sabha*. Calcutta, Communist Party of India-Marxist.

Daalder, H., 1973, Building Consociational Nations, *in* Eisenstadt, S.N., Rokkan, S. (eds.), *Building States and Nations*, vol. II, pp. 14–31. Beverly Hills, Sage.

De, N.R., 1984, Toward an Appreciation of Quality of Life and Quality of Work Life, *Economic and Political Weekly* 19(20–21): M46–M57.

Drewnowski, J., 1974, *On Measuring and Planning the Quality of Life*. The Hague-Paris, Mouton.

Duncan, O.D., 1969, *Toward Social Reporting: New Step*. New York, Russel Sage Foundation.

Durkheim, E., 1897, 'Review' of A. Labriola: *Essais sur la conception materialiste de l'histoire* in *Revue Philosophique:*December issue (quoted by Winch, P., 1958, *The Idea of a Social Science*, pp. 23–24, London, Routledge and Kegan Paul).

————, 1938, *The Rules of Sociological Method*. Glencoe, The Free Press.

Einstein, A., 1916, 'Obituary' on Ernst Mach, *Phys. Z.* Vol. 17 (quoted by Born, M., 1956, *Physics in my Generation: A Selection of Papers*, p. 90, London, Pergamon Press).

Engels, F., 1939, *Herr Eugen Duhring's Revolution in Science (Anti-Duhring)*. New York, International Publishers.

————, 1948, *The Origin of the Family, Private Property and the State*. Moscow, Foreign Languages Publishing House.

Fanchette, S., 1974, Social Indicators: Problems of Methodology and Selection, *in* Methods and Analysis Division, Department of Social Sciences (ed.), *Social Indicators: Problems of Definition and of Selection*, pp. 7–10. Paris, UNESCO.

Firth, R., 1946, *Malay Fishermen: Their Peasant Economy*. London, Routledge and Kegan Paul.

Fisher, R.A., 1949, *The Design of Experiment*. London, Oliver and Boyd.

Frank, A.G., 1970, *Latin America: Underdevelopment or Revolution*. New York, Monthly Review Press.

————, 1972, *Lumpen Bourgeoisie: Lumpen Development*. New York, Monthly Review Press.

————, 1975, *On Capitalist Underdevelopment*. Bombay, Oxford University Press.

Galtung, J., Wirak, A., 1977, Human Needs, Human Rights and Theories of Development, *in* UNESCO (ed. and pub.), *Indicators of Social and Economic Change and Their Applications*, pp. 7–34. Paris, UNESCO Papers and Reports in the Social Sciences No. 37.

Gerth, H.H., Mills, C.W., 1970, *From Max Weber: Essays in Sociology*. London, Routledge and Kegan Paul.

Gillingham, R., Reece, M.S., 1980, Analytical Problems in the Measurement of the Quality of Life, *Social Indicators Research* 7(1–4): 91–101.

Glass, D.V. (ed.), 1954, *Social Mobility in Britain*. London, Routledge and Kegan Paul.

Golant, S.M., McCutcheon, A.L., 1980, Objectivity of Life Indicators and the External Validity of Community Research Findings, *Social Indicators Research* 7(1–4): 207–35.

Goldthorpe, J.H., Hope, K., 1974, *The Social Grading of Occupations: A New Approach and Scale*. Oxford, Clarendon Press.

Gough, K., 1981, *Rural Society in Southeast India: Part 1. Thanjavur*. Cambridge (U.K.), Cambridge University Press.

Hankiss, E., 1978, Quality of Life Models, *in* UNESCO (ed. and pub.), *Indicators of Environmental Quality and Quality of Life*, pp. 57–88. Paris, UNESCO Reports and Papers in the Social Sciences No. 38.

Hellwig, Z., 1974, A Method for the Selection of a 'Compact' Set of Variables, *in* Methods and Analysis Division, Department of Social Sciences (ed.), *Social Indicators: Problems of Definition and of Selection*, pp. 11–20. Paris, UNESCO.

Herrera, A., et al., 1976, *Catastrophe or New Society? The Bariloche Report*. Ottawa, IDRC.

Hobhouse, L.T., 1938, *Social Development: Its Nature and Conditions*. London, George Allen and Unwin.

Hope, K. (ed.), 1972, *The Analysis of Social Mobility: Methods and Approaches*. Oxford, Clarendon Press.

Hopkins, T.K., 1977, Notes on Class Analysis and World-System, *Review* 1(1): 67–72.

——, 1978, World-systems Analysis: Methodological Issues, *in* Kaplan, B.H. (ed.), *Social Change in the Capitalist World Economy*, pp. 199–217. Beverly Hills, Sage.

Hopkins, T.K., Wallerstein, I. (eds.), 1980, *Processes of the World-System*. Beverly Hills, Sage.

Hume, R.E., 1958, *The Thirteen Principal Upanishads Translated from the Sanskrit with an Outline of the Philosophy of the Upanishads and an Annotated Bibliography*. London, Oxford University Press (2nd. ed.).

Indian National Congress-Indira (Cong I), 1972, *Election Manifesto*. New Delhi, Indian National Congress.

——, 1977, *Congress Election Manifesto*. New Delhi, Indian National Congress.

Inkeles, A., Diamond, L., 1980, Personal Development and National Development: A Cross-national Perspective, *in* Szalai, A., Andrews, F.M. (eds.), *The Quality of Life: Comparative Studies*, pp. 73–109. Beverly Hills, Sage.

International Centre for Development, 1979, *Circular Letter, 15 October*. Paris (issued by J.C. Aruna Sanchey).

Ivanovic, B., 1974, A Method of Establishing a List of Development Indicators, *in* Methods and Analysis Division, Department of Social Sciences (ed.), *Social Indicators: Problems of Definition and of Selection*, pp. 21–26. Paris, UNESCO.

Janata Party (JP), 1977, *Election Manifesto*. New Delhi, Janata Party.

Johansson, S., 1973, The Level of Living Survey: A Presentation, *Sartryck ur Acta Sociologica* 3: 211–19.

Kiurnov, C., 1980, An Integral Indicator of the Quality of Work and Quality of Life, *in* Szalai, A., Andrews, F.M. (eds.), *The Quality of Life: Comparative Studies*, pp. 171–88. Beverly Hills, Sage.

Land, K.C., 1971, On the Definition of Social Indicators, *The American Sociologist* 6 (November): 322–25.

———, 1978, Theories, Models and Indicators of Social Change, *International Social Science Journal* 27(1): 7–37.

Leach, E., 1963, The Political Future in Burma, *in* Jouvenel, B. de (ed.), *Futuribles*, pp. 121–53. Geneva, Droz.

Lenin, V.I., 1894, *What the 'Friends of the People' are and How They Fight the Social Democrats* (English translation 1946). Moscow, Foreign Languages Publishing House.

———, 1899, *The Development of Capitalism in Russia* (English translation). Moscow, Foreign Languages Publishing House.

———, 1951, The Marxian Doctrine: The Materialist Conception of History, *in* Lenin, V.I., *Marx, Engels, and Marxism*. Moscow, Foreign Languages Publishing House.

Leontief, W., et al., 1977, *The Future of the World Economy*. Oxford, Oxford University Press.

Linz, J.J., Miguel, A. de 1966, Within-nation Differences and Comparisons: The Eight Spains, *in* Merritt, R.L., Rokkan, S. (eds.), *Comparing Nations*, pp. 267–319. New Haven and London, Yale University Press.

Loomis, C.P., Loomis, Z.K., 1969, *Socio-economic Change and the Religious Factor in India: An Indian Symposium of Views on Max Weber*. New Delhi, Affiliated East-West Press; New York, Van Nostrand Reinhold Company.

Mahalanobis, P.C., 1944, On Large Sample Survyes, *Philosophical Transactions of the Royal Society of London*. Series B, 231(584): 329–451.

———, 1950, Why Statistics?, Address of the General President, *Proceedings of the 37th Indian Science Congress*. Calcutta, Indian Science Congress.

Malinowski, B., 1922, *Argonauts of the Western Pacific*. London, Routledge and Kegan Paul.

———, 1944, *A Scientific Theory of Culture and Other Essays*. North Carolina, North Carolina University Press.

———, 1947, *Freedom and Civilization*. London, George Allen and Unwin.

Manghahas, M., 1983, Measurement of Poverty and Equity: Some Asean Social Indicators Experience, *Social Indicators Research* 13(3): 253–79.

Markides, K.S., Martin, H.W., 1979, A Causal Model of Life Satisfaction Among the Elderly, *Journal of Gerontology* 34: 86–93.

Marx, K., 1844, Critique of Hegel's Philosophy of Right, *Deutsch-Franzosische Jahrbucher* (quoted in Bottomore, T.B., 1966, *Classes in Modern Society*, pp. 82–83, New York, Vintage Books).

———, 1859, Preface, *in A Contribution of the Critique of Political Economy* (Published in *Selected* and *Collected Works* of K. Marx and F. Engels).

———, 1942, *Theses on Feuerbach*. Appendix to *The German Ideology*. London, Lawrence and Wishart (also published in *Selected* and *Collected Works* of K. Marx and F. Engels).

Marx, K., Engels, F., 1848, *Manifesto of the Communist Party* (published in *Selected* and *Collected Works* of K. Marx and F. Engels).

Maslow, A.H., 1971, *The Farther Reaches of Human Nature*. New York, Viking Press.

McGinnis, R., 1979, Science Indicators/1976: A Critique, *Social Indicators Research* 6(2): 163–80.

McGranahan, D., Pizarro, E., Richard, C., 1985, *Measurement and Analysis of Socio-economic Development*. Geneva, United Nations Research Institute for Social Development.

Meadows, D., et al., 1972, *The Limits to Growth*. New York, Universe Books.

Mende, T., 1959, Southeast Asia and Japan, *Bulletin of the International House of Japan, Inc.*, Winter, No. 3.

Mesarovic, M., Pestei, E., 1974, *Mankind at the Turning Point*. New York, Dutton/ Readers Digest Press.

Michalos, A.C., 1974, Strategies for Reducing Information Overload in Social Reports, *Social Indicators Research* 1(1): 107–31.

————, 1980, Satisfaction and Happiness, *Social Indicators Research* 8(3): 385–422.

————, 1982, The Satisfaction and Happiness of Some Senior Citizens in Rural Ontario, *Social Indicators Research* 11(1): 1–30.

————, 1985, Multiple Discrepancies Theory (MDT), *Social Indicators Research* 16(4): 347–413.

Milbrath, L.W., 1978, Indicators of Environmental Quality, *in* UNESCO (ed. and pub.), *Indicators of Environmental Quality and Quality of Life*, pp. 33–56. Paris, UNESCO Reports and Papers in the Social Sciences No. 38.

Miles, I., 1986, *Social Indicators for Human Development*. London, Frances Pinter.

Miller, S.M., 1974, Policy and Science, *Social Policy* 3 (January).

Moore, W.E., 1967, *Order and Change*. New York, John Wiley.

Morgan, L.H., 1964, *Ancient Society*. Cambridge (Mass.), the Belknap Press of Harvard University Press.

Morris, D.M., 1977, A Physical Quality of Life Index (PQLI), *in* Sewell, J.W., et al., *The United States and the World Development Agenda 1977*, pp. 147–54. New York, Praeger.

Moum, T., 1981, Social Inequality, Social Status, and Quality of Life, *Psychiatry and Social Science* 1: 177–95.

Mukerjee, Radhakamal, 1938, The Sociological Analysis and Forecast of Population Increase, Presidential Address, *Proceedings of the Second All-India Population and First Family Hygiene Conference*. Bombay, Karnatak Publishing House.

Mukherjee, M., Ray, A.K., Rajyalakshmi, C., 1979, Physical Quality of Life Index: Some International and Indian Applications, *Social Indicators Research* 6(3): 283–92.

Mukherjee, R., 1957, *The Dynamics of a Rural Society*. Berlin, Akademie-Verlag.

————, 1965, *The Sociologist and Social Change in India Today*. New Delhi, Prentice-Hall.

————, 1974, *The Rise and Fall of the East India Company*. New York, Monthly Review Press.

————, 1975, *Social Indicators*. New Delhi, Macmillan.

————, 1976, *Family and Planning in India*. New Delhi, Orient Longman.

————, 1978, *What Will it be? Explorations in Inductive Sociology*. Durham (N.C.), Carolina Academic Press; New Delhi, Allied (1979).

————, 1980, Commentary, pp. 314–316, on Bach, R.L., On the Holism of a World-system Perspective, *in* Hopkins, T.K., Wallerstein, I. (eds.), *Processes of the World-System*, pp. 289–310. Beverly Hills, Sage.

————, 1981a, On the Use of Social Indicators for Planning, *Social Indicators Research* 9(2): 183–95.

———, 1981b, Realities of Agrarian Relations in India, *Economic and Political Weekly* 16(4): 109–16.

———, 1983, *Classification in Social Research*. Albany, State University of New York Press.

———, 1985, *Uganda: An Historical Accident? Class, Nation, State Formation*. Trenton, Africa World Press.

Myrdal, G., 1971, *The Challenge of World Poverty*. London, Penguin International.

Nerfin, M. (Project Director, 1975, 'The 1975 Dag Hammerskjold Report: What now?'), *Development Dialogue* (Uppsala), Nos. 1/2.

Ossipov, G.V., Kolbanovsky, V.V., 1974, *Social Indications and Indicators of the Social Development Planning*. Moscow, Soviet Sociological Association.

Oyebanji, J.O., 1982, Quality of Life in Kwara State: An Exploratory Geographical Study, *Social Indicators Research* 11(3): 301–18.

Pareto, V., 1963, *The Mind and Society: A Treatise on General Sociology*. New York, Dover.

Parsons, T., 1954, *Essays in Sociological Theory*. Glencoe, The Free Press.

Plekhanov, G. (Beltov, N.), 1895, *The Development of the Monist View of History* (English edition, 1956). Moscow, Foreign Languages Publishing House.

Popper, H., 1968, *The Logic of Scientific Discovery*. New York, Harper and Row.

Ridge, J.M. (ed.), 1974, *Mobility in Britain Reconsidered*. Oxford, Clarendon Press.

Rossi, P.N., Wright, S.R., 1979, *Evaluation Research: An Assessment of Current Theory, Practice and Politics* (mimeo.). Paris, UNESCO (SS. 79/WS/16).

Rostow, W.W., 1962, *The Stages of Economic Growth: A Non-communist Manifesto*. Cambridge (U.K.), Cambridge University Press.

Rudolph, L.I., Rudolph, S.H., 1967, *The Modernity of Tradition: Political Developments in India*. Chicago, University of Chicago Press.

Russel, B., 1931, *The Scientific Outlook*. London, George Allen and Unwin.

Ryabushkin, T.V., Levykin, I.T., Reizema, Ya. V., 1983, *Methodological Problems of Studying the Way of Life* (mimeo.). Paris, UNESCO (SS. 83/Conf/CS/13/5).

Sajogyo, 1977, Garia kemiskinan kebutuhan minimum ('The Poverty Line and Minimum Food Needs'), *Kompas* 4 (November).

Scott, W., 1978, *Measurement and Analysis of Progress at the Local Level: An Overview*. Geneva, United Nations Research Institute for Social Development.

Seashore, S.E., 1978, Indicators of the Quality of Working Life, *in* UNESCO (ed. and pub.), *Indicators of Environmental Quality and Quality of Life*, pp. 9–31. Paris, UNESCO Reports and Papers in the Social Sciences No. 38.

Seers, D., 1972, What are we Trying to Measure?, *The Journal of Development Studies* 8(3): 21–36.

Sen, A., 1983, *Choice, Welfare and Measurement*. Delhi, Oxford University Press.

———, 1986, The Concept of Well-being, *in* Guhan, S., Shroff, M. (eds.), *Essays on Economic Progress and Welfare*, pp. 174–92. Delhi, Oxford University Press.

Servoise, R., 1963, Whither Black Africa? *in* Jouvenel, B. de (ed.), *Futuribles*, pp. 181–294. Geneva, Droz.

Sheer, L., 1980, Experience with Quality of Life Comparisons, *in* Szalai. A., Andrews, F.M. (eds.), *The Quality of Life: Comparative Studies*, pp. 145–55. Beverly Hills, Sage.

Sheldon, E.B., Land, K.C., 1972, Social Reporting for the 1970s, *Policy Sciences* 3(2): 137–51.

Sheldon, E.B., Moore, W.E. (eds.), 1968, *Indicators of Social Change: Concepts and Measurements.* New York, Russel Sage Foundation.

Shils, E., 1962, *Political Development in the New States.* 's-Gravenhage, Mouton.

Silverstein, J., 1959, Burma, *in* Kahin, G.M. (ed.), *Governments and Politics of Southeast Asia,* pp. 75–152. New York, Cornell University Press.

Singh, Y., 1973, *Modernization of Indian Tradition: A Systemic Study of Social Change.* Delhi, Thomson Press (India) Ltd.

Socialist Party of India (SP), 1972a, *All Power to the People: Election Manifesto.* Bombay, The Socialist Party.

————, 1972b, Platform of the Socialist Party, *Janata* (Bombay) 27(35): 1–49.

Spender, D. (ed.). 1981, *Men's Studies Modified: The Impact of Feminism on the Academic Disciplines.* Oxford and New York, Pergamon Press.

Stone, P.J., 1980, Organic Solidarity and Life Quality Indicators, *in* Szalai, A., Andrews, F.M. (eds.), *The Quality of Life: Comparative Studies,* pp. 211–19. Beverly Hills, Sage.

Szalai, A., 1980, The Meaning of Comparative Research on the Quality of Life, *in* Szalai, A., Andrews, F.M. (eds.), *The Quality of Life: Comparative Studies,* pp. 7–21 Beverly Hills, Sage.

Tonnies, F., 1955, *Community and Association (Gemeinschaft und Gesellschaft),* London, Routledge and Kegan Paul.

Tunstall, D.B., 1979, Developing Indicators of Environmental Quality: The Experience of the Council of Environmental Quality, *Social Indicators Research* 6(3): 301–47.

Tylor, E.B., 1898, *Primitive Culture.* Vol. I. London, John Murray.

UNESCO, n.d., *Long Term Educational Planning: Module I. The Context of Long Term Educational Planning.* Paris, UNESCO, Division of Educational Policy and Planning.

————, 1978, Final Report, *in* UNESCO (ed. and pub.), *Indicators of Environmental Quality and Quality of Life,* pp. 89–96. Paris, UNESCO Reports and Papers in the Social Sciences No. 38.

United Nations, 1951, *Enquiries into household standards of living in less-developed areas.* New York, UN Publications Sales No. 1950. IV.7.

————, 1954, *Report on International Definition and Measurement of Standards and Levels of Living.* New York, UN Publications Sales No. 54.IV.5.

————, 1975, *Towards a System of Social and Demographic Statistics.* New York, United Nations.

United States Department of Health, Education and Welfare, 1969, *Toward a Social Report.* Washington, D.C., U.S. Government Printing Press.

Vidwans, S.M., 1985, A critique of Mukherjee's Index of Physical Quality of Life, *Social Indicators Research* 17(2): 127–46.

von Dusen, R.A., 1974, *Social Indicators, 1973: A Review Symposium.* Washington, D.C., Social Science Research Council (Center for Coordination of Research on Social Indicators).

Wallerstein, I., 1974, *The Modern World-System.* New York, Academic Press.

————, 1979, *The Capitalist World-Economy.* Cambridge (U.K.), Cambrdige University Press.

Warren, R.D., Fear, F.A., Klonglan, G.E., 1980, Social-indicator Model Building: A Multiple-indicator Design, *Social Indicators Research* 7(1–4): 269–97.

Weber, M., 1949, *The Methodology of the Social Sciences*. New York, The Free Press.
——, 1958a, *The Protestant Ethic and the Spirit of Capitalism*. New York, Charles Scribner's Sons.
——, 1958b, *The Religion of India*. Glencoe, The Free Press.
Weiner, M., 1966, Preface, *in* Weiner, M. (ed.), *Modernization: The Dynamics of Growth*. New York, Basic Books.
Weldon, W.F.R., Pearson, K., Davenport, C.B., 1901, Editorial, *Biometrika* 1: 1–6.
Wolf, K.H., (tr.), 1950, *The Sociology of Georg Simmel*. New York, The Free Press.
Young, R.C., Maccannell, D., 1979, Predicting the Quality of Life in the United States, *Social Indicators Research* 6(1): 23–40.

• Author Index •

· Subject Index ·